ISBN 978-0-259-50820-5
PIBN 10820700

This book is a reproduction of an important historical work. Forgotten Books uses state-of-the-art technology to digitally reconstruct the work, preserving the original format whilst repairing imperfections present in the aged copy. In rare cases, an imperfection in the original, such as a blemish or missing page, may be replicated in our edition. We do, however, repair the vast majority of imperfections successfully; any imperfections that remain are intentionally left to preserve the state of such historical works.

For support please visit www.forgottenbooks.com

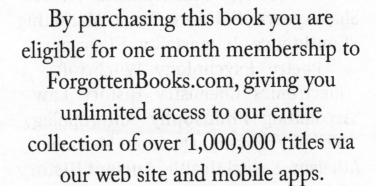

English
Français
Deutsche
Italiano
Español
Português

www.forgottenbooks.com

Mythology Photography **Fiction**
Fishing Christianity **Art** Cooking
Essays Buddhism Freemasonry
Medicine **Biology** Music **Ancient
Egypt** Evolution Carpentry Physics
Dance Geology **Mathematics** Fitness
Shakespeare **Folklore** Yoga Marketing
Confidence Immortality Biographies
Poetry **Psychology** Witchcraft
Electronics Chemistry History **Law**
Accounting **Philosophy** Anthropology
Alchemy Drama Quantum Mechanics
Atheism Sexual Health **Ancient History**
Entrepreneurship Languages Sport
Paleontology Needlework Islam
Metaphysics Investment Archaeology
Parenting Statistics Criminology
Motivational

RECORDS OF THE LUMLEYS OF LUMLEY CASTLE

LUMLEY CASTLE, EAST FRONT

RECORDS OF

⌐E LUMLE⌐

OF

LUMLEY CASTLE

BY

EDITH MILNER

EDITED BY

EDITH BENHAM

LONDON

GEORGE BELL AND SONS

1904

CHISWICK PRESS: CHARLES WHITTINGHAM AND CO.
TOOKS COURT, CHANCERY LANE, LONDON.

PREFACE

CHRONICLERS are useful people, and are not as plentiful as they might be. Many interesting stories are thus lost, and tradition will perhaps in the near future become literally a thing of the past. It was due to the fact that one member of the Lumley family had a tenacious memory that this book came to be written. These memories were gathered together, and soon grew into a considerable record.

It then became necessary, if the book was to be of any public value, to verify the traditions. Family papers were put in order, searched and translated. The task outgrew the modest capacities of the author, and then the editor came to the rescue. After translating the family papers, searching the British Museum and the Record Offices, besides obtaining access to valuable papers in other families, notably those belonging to the See of Winchester, Miss Benham was able to give the book value and authority; and if it should appeal to the thoughtful and learned, the thanks of the family and the author are due to her for the invaluable service she has rendered. The Appendix is chiefly her

work. Both author and editor are greatly indebted
to Mr. Algernon Graves, F.S.A., for the assistance
he rendered in identifying the various portraits
which illustrate the book, and beg to tender him
their best thanks.

CONTENTS

LIST OF ILLUSTRATIONS

RECORDS OF THE LUMLEYS
OF LUMLEY CASTLE

CHAPTER I

Liulph, the founder of the family.—Uchtred.

TO write the record of a family intimately asso-
ciated with the history of the great English-
speaking race from Anglo-Saxon times down
to the present day is a task of no small magnitude. When the present writer began, it was
her intention to embody the early records in a preface, or
at most an introductory chapter, and write a chatty account
of the recent events in the Lumley history. When, however,
the mass of family documents was put into her hands, she
found so much material out of which to weave a veracious
story, thrilling as any romance, that she attacked the work
in a different spirit, and with the assistance of a friend who
translated and arranged the documents at Sandbeck, and
found others in the Record Office and at the British Museum,
she has gathered together a consecutive history, which she
hopes will be found full of interesting matter.

The earlier records gather round Lumley Castle, which
for long was the only family seat. In Camden's "Britannia,"
first translated into English by Philemon Holland in 1610,
we find the following: "From thence *Were* passeth by
Lumley Castle, standing within a park, the ancient seat
of the *Lumleies*, who descended from *Liulph*, a man in this
tract of right great nobility in the time of King Edward the
Confessour, who married *Aldgitha*, the daughter of *Aldred*

Earle of Northumberland. Of these *Lumleies*, Marmaduke assumed unto him his mother's coate of Armes (in whose right he was seized of a goodly inheritance of the *Thwengs*), namely, *argent of Fesse Gueles between three Popinjaes Vert*, whereas the *Lumlies* beforetime had borne for their Armes, *Six popiniayes Argent, in Gueles*. For shee was the eldest daughter of Sir Marmaduke *Thweng*, Lord of Kilton, and one of the heires of Thomas *Thweng* her brother. But Ralph sonne to the said Marmaduke was the first Baron *Lumley* created by King Richard the Second: which honour John the Ninth from him enjoied in our daies a man most honourable for all the ornaments of true nobility." (In one edition he is described as a "most respectable old man."— Ed.)

"Just over against this place, not farre from the other banke of the river standeth *Chester upon the Street*, as one would say, *the Castle or little City by the portway side* : the Saxons called it *Concester* : whereupon, I would deeme it to bee *CONDERCUM*. . . . The Bishops of Lindifarre lived obscurely heere with the corps of Saint Cuthbert, whiles the raging stormes of the Danes were up, for the space of an hundred and thirteene yeeres. . . . Anthony Bec, Bishop of Durham and Patriarch of Jerusalem, erected here a Collegiat Church, a Deane, and seven Prebends. In which church, the Lord *Lumley* aboue said placed and ranged in goodly order the monuments of his Ancestors in a continued line of succession even from *Liulph* unto these our daies ; which he had either gotten togither out of monasteries that were subverted or caused to bee made anew."

In later editions of this same book (Camden) Lumley is also briefly mentioned in connexion with other families, and in the notice of Scarborough town it is stated " that the Right Honourable Richard Lumley has from this place his title of Earl of Scarborough." [2]

In the mention of the last Earl of Arundel, John, Lord

---

[1] A considerable jump is here made to Marmaduke in the fourteenth century from Liulph in the eleventh.

[2] Spelt thus here and in the patent, but in the last century changed to Scarbrough.

Lumley, is said to receive or rather to give himself honourable mention as having erected a very fulsome monument to his father-in-law's memory. After setting forth his virtues and exploits in a long Latin inscription, this post-scriptum is added :

"John Lumley, Baron of Lumley, his most dutiful and disconsolate son-in-law, and executor, with the utmost respect put up this statue with his own armour (after he had been buried in great pomp) for the kindest of fathers-in-law and the best of patrons, as the last office he was able to pay him: not to preserve his memory which his many virtues had made immortal; but his body in hope of a joyful Resurrection."

It may be mentioned here that John, Lord Lumley, though nominally heir to this great earl, had paid dearly for the honour, in discharging the numerous debts that had resulted from his many achievements and high offices.

Arthur Collins gives a fairly accurate account of the history of the family in his peerage from early times to 1779. The Rev. Frederick Barlow, M.A., gives much the same account, but carries the pedigree one step further back, beginning thus : " This noble family derive their descent, both on the male and female side, from no less ancient than illustrious ancestors. Liulph lord of Lumley-Castle, son of Osbert de Lumley, married Algitha, daughter of Aldred, Earl of Northumberland, by Edgina, younger daughter of King Ethelred II., which Liulph lived in the time of King Edward the Confessor; and was at length murdered by means of Leofwin, chaplain to Walcher, bishop of Durham."

The name of Aldred was also borne by Liulph's contemporary, the Bishop of Worcester and Archbishop of York in 1060. (He held both sees for a short time, but was compelled by the Pope to resign the see of Gloucester.) To this Aldred, Florence of Worcester, who died in 1118, was doubtless indebted for the account he gives of the murder of Liulph, translated from the original as follows :

"A.D. 1080. Walcher, Bishop of Durham, a native of Lorrain, was killed by the Northumbrians on Thursday, the 2nd of the Ides of May (May 14), at Gateshead, in revenge of the death of Liulph, a noble and generous thane. This same man had many possessions far and wide throughout England by hereditary right, but because the Normans gave vent everywhere to their cruelty at that time he betook himself with all his people to Durham, because with a sincere heart he loved S. Cuthbert; for this saint, as he was wont to relate to Aldred, Archbishop of York, and other religious men, appeared to him very often both when he was sleeping and waking and revealed to him as to a faithful friend what he wished to be done; under whose protection, now in the town, now on those possessions which he had in those parts, he had lived for a long time. His coming was not unpleasing to Bishop Walcher, who greatly loved this same saint in all things. For this reason Liulph was so greatly beloved by the bishop that he would by no means act or arrange weightier affairs of his secular business without his advice. Wherefore the chaplain Leobwin, whom he had so much exalted that both in the bishopric and in the country scarcely anything could be done without his advice, inflamed with the incentive of envy, and puffed up with excess of pride because of his power, set himself arrogantly against the aforementioned man; so that he regarded some of his judgements and coun- sels as of no value, striving in every way to annul them. Frequently also, when disputing with him in the presence of the bishop, not without threats he would provoke him to anger with opprobrious words. Thus one day when this man Liulf, being summoned by the bishop to the council, had in all cases ruled legally and wisely, Leobwin withstood him obstinately, and exasperated him with contumelious speeches. But because he was answered more roughly than usual he at once left the place of judgement, and calling to him Gilebert, to whom the bishop had committed the government of the county of Northumbria, because he was his own kinsman, prayed him earnestly to avenge him and to put Liulf to death as soon as possible. He, at once acquiescing in the iniquitous request, having gathered to- gether the soldiers of the bishop and of Leobwin himself, proceeded one night to the town where Liulf was then dwelling and wickedly slew him and nearly all his family in

LIULPHUS

his own house. When he heard this the bishop sighed heavily from the bottom of his heart, and having pulled his hood off his head and thrown it to the ground, he said sadly to Leobwin, who was present: ' These things are thy doing, Leobwin, with thy crafty doings and most foolish wiles; therefore I would have thee know for certain that thou hast destroyed me, thyself, and all my household with the sword of thy tongue.' Having said this he hastened into his castle, and having at once sent messengers throughout Northumbria, he took care to announce to all that he was not privy to the murder of Liulf, but rather that he had outlawed from Northumbria his murderer, Gilebert, and all his associates, and he was prepared to purge himself according to pontifical judgement. Then, interceders having gone between them and peace having been given and accepted, he and the relations of the murdered man were able to fix place and day where they could meet and confirm the peace.

" The day having arrived, they met together in the appointed place; but the bishop did not wish to plead with them in the open air, so he entered into the church there with his clergy and the more honourable of his knights, and having held a council he sent out to them from among his people those whom he would to make peace with them. But they would by no means acquiesce in his conditions, because they believed for certain that Liulf had been murdered at his demand, for not only had Leobwin in the very night after the murder committed by his relative received Gilebert and his allies familiarly and amicably into his house, but even the bishop himself had received him as at first in his grace and favour. Wherefore they first killed all who were found out of doors on the side of the bishop, a few having saved themselves by flight. Having seen this, in order to satisfy the fury of the enemy the bishop commanded his kinsman, the aforesaid Gilebert, whose life they were seeking, to go out of the church, upon whose exit the guards followed closely; but being quickly assaulted by the hostile swords and lances, they were destroyed in a moment, but they saved two English thanes on account of consanguinity. They also killed Leobwin,

Dean of Durham, because he had often given many attacks against them to the bishops, and the other clergy as soon as they went forth. But the bishop, when he understood that their fury could in no way be mitigated unless Leobwin, the head and author of all this calamity, was killed, asked him to go out to them. But when it was impossible to force him to go out, he himself gained the doors of the church and prayed that his own life might be saved. They, however, refusing, he, covering his head with the border of his cloak, went out and was instantly killed by his enemies' swords. Then they commanded Leobwin to go out, and when he would not they set the church and other buildings on fire. He, choosing to end his life rather by burning than by slaughter, sustained the flames for some time; but when he was half burned he rushed out, and being cut to pieces received the punishment of his crimes and perished miserably. In revenge for which detestable murder King William in that year devastated Northumbria."

Simeon of Durham gives exactly the same account, except that instead of the story about St. Cuthbert's appearing to Liulph, which, as we have said, Florence probably heard from Aldred at the time when he was Bishop of Worcester, we find the following passage:

"He married Algitha, daughter of Earl Aldred, by whom he had two sons, Uchtred and Morekar.[1] The sister of this Algitha was Elfleda, mother of Earl Waltheof. This earl gave his little aforementioned cousin, Morekar, to the monks of Jarrow. At which time this earl was at Tynemouth, which place he gave over to the monks at the same time as the aforementioned youth."

From this translation we gather that Liulph, spoken of in the family Red Velvet Book (of which more anon), as "noble generous man," left by his wife Algitha two sons. Morkar, as we see, was given by his kinsman, the Saxon

---

[1] There is another Liulph about this period who is evidently confused with Liulph of Lumley; but he was of Greystock, and there was no connexion beyond the fact that the two men bore the same name. Liulph of Greystock had four sons, two of whom are erroneously given to Liulph of Lumley in one or two old peerages.

Earl, to the monks of Jarrow; while Uchtred, the elder, succeeded to his father's estates.

Uchtred of Lumley left two sons, William and Matthew. Both these names appear frequently in old deeds, as they gave rich endowments to the neighbouring abbey at Finchale, and were witnesses in many matters both civil and ecclesiastical.

The original deeds are lost, but notices of them are contained in Robert Surtees' "History of Durham," from which we have obtained our information. Thus in vol. ii., p. 165 (ed. 1820), we have a deed, dated at Durham, by which Matheus de Lumleya left two acres of land in Lumley to the monks of Finchale. This Matthew or his son is the one named in this following deed: "Matthew de Lumley . . . sendeth greeting. . . . Know that I have conceded and by this present charter confirmed to Uchtred son of Uchtred de Wodeshende the vill of Wodeshende which my father and uncle had given to him," etc. Wodeshende is in the parish of Chester-le-Street. The seal affixed was a very fine one, representing a knight in armour on horseback, the left arm extended, carrying a popinjay on his finger.

These endowments were certainly conferred within fifty years of the time when Henry de Pudsey established his monks at Finchale, and less than one hundred years after the death of Liulph.

Sir William Lumley, knight, also stood as witness with others of his name in charters of Finchale dated 1250-1260, and with Matheo and Henrico de Lumley he witnessed the "Carta de Ferimanside." One deed of this period is witnessed by Matheo de Lumley, Emerico son of Henrici de Lumeley, and Matheo son of Mathei de Lumley.

In these documents the Lumley name is spelt in various ways, and in a curious deed in old English, "mayd betwyxt Sir Georg Lumley and Robert Werdall, Prior to Finchale," dated 1483, the name is also spelt Lumble. Of this Sir George we shall treat further in order of descent.

Surtees' history contains so many bequests from various Lumleys that they would fill many chapters, and would, it is feared, prove somewhat tedious reading, but enough have been given to prove the antiquity of the family.

CHAPTER II

The three Sir William Lumleys.—Sir Robert.—Sir Marmaduke Lumley and the Thweng arms.—Sir Ralph, first Baron Lumley.—The rebuilding of Lumley Castle.

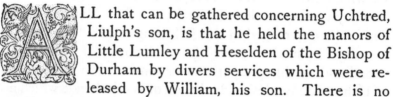LL that can be gathered concerning Uchtred, Liulph's son, is that he held the manors of Little Lumley and Heselden of the Bishop of Durham by divers services which were released by William, his son. There is no mention of his wife in any pedigree. His brother, Morkar, being given in early youth, as we have seen, to the monks of Jarrow, doubtless became a monk. There is a mutilated figure in the churchyard of Durham Cathedral which is called Uchtred, but there is no evidence to prove that it is Uchtred of Lumley.

Sir William de Lumley, son of Uchtred, married Judith, daughter of one Hesilden of Hesilden.

Uchtred's younger son, Matthew, already mentioned as a great benefactor to Finchale, and whose name appears in numerous deeds as witness to various wills and benefactions, is the ancestor of the younger branch who settled at Great Lumley and held the manor there. A house is still in existence which is supposed to have formed part of Matthew de Lumley's manor-house.

Sir William de Lumley left one son, William, of whom nothing is known. He left two sons, William and Marmaduke. It is said in Collins's "Peerage" that the "John Fitz-Marmaduke, Baron of Horden, who on Feb. 12, 1300-1, was among those barons that subscribed a memorable letter to Pope Boniface VIII.," was a son of Marmaduke de Lumley; but this is a mistake, as the barons of Horden

belonged to the Thweng family. Collins was probably mis-
led by the seal bearing the Thweng arms which a later
Marmaduke Lumley assumed.

Sir William Lumley, the elder brother, married the
daughter and co-heir of Walter de Audre, of Molton-audre
in the bishopric of Durham. There appears little doubt,
from the slender records which are extant, that these Lumleys were men of great weight in the important and powerful
County Palatine of Durham. At least one member, if not
more, sacrificed much in the cause of the Crusades, and
risked life and health against the forces of the Crescent in
the far East. One longs to lift the veil, to catch one real
glimpse of the domestic life of our own ancestors, to know
what were their thoughts, their wishes, their anxieties. The
few bare facts recorded prove them to have been men with
generous instincts, who performed noble needs; with this
knowledge the chronicler of a veracious history must rest
content.

Sir William left a son, says Collins, "Sir Roger de
Lumley, Knt., who wedded Sibil, daughter and co-heir of
Hugh de Morewic,[1] an ancient baron in Northumberland,
who left the said Sibil, Theophania, and Beatrix, his co-
heirs, and then in minority, whose wardships and marriages,
without disparagement to them, were obtained of the King,
by William de Latimer, for MCC marks." A close connexion with royalty is thus apparent in marriages subsequent to those of Liulph and his father Osbert. The authority
for the above statement is to be found in Rot. Pip. 45
Henry III. Ebor.

Roger and Sibil de Lumley left two sons, Sir Robert de
Lumley and Sir Roger de Lumley, who was ancestor to the
Lumleys of Harleston and Clipston in Northamptonshire.

Sir Robert de Lumley in 1298, on the death of his mother
(then the widow of Lawrence de St. Maur), succeeded to
the lands of her inheritance—West Chivington, Morewicke
and Bamburgh Castle, with other vast possessions—besides
his paternal inheritance. He was then in his twenty-sixth

[1] See the pedigree, taken from Baker's "Chronicles," at the end of the
chapter.

year. He married Lucia, eldest daughter of Marmaduke de Thweng, Lord of Kilton Castle and Thweng, with divers other manors in Yorkshire, Lancashire, and Westmoreland. The following account of this family is taken from Whitaker's " History of Richmondshire and Lonsdale," vol. ii., p. 291:

" Here may be the proper place to introduce a short account of a family, on whom, collaterally, descended large possessions in this neighbourhood from the old barons of Kendal. These were the Barons of Thwenge, once of great account in the East Riding of Yorkshire. Of these, Marmaduke de Thwenge, so highly distinguished for his bravery in the battle of Strivelyn, as it is called, 25th Ed. I. (1297), gave to William, his son, certain lands in Helsington, Kirkby in Kendal, Warton, Kerneford and six other towns, which he must have obtained in marriage with Isabel, daughter of William de Ros, of Ingmanthorpe. . . . William de Thwenge, however, died without issue, Feb. 25, 15th Edw. III. (1341), and was succeeded by Robert, his brother, a priest, and he by Thomas, a third brother, and a priest also, who dying on Trinity Sunday, 48th Ed. III. (1374), was found to be seized of Thirnum (Thurnham) and Ellel, of Kirkby Kendal (meaning I suppose the lands already mentioned, for the Thwengs do not appear to have been at any time seized of that barony), and many other large possessions. Thomas de Thwenge dying, of course, without issue, his estates were divided between his three sisters, namely, Lucy, wife of Sir Robert de Lumley, Margaret, wife of Sir Robert de Hilton, of Surno in Holderness, and Katherine, wife of Sir Raafe Dawbeny."

The son of Sir Robert and Lucy, Sir Marmaduke Lumley, first assumed the arms of Thweng, which have ever since been retained by his descendants. He married Margaret, daughter and co-heir of — Holland, by whom he had issue four sons, Robert, Ralph, Thomas, and William, as also a daughter, Isabel, married to Sir William Fulthorp, Knt.

Robert died young, unmarried, and Ralph, still under age, succeeded to the honours of the family. He must have been well and wisely brought up by his widowed mother, for he proved worthy of his high estate and vast possessions. Tradition asserts that he leaned strongly to the doctrines of Wycliffe; he was high in favour with King Richard II. Perhaps the known tendencies of Queen Anne of Bohemia, Richard's tenderly loved consort, may have caused the King to ignore any rumours not actively confirmed. There is also a legend of a murdered Lady of Lumley, who cannot be traced in any of the genealogical tables. This is taken advantage of by the author of "The Lily of Lumley," a romance of this period mingling fact with fiction, in which the murdered lady is made the first wife of Ralph of Lumley.

Sir Ralph was summoned to Parliament from the eighth year of Richard III. till the first of Henry IV. inclusive, 1385-1400, when he was attainted, of which more anon. He was a knight, and in the retinue of Henry of Percy, Earl of Northumberland, in that expedition made into Scotland in 1386, and was so well behaved that he was made Governor of Berwick-upon-Tweed in 1387; but in 1388 he was made prisoner by the Scots. In 1391 he was made Deputy-Governor of Berwick, under Henry de Percy, and the year after, 1392, obtained licence to make a castle of his manor-house of Lumley.

He married Eleanor, daughter of John, Lord Neville, by Maud, daughter of Percy, Earl of Northumberland, and sister of Ralph, Lord Neville, created first Earl of Westmorland. The Lady Eleanor was beautiful and clever, and the proximity of Brauncepeth, her maiden home, would have doubtless thrown the young heir of Lumley into her company. His being in the retinue of her relation, Henry de Percy, might also conduce to intimacy between the families. The whole surroundings of this picturesque period provided subject and matter for a thrilling romance. The craving for a purer, simpler faith was stirring in the hearts of gentle and humble. The half savage feudal system was giving way to a fairer and nobler state of affairs, and though education was still looked upon as the exclusive possession of the clergy, knights and squires were beginning to realize that it was not beneath their dignity to be able to sign their names instead of affixing the hitherto rude mark to public and private documents. That Sir Ralph, first Baron Lumley, by summons to Parliament, was a man of some culture is proved by many facts; notably the building of the stately castle which is still the pride of the county of Durham, as well as his high appointments, his marriage with the almost royal house of Neville, and not least his loyalty and devotion to the unfortunate, gifted, if misguided King, in whose cause he was to lose his life. All contemporary documents bear witness to the worth and nobility of Sir Ralph, the architect (as he is sometimes called) of Lumley Castle, and tradition associates the Lady Eleanor with all his best acts.

He died as he had lived, fighting for the King to whom he had sworn fealty, and the picture of King Richard II. in the great Barons' Hall of Lumley represents Sir Ralph kneeling at his royal master's feet, receiving the patent of nobility. The picture in question is a replica or a very early copy of the one in Westminster Abbey. The figure of Sir Ralph is supposed by some to have been painted in by order of John, Lord Lumley, in the reign of Queen Elizabeth; for the knight is portrayed as burly and past his prime, and does not accord with the appearance of the youthful King, whose contemporary Sir Ralph must have been. Lord Lumley was only in his thirty-ninth year when he died on the field of battle, bearing the royal standard—more fortunate in this than the other lords concerned, who were overpowered by the inhabitants of Cirencester to the number of twenty-eight, lords, knights, and gentlemen, chief leaders of the expedition, and brought from thence to Oxford to the King (Henry IV.), who immediately caused them to be executed there. Sir Ralph's widow lived to see their second son, John, restored to the honours earned in life and forfeited by his loyal death by her noble husband, Sir Ralph Lumley.

Among the few early deeds still in existence are two bearing the signature of Sir Ralph Lumley, with very fine seals attached, bearing the Lumley arms, which were discovered by the Rev. Canon Greenwell amongst some papers in a waste-paper basket at a lawyer's office in Durham. He gave one concerning the repayment of certain moneys to the present Lord Scarbrough and retained the other in his own possession. There are many Lumley deeds in the Durham Cathedral Library.

KING RICHARD II. CONFERRING PATENT OF
NOBILITY ON RALPH LUMLEY

CHAPTER III

UBSEQUENT events prove that Eleanor, Lady Lumley, mourned her gallant husband during a long widowhood, and brought up their large family well and wisely.

There is a curious mistake in a quaint old MS. pedigree in the British Museum (Harl. MS. 2289) making Sir Ralph de Lumley marry Margaret, daughter of Ralph Neville, Earl of Westmorland, and of Joan Beaufort, daughter of John of Gaunt. This same error occurs in Edmondson's "Peerage," but is corrected in the copy of this work at the British Museum in a marginal note. From this error must have arisen the tradition which named the wife of Ralph, first Baron Lumley, "the Rose of Raby." The lady historically entitled to bear the name was certainly Cecily, Duchess of York, mother of Edward IV. and of Richard III., niece of Eleanor, Lady Lumley, who was sister and not daughter to the first Earl of Westmorland.

Lady Lumley had the pain of parting with her eldest son, Thomas, who died during his minority on the 31st of May, 1404. There is a document dated May 24, 1379, at the Record Office, revoking the protection *with clause volumus* for one year granted to Thomas de Lumley, believed to be staying with Henry de Percy, Earl of Northumberland, warden (*custos*) of the castle and town of Berwick-on-Tweed upon its defence; the said earl testifies that he is not so staying. He, however, in part at all events, seems to have been in possession of his father's estates; but the title was only restored to his brother John, partly by the widowed

Lady Lumley's unwearied exertions and spirited appeals to obtain the reversal of her husband's attainder, and partly in recognition of John's great services in Scotland, and also for the fidelity with which he served the King in France, where he ultimately lost his life. It seems easy, even through so long a vista of years, to conjure up the picture of the proud and devoted mother thus emerging from her widowed retirement to secure her son's re-establishment in the stately home which had been so enlarged and beautified by her husband. We find in an old chronicle that the sum of £20 a year was secured to Lady Lumley for her life in the second year of the reign of Henry IV. (1401), which was confirmed to her by Henry V. in 1413, together with various manors, tenements, and appurtenances. From her father John, Lord Neville, she also inherited the following bequests: He leaves to his daughter, Eleanor de Lumley, wife of Sir Ralph Lumley of Lumley Castle, "ij banaret beddis de Norfolk cum curtinis xij dis cos vj saucers et ij ollas ij potz poletters ij pelves cum ij lavatoriis argenteis xi vaccas et xx stottos iiij annorium."

Surtees goes on to say: "She is probably the person represented by the recumbent female effigy in the Cathedral Yard at Durham, erroneously attributed to the man who broke his neck for a purse of gold." This, however, is not very probable considering the trouble John, Lord Lumley, in the reign of Elizabeth, took to gather together even the reputed effigies of his ancestors.

Marmaduke, another son of this remarkable couple, who certainly stand out in their generation, received a learned education, was Rector of Stepney, and Bishop of Carlisle for twenty years, from which see he was translated to Lincoln, which he scarce enjoyed a year, dying in London in 1451, when in attendance on King Henry VI. He was constituted Treasurer of England, and was a great benefactor towards the building of Queen's College in Cambridge, and bestowed 200 marks (a great sum in those days) on the library of the College, together with a great many good books.

John, second Baron Lumley, married Felicia, daughter

of Sir Matthew Redman, who succeeded Sir Ralph as
Governor of Berwick in 1388, and fought in that capacity
in the battle of Otterbourne, which is perhaps more familiar
to the ordinary reader as the battle of Chevy Chace, of
which both Lord Berners and Froissart give such vivid de-
scriptions. Such deeds of prowess were then performed as
those of the hero who,

> When his legs were smitten off
> He fought upon his stumps.

Sir Matthew apparently resorted to the other expedient of
the man who chose the better part, that

> He who fights and runs away,
> Will live to fight another day.

Here we will let Sir John Froissart tell his own tale :

"When Douglas was dead, and Sir Henry Percy and
many notable knights were prisoners, Sir Matthew Redman,
when he saw the English army was defeated without hopes
of recovery, and that his brother knights were surrendering
themselves to the Scots, mounted his horse and rode off.

"He was, however, noticed by Sir James Lindsay, a
valiant Scot knight, who was desirous of gaining renown by
the capture of a notable Englishman, and so he mounted
his horse and pursued him. When he got near enough to
pierce him with his lance, he forbore and said :

"'Ha, Sir Knight, turn about; it is disgraceful thus to
fly; I am James Lindsay, and if you do not turn, I will
drive my spear into your back.'

"But Sir Matthew struck spurs into his horse, and fled
away harder than before. After a three miles' chase, the
horse stumbled under him, so Sir Matthew leapt off and
put himself in an attitude of defence. After a gallant
struggle Sir Matthew, getting the worst of it rather for lack
of breath than of skill, surrendered his sword, which Sir
James Lindsay returned, and allowed Sir Matthew to continue his journey to Newcastle on condition that he gave
his parole to surrender himself to Sir James at whatever
time he should appoint. To this Sir Matthew consented;
but Sir James himself mistook his road through the dark-

ness on his return to the camp, and fell into the hands of the Bishop of Durham. Sir James recounted to the Bishop his capture of Sir Matthew Redman, into whose care the Bishop confided him when they reached Newcastle."

Doubtless the two knights agreed to an exchange of paroles while Lindsay enjoyed Redman's hospitality at New-castle.

Sir John, after distinguishing himself in various ways under Henry IV. and Henry V., was slain at the battle of Beaujé on Easter Eve, April 13th, 1421, together with Thomas, Duke of Clarence, the King's brother, the Earls of Tanqueville and Angus, and the Lord Ross. "These noblemen all disapproved of the rash action of the Duke of Clarence in thus attacking a force superior to their own by four to one, but yet made proof of their duty and valour, no men ever behaving more courageously" (Old Chronicle).

Among the deeds at Sandbeck is one dated "St. Dunstan's Day in March, in the sixth year of the reign of King Henry V." (March 20th, 1419), in which Ralph de Neville, Earl of Westmorland, concedes to John de Lumley, Knight, his nephew, all his lands which had come to him at the death of Robert Umfraville in the town of Seton-kerrowe.

This chapter may fitly conclude with the codicil to the will of the said Sir John Lumley, being a most interesting example of the ability of the testator, and proving that men of arms could even thus early be men of education.

CODICIL to will of "Sir John Lumley of Lumley Castle, Knight, son and heir of Sir Ralph Lumley, who died in battle at Cirencester against Henry IV., by Eleanor, daughter of John Lord Neville of Raby and sister of Ralph, first Earl of Westmorland.

"*Codicilium*. Be it known till all men yat yis is ye last wille of me Sir Johan of Lumley Knyght. I wille yat my testament yat I made in England stande in his strenth with yis that I wylle on alle wyse bee fulfillet. I wille yat my brothre Marmaduc bee oon of ye chief executors and chief surueiour not withstonding any othir surueiour maade before yis tyme. And as touchant ye goodes of myn in Normandy and in ffrance I wille yat yei be disposet and gouernet bee

D

family is indebted for much interesting information; and from this time there will be less difficulty in following the fortunes of the family in which this worthy Baron of Elizabeth's reign took so much interest and pride.

APPENDIX TO CHAPTER V

An account of the Rebellion, commonly called "Aske's or Bigod's Rebellion," and of George Lumley's share in it, will best be given by quoting the following account from a MS. in the Record Office:

(In Latin.) "Examination taken in the Tower of London 8 Feb. 1536 (1537), by Lord Thomas Cromwell lord Cromwell and Masters John Tregonwell, Rich. Layton and Thomas Legh, Doctors, in the presence of me Jo. Rice," etc.

(In English.) "George Lumley, soonne & heire to the Lorde Lumley, examined saith that hering first that they were up in Lincolnshire and that Aske was gon to Holdernes to feire theym there, his father and he fledde into Newcastell and there being my lord his father and he fering lest they shulde be betrayed of the commons of the towne as Sir Thomas Hilton said and by his persuasion went to the same Mr. Hiltons house and this exa^t went to a house of his fathers called thisle. And as he was there came to hym certain souldiors out of Richmondeshire and asked hym whether he wolde not come to my lorde Latomer or els the people would spoyle all his fathers goods. And thereupon this ex^t came to my lorde Latomer which was then mowstering with a greate company toward the nomber of viii or x thousand afore Awklande the busshop of Duresmes house, from whome was sent a little before Mr. Bowes to my Lorde of Westmorlande and was come agen therehens with an answer from my Lorde of Westmorland." (In margin: "Thether cam in the same tyme Sir James Strangwise with a greate company. yong Bowes a nother company with him both about the nomber of M men Sir Rauff Bowmer with a nother company, and a knight that entred (?) with my lord latomer whose name he can [knows] not but he dwelleth nygh my lorde latomer with a nother company with hym.") "And there as this exaᵗ was come, my Lorde Latomer said to this examinante and asked hym where my lorde his father was. And he answered hym faynedly bicause he thought it best for the sauftie of his father that he was in Northumbreland making mery with his friends. And he said agein. that he thought my lorde had no warnyng of their assemblie there. And doubted not but upon convenient warnyng he wolde come in or sende a reasonable answere. & asked this exaᵗ whether he had sent his father any worde, and he said noe, And thereupon willed this exaᵗ to sende his father worde that he shulde come in or els the commons wolde spoyle his house. Than my said lorde Latomer gave thothe to this exaᵗ. And after that this exaᵗ sent the said message to his father by a tenant of my lorde his father whose name he remembereth not. And this exaᵗ went agein to the said Isle & afterward upon worde brought hym by one Christophere Arnolde that his owne house was in grete daunger to be spoyled & his wif in greate fere to his owne house on the next morowe where he understode that Sir Thomas Percy had reysed and mowstered all the people of that quarter of Yorkswolde. & there taried this exaᵗ ii dayes, & from thens this exaᵗ went to yorke with ii of his servants to one Becks wifs house, & there being resorted to Sir George Lawsons house where he mett with Sir Thomas Percy. Sir Nicholas Ferffox. Sir Oswalde Wolsethorpe. and divers other gents thinking to this exaᵗ that he shulde have mett with his father there., bicause it was said in the countrey that all the gents shulde there mete about that tyme. And there being he harde Sir Thomas Percy geve grete preyse to the Prior of Byrlington for that he had sent ii of his brethren the tallest men that he sawe unto theym. And also Mr. Ferffox said that the same matier that they rose for was a matier for the defense of the faith & a spirituall matier (;) wherfore he thought mete that the Priors & Abbots and other men of the churche shulde not only sende ayde unto theym but also goo foorth in their owne person whereupon the said Sir Nicholas Ferffox went to thabbot of Sainct marie Abbeyes & this exaᵗ at Sir

Thomas Percyes commandment went to Sainct Saviors of Newburgh/ to Bylande/ Revieulx/ Whitby/ Malton, and Kirkeham and he sent one John Lambert his servant to Mountgrace/ Birlington/ and Guysborough: to move thAbbots or priors & two monks of every of those houses with the best crosse to come forwards in their best araye. & saith that he had xl^s of a pece of eche of the Abbots of Bylande/ of Newburgh/ & of Whytby: of their owne offer without any request made of this exa^{ts} behalf; And all they answered that they could not come theymself/ but they had & wolde send theym all the furtherance and ayde they coulde. & saith that there were sent afore that a certain of their brethren to the rest of the rebells at yorke out of every house. And thabbot of Ryvieulx/ & the Prior of Guys-borough promisede to come theymself, but afterward as they wrote to this exa^t/ they were countermaunded by Mr. Robert Aske to tarie at home theymself/ and to sende their provision & cariage by some other which they did in dede. & the Prior of Guysborough cam hymself to yorke. where this exa^t shewed hym of the countermaundment that other fathers had to goo home. and therefore willed hym to go home to. And as this exa^t was at Whytby Aske sent a letter to this exa^t moving hym to speke to Thabbot there that he shulde sende unto hym cariage with his benevolence and tarie hymself at home. And than retorned this examin-ante & shewed to Sir Thomas Percy whome he found with all the hole company beside Pomefrete that he had doon his message. & there this exa^t taried with his father. till my lorde of Norfolk came thether/ & drewe a treuse among bothe parties. And the causes alledged of the said insur-rection were thies. that is to saye. The pulling downe of thabbeys and tales went about that there shulde be money paid for every childe that shuld be christened. & for every wedding. & that no poore man shuld eate white bredde. & divers other which he doth not nowe remember. And saith Robert was the cheffe ringleder & cheffe feyrer of that insurrection.

"And saith that there was an Abbot a tall lusty man at the said mowster before Aukelande which said. that. I here

saye that the King doth crie xviii^d a daye. And I truste
we shall have as many men for viii^d a daye. and as he
troweth it was thabbot of Jervieulx. & his chaplen had a
bowe and a sheffe of arowes.

"And Sir Thomas Percy/ and one Rudston were next
Aske the cheffe doers & promoters of that busynes. as he
saieth.

"To the seconde article. he thinketh that there was never
a spirituall man in all the countrey but he gave theym bothe
money & sent to theym strength. for he harde the said
Abbots that he was with all saye that they had sent before
that to Sir Thomas Percy money and ayde. Also he saieth
that every towneshippe delivered to suche souldiers as went
out from theym xx^s to a pece which served theym for so long
as they were foorth. And so had this exa^{ts} servants of the
towne of Thwyng whereof this exa^t was hymself. And
gents had no wages as furre as he knoweth. for he had none.
& saith that Sir Thomas Percy can saye more who sent
money & ayde unto theym. Also he harde Robert Aske
saye at my lorde Darcys house called Templehurst. that he
had delivered or sent a copie of thothe to a gent of Norfolk
whose name he can not tell which wolde sett as he troweth
the matier forward in the South parties.

"To the third article he saith. that the brute [bruit]
was among theym that if they had gon forwarde past
Doncastere the South parties wolde not fight against theym.
And saith that Robert Aske wrote moste letters & devysed
them to feire the people. & he can not tell as he saieth of
any other writers but the said Askes servants. nor of any
other message or letters he can not depose.

"To the iiiith article/ he saieth that he harde Robert
Aske saye that he had devysed thothe hymself. And as for
tharticles he knoweth not who devysed theym. for this exa^t
was sik in his bedde when those articles were putt foorth
and a greate while after.

"To the vth article. he saith that upon a tuesdaye in the
mornynge after this exa^t had ben with Sir Rauf Yvers, as
this exa^t was at his house at Thwyng in his bedde came to
hym to his bedside one Richarde Sympson Constable of

and redde the same openly. And than said. it is no more
but as if I wolde saye unto you. the kings grace will geve
you a pardon and badde you go to the Chauncerye &
fatche it. And yet the same is no pardon. Also here ye
are called Rebells, by the which ye shall knowledge yo^{r}self
to have doon ageinst the king which is contrarie to yor
othe." (In margin: "And therewith he feired the people
so moche that one of the commons whose name he can not
tell. said openly. the King hath sent us the fawcet and
kepeth the spigot hymself. & a nother said. as for the
pardon it makes no matier whether they had any or not for
they nev^r offended the king nor his lawes. Wherefore they
shulde nede to have any pardon. Also he said a parliament
is apoynted as they saye. but neither the place where. nor
the tyme whan it shulde be kept as appoynted.") " And also
here is that the King shulde have cured bothe of yor body
& soule/ which is playne false for it is ageinst the gospell
of christ/ & that will I Justifie even to my deth. And
therefore if ye will take my parte in this & defende it I
will not faille you so long as I live to thuttermoste of my
power. & who will so doo adsure me by yor hands & holde
theym up. And they with that helde up their hands with a
greate shoote. and said who so ever wolde not so doo strike
of his hed. Than departed the said bygod towarde Hull.
And this exa^t with a nother company to the nomber of xl
persons went towarde Scarborough.

" And being examined what notable persons were with
bygod said. that there was one tall man that went like a
preste in company with hym. which was a greate feyrer of
that busynes. and said if they went not forwarde. all was
loste that they had doon before. for all was but falsehod
that was wrought ageinst theym." (Inserted: "whose name
that exa^t can not tell.") "Also he saith that bygod in his
said declaracion made to the people said that the fatt
prestes benefices of the South that were not resident upon
the same and money of the suppressed Abbeys shulde finde
the poore souldiors that were not able to beare their owne
charges

" Further the said Bygode commaunded at the same tyme

& place the souldiors that were with this exa^t to see that this exa^t shulde reyse the reste of the countrey & by name that parte called Dykring to go with this exa^t & ayde hym at Skarborough. Than this exa^t went to a place called Monyhouse and there toke the mowster of those men of Dickring which were named to rise byfore by Sir Francis Bygods commaundement. And where as they wolde have gon all hoolly with this exa^t to Scarborough. he discharged theym all home sauf only ii of every towne which he thought he might best rule & order. And so went towards Scarborough. And by the weye going the commons were not contented with this exa^t bicause their company was no greter. & so commaunded this exa^t to sende warnynge to Pikryng Lithe to rise up the contrey there & come to Scarborough to ayde them. And so this examinante by the commaundement of the commons gave warnyng to the constable of Semere that he shulde commaunde the contreye of Pikering Lithe to mowster on the next daye at a place called Spittels as this ex^t shulde come agein from Scarborough where this exa^t appoynted to be at that mowster. Than this exa^t entered into Scarborough with the nomber of a syx or seven score persons as he estemeth. And there this exa^t caused a proclamation to be made. that no man shulde take nothere mete nor drinke there but that he shuld honestly paye for. Nor make no quarrel ageinst any that belonged towarde yonge Sir Rauph Yvers upon any olde grudge for keping of the castell in tymes paste. nor yet for none occasion doon at that tyme without they had made this exa^t privey to it first. And so this exa^t departed to his lodging. Than the same nyght the commons sent worde to this ex^t saing that they fered leste the castell shulde be entred by Force ageinst theym that night/ except it were watched. Wherupon they desired that they might enter into the castell that night. And than this exa^t answered theym that he wolde not be of their counsaill to enter into the Castell for it was the kings house: & there had they nor he nothing to doo. And their othe was to doo no thing ageinst the king. Wherefore they determyned than to kepe a watche that nyght about the castell that no other man shulde enter.

which this exa^t affirmed it was better to doo." (Inserted: "And in the meane tyme the same night about midnight this ex^t sent worde by his servant Christopher Lambert to old Sir Rauf Yvers to geve hym warnyng that if yong Sir Rauf Yvers were there he shulde not come to the Castell that night for the watche was sett about the same leste he shulde be taken of the watche/& that this ex^t trusted shortely to dispatche the company that was there whereby Sir Rauf Yvers might come afterwarde more quietly to the Castell.") "And on the morowe this exa^t & his company went to the graye friers & there spake with the baylyfs & other officers of the towne. and sware theym according to Sir Fraunces Bygods letter. theffect wherof was in all things like the former othe with this addicion. that no man shulde geve counsaill to any man to sitt still untill suche tyme as they had obteyned their former articles. Than the commons demaunded to have one Guye Fishe & a nother called Lockwood,/ & Lancelot Lacye all servants to yong Sir Rauph Yvers to be killed & heded bicause they had kept the Castell with Sir Rauph Yvers bifore. for whose savegarde this exa^t made fervent request to the commons & with long entrety stayed theym from doing any harm unnto theym. That doon the commons determyned utterly eftsones to enter agein into the Castell and at the persuasion of this exa^t & the baylifs of the towne they were stayed agein from attempting the same. Lockwoode aforesaid being there and then present. Than bicause this exa^t said he muste neds departe thens saing there were company ynough to kepe the towne & he had busynes at home they condescended that one Wyvel shulde be lefte there for the keping of the towne & to be their Capitain. Which Wyvel said afterwarde to this exa^t that he was lefte very sklender there for this exa^t had taken aweye all the souldiors that came to the towne with hym, And said that seing this exa^t had all the souldiors with hym it shulde be necessarie for hym to have ayde of the next townes adioynynge for that night/ & required this exa^t to sende hym on the morowe suche other ayde as shulde be thought convenient to be there continually with hym for the defense of the towne. Which thing for satisfying of his mynde this ex^t promiśed hym to do. And so this ex^t departed out of Scarborough with his company towarde the place where the mowster shulde be of Pikering Lithe. And by the weye he met divers of that partes. to whome he declared that the commons were in doubt leste Scarborough & other holdes shulde be kept from theym to their destruction. Which thing this ex^t thought they wolde defende to the uttermoste of their power. willing theym that night to sende ayde sufficient to Scarborough till the morowe that this ex^t wolde sende other souldiors sufficient for defense of the towne & castell. & so departed from that company & cam to the place appoynted called the Spittels where as there were none assembled for they were all departed before bicause this ex^t taried so long er he wolde come thether. In which place this ex^t made proclamacion to the souldiors being in his company/ that every man shulde go home to his house and not to rise at the commaundement of any lewde person. Nor upon the sight of any bekon untill they knewe this exa^{ts} plesure. And in the meane tyme this exa^t said he wolde either sende or go to the Duke of Norfolk, & show him their doubts, & knowe his plesure therin. And so they assured this exa^t that they wolde rise at no mans calling but either at this exa^{ts} calling or Sir Thomas Percyes. than said this exa^t if ye shulde rise at his calling or any other mans than were I, said this ex^t, in a sure case for than shulde I be lefte alone. Than they made answere agein they wolde rise for no man but upon speciall commaundement had from one of theym both. Launcelot Lacy servant to yong Sir Rauf Yvers being theire & then present. And so they departed every man homewarde. & this exa^t to his owne house. And on the morowe which was other " (either) "upon thursedaye or fryedaye so this exa^t sent a letter to Wyvel & his company lefte at Scarborough showing theym that he had hardé saye that the kings plesure was to come to yorke about Whitsontide & there to kepe his parliament and to have the Quenes grace crowned and that he had harde by good credit that my lorde of Norffolk was come downe with no such company as was reported but only with a trayne mete for a duke to come with. & to pacifie the country wherefore this exa^t willed theym to departe from Scarborough & go every man home. Which letter he sent by a servant of his called John Corte to the said Wyvel & his company. And saith that he had learned the said tydings of the parliament & coronacion by a letter which Sir Robert Constable had sent to yong Sir Marmaduke Constable & brought to this exa^t by a servant of Sir Robert Lacyes. After which letter sent this exa^t bicause he wolde be from the commons whereby they shulde have the lesse occasion to rise agein seing they promised bifore not to rise except this exa^t wolde commaunde theym went to yorke and there heringe that my Lorde Mayor had a commaundement to attache " (attack) " this exa^t or some of his servants, on the morowe after he cam thether he sent for Sir Oswalde Wolse-thorpe, which came to this exa^{ts} lodging to one becks wifs house. And there the said Sir Oswalde bade this exa^t wel-come. to whome answered this exa^t. if I be welcome unto you I wote not whether I be welcome to all other. for I am informed my Lorde mayor hath a commaundement to attache me or any of my servants. And for that it maye be perceaved that I will not flee. I well remayne still here to see what wolbe layde to my charge. Where as I was pur-posed bifore to goo to my Lorde of Norfolk. And so this ex^t taried & went up & downe in the towne two or thre dayes together. Then my lady his mother sent for hym. for she had not seen hym long bifore. And so this exa^t went to her to my lorde Scropes house at Bolton. And there taried but one daye and showed my lord the maner of the commo-tion that bygod had feired & howe he was troubled there-with. & howe he wolde for feare of suspicion in that matier repare to yorke agen. & on the morowe so he did. & there taried a daye. Than on the next morowe this ex^t thought to go to his owne house for a season. And lying at Stam-forde Bridge in the weye homewarde that night cam a servant of this exa^t with a letter from Sir Oswalde Wolsethorpe ad-vysing this exa^t to retorne backe to yorke agen/ And so this exa^t did the same night without any taring. And so this exa^t kept company with hym till suche tyme as he was attached by the said Sir Oswalde Wolsethorpe & afterwarde he was brought to my lorde of Norfolk to whome he tolde all. the promisses in effect.

"To the rest of tharticles. he saieth. that the same daye that bygod was departed from this ex^t & his company he harde the commons saye among theym. Blessed was the daye that Sir Frances Bygod/ Rauf Fenton/ John Halom/ & the frier of Saint Roberts mett together for and if they had not sett their hedds together this matier had never ben bulted out.

"Also he saieth that he being at olde Sir Rauf Yvers house he harde Sir George Conyers saye that Boynton had a boke or a copie of a boke that Sir Frances bygod had made to feire & move the people to an Insurrection.

"Than being further ex^d what moved my lorde his father to go from his owne house first to Newcastell. saith that my said Lorde was a hunting of the hare about thile cam one of his owne servants with worde from Sir Thomas Hilton that the busshop of Duresme was fledde from Awklande at midnight before. And therfore the said Sir Thomas Hilton willed hym as he regarded his honor & savegarde of his substance that he shulde remove & gete hym to some sure place for feare of the commons leste he shulde be taken of them. Than he seing that the strongest house that he knewe was the Maison Dieu at newe castell went immediately to his house & packed up his plate and juells. & gate hymself to Lumley Castell that night & sent this ex^t by night to newcastell with his plate. & on the morowe cam thether hymself. & there taried two dayes. till Sir Thomas Hilton came thether." (In margin: "Whan examined what moved his father seing the town was then in quietnes to feare any commotion there & to departe thens, saith that") "Sir Thomas Hilton sent ii of his servants about the towne to serche the myndes of the commons which reported that theyr myndes were if the other commons cam thether not to withstande theym. Saing to theym that had layd the goones on the walls. that they might laye the goones where they wolde but they wolde torne theym whan the commons cam whether they wolde. And thereupon by the suasion of the said Sir Thomas Hilton his father departed out of New-

castell, to Sir Thomas Hiltons house. & further he knoweth
not what they did nor what they intended to doo further:
nor had any other convention or consultation with theym
nor sawe not his father till he sawe hym on the hethe before
Doncaster.

"Also exa^d whether he rec. any letters or private message from his father or any other to come to yorke. saith No.
but one of the speciallest causes that moved hym to go thether was that his wif had promised that by the same daye at
the furthest this exa^t shulde come home, for they had thret-
ened els to spoyle his house, & bicause he wolde shewe
hym self that he was gone home he went thether than as
he saieth

"Also examined why did he not sende his servant/ to the
company assembled beside Setterington where he met with
bygod as he was ones mynded. saith bicause he thought
he shulde doo more good hymself with theym to bring theym
to a staye than he thought his servant coulde doo/ if they
were sett upon any ill purpose.

"Further exa^d for what cause said he that Sir Thomas
Percy was the locke/ keys and wardes of this matier: saith
bicause he harde people saye. whan he moved theym to rise
at no mans calling but at his. that they wolde rise at no
mans but othre" (either) "at his calling or Sir Thomas
Percyes. And ryding to my lorde Scropes house harde the
people bente about those quarters specially in a towne wher
as he bayted betwyxt yorke and bolton castell, that the
countrey there was redy to rise agen if Sir Thomas Percy
wolde have sett forwarde for they trusted hym bifore any
other man. And thirdely the said letter that bygod sent
to myne olde lady of Northumbreland which he thought
she wolde sende to the said Sir Thomas Percy/ made this
ex^t believe that the same wolde feire hym ther rather to
come forwarde. And fourthely bicause at the first insurrection the people were more glad to rise with hym than with
any other, & there proclaymed hym twyes a lorde Percy:
and showed suche affection towardes him as they showed
towards none other man that he knewe.

"And bicause he was the best of the Percyes that were

lefte next to my lorde of Northumberland. & no other
causes saith he that moved to saye so of Sir Thomas
Percye.

" And he appercenyinge the peoples myndes muche in-
clyned towarde hym for the causes above rehersed therefore he said so of hym. bicause he wolde have hym the
rather stayed to thintent that no further insurrection shulde
be feared hereafter."

(Endorsed) " Thansweres of G. Lumley."

There is a series of three papers in the Record Office
with alterations in Thomas Cromwell's hand, the first being
endorsed, " The names of the lords for the arraignment of
the Northern."

They were as follows:
" My lord Marquis of Exeter
" Therle of Oxenford
" Therle of Shrewsbury
" Therle of Sussex
" Therle of Rutland
" * Therle of Wiltshire *
" * Therle of Essex *
" The Visconte Beauchamp

" The lord Cobham
" The Lord Wyndesore
" The lord Mordaunt
" The lord Borough
" The lord Clynton *
" * The lord Matravers
" The lord Morley *
" * The lord Lawarre *
" * The lord Dacres of the South." *

The second is a list of the prisoners and is headed:
" Tuesday
" The lorde Husseye
" Thomas Darcy late of Tempylhurst in co. York, knight.
" Robert Constable ,, Flamburgh ,, ,, ,, ,,
" Francis Bigot ,, ,, Sedryngton ,, ,, ,, ,,

This was indeed a truly noble oath, and if carried out ever so imperfectly, the men who took it must have felt constrained to act up to a higher standard than was, or for that matter is, realized by ordinary men.

Lord and Lady Lumley were at the coronation, he attending among the barons, and she, Jane, the elder daughter and co-heiress of the clever and unscrupulous Earl of Arundel, being one of the six principal ladies that sat in the third chariot of state, dressed in crimson velvet, next to whom rode ten ladies in crimson velvet, their horses trapped with the same. The only chariots at the beginning of the sixteenth century were horse-litters, and were not used except for purposes of state and for the sick and aged. During the reign of Mary they were slightly improved, but even then were like huge timber arks without springs. The coach was introduced into England by William Bomen, a Dutchman, who was Queen Elizabeth's coachman in the year 1564.

Lord Lumley was among those who attended the Prince of Spain at his marriage at Winchester on July 25th, 1554; and on April 24th, 1556, he and Lord Talbot introduced Osep Napea, ambassador from the Emperor of Russia, to his audience of leave of the Queen, who brought several rich presents from his master, and concluded a treaty of amity and commerce; being the first ambassador who came here from that court. In 1558 and later he is mentioned as one of those members of the Council in the north who were "not bounden to attendance."

From the family records we only hear of John, Lord Lumley, as devoting his leisure to the improvement and beautifying of his noble castle in County Durham, and collecting the records of his family from all known sources to which he could have procured access. It was in his time that the Red Book was written and all the other valuable MS. books now in Lord Scarbrough's possession. But there was a darker side to the picture. In 1557 the second wife of the Earl of Arundel died, and Lord and Lady Lumley came to live with him at Nonsuch. The Earl had a very bad influence on his more upright but weaker son-in-law, and implicated him in many intrigues connected mainly with Mary, Queen of Scots. The greater number of the following extracts are taken from Mr. Hume's edition of the Spanish State Papers of this time, most of them being the letters from the Spanish Ambassador in London to his master, the King of Spain, and the answers. These have mostly been lately discovered in Simancas, and a great many of the originals are in cipher. They reveal a terrible undercurrent of intrigue. The first quoted is from Don Gomez Suarez de Figueroa, Count de Feria, who had accompanied Philip when he came to be married to Queen Mary and had settled in London, and is dated December 29th, 1558: "The Earl of Arundel has been going about in high glee for some time and is very smart. He has given Jewels worth 2,000 crowns to the women who surround the Queen and his son-in-law Lord Lumley has been very confidential with her. I was rather disturbed at this for a time as an Italian merchant, from whom he has borrowed large sums of money, told others here that he heard that he was to marry the Queen, but I did not lose hope *as the Earl is a flighty man, of small ability.*"

Lord Lumley is mentioned as having been present on January 12th, 1561, when Shane O'Neill gave his submission to the Queen, which was to the following effect:

"O my most drad soveraine lady and Queene, lyke as I Shane Oneill your Ma^{ts} subiect of your Realme of Ireland have of long tyme desyred to com into the presence of yor Ma^t, to acknowledge my humble and bounden subiection: So am I now heere upon my kneese by your gratious permission, and do most humbly acknowledge your Matie to be my souverayne Lady and Queene of England France & Ireland. And do confesse that for lacke of civill educacion I have offendid your Matie and your lawes. for the wch I have requyred and obteyned your Ma^{ts} pardone. And for that, I most humbly from the bottome of my harte thanke your Ma^{te} and still do w^t all humblenesse requyre the contynuance of the same. And I faithfully promesse here before almighty god" (hole) "Matie and in the presence of all these your nobles, that I entend by gods grace, to lyve hereafter in the obedience of your Ma^te, as a subiect of your land of Ireland or eny of my predecessowers have or ought to do. And because my speeche being Irishe, is not well understood, I both caused this my submission to be writen in Englishe and Irishe. And therto have sette my hand and Seale. And to these gentlemen my kynsemen and freends, I most humbly beeseech your Ma^te to be mercyfull and gratiouse lady.

(Signed)   "SHANE ONFILL."

After this we hear nothing more of Lord Lumley till August 6th, 1565, when Don Guzman de Silva, who had become Ambassador in January, 1563-4, wrote to the King as follows: "On the 29th I wrote to your Majesty that the Emperor's Ambassador was at Richmond with the Queen. When he was there the Earl of Arundel, who had also gone to take leave of the Queen on his departure for his estates at Arundel for a few days, invited him to see his house of Nonsuch before he left it, and to ask me to accompany him, as I had already promised to go. He answered that he should be pleased to do so if his engagements allowed him, and if not that I would go. The Ambassador found he could not spare the time, and I accordingly went on the 31st. The house is excellently embellished and fitted and has beautiful gardens. The Earl has brought water thither which King Henry could not find. As soon as I got there Sidney arrived, and as the Earl was somewhat troubled with gout, one of his sons-in-law called Lumley, and Sidney took me over the house and gardens, etc." This is all in cipher.

On November 5th, Guzman de Silva writes to the King: ". . . On the night before his departure from London the Earl of Arundel invited the Swede" (the King of Sweden's sister) "and all the Court to supper, and even the Queen was to go uninvited as she sometimes does out of compliment, but she was unwell. The Earl begged me to attend the feast and told me that nothing could be done in the matter of commerce with Flanders even if the Conference

met again. He assured me that if your Majesty desired a
satisfactory solution to be arrived at the way would be to
send to me some person from the State who was well informed on the business, and let me arrange the affair with
them. Nothing could be done otherwise, as the changes
here were so continual that by the time answers came to the
instructions sent to the representatives something new occurred. I really believe that the Earl wishes to see the
question settled, and have no doubt of his desire to serve
your Majesty and maintain the Kingdom in its old friendship, as all the principal men understand that such a course
is the most advantageous to them. The decision adopted,
as I wrote your Majesty, to send a person to negotiate with
that Queen [of Scots] is confirmed, and they have appointed
Lord Lumley, who is married to a daughter of the Earl of
Arundel. He is a very worthy gentleman, a good Catholic,
and a devoted adherent to your Majesty, as indeed are all
good people in the Realm. The appointment has not yet
been announced, unless it was done after I left."

On January 28th, 1565-6 he writes that he has been trying to persuade Elizabeth "to make terms with her cousin
and neighbour and live in amity with the Scots. . . . She
said she felt sure peace would be settled, and she had appointed representatives with that object who would meet at
Berwick those who had been nominated by the Scotch
Queen. This is true, as the Queen has appointed the Earl
of Bedford, who is governor there, and another person who
is on the frontier with him, and Lord Lumley's mission has
therefore been suspended, although he was ready to start.
They tell me that the cause of this was that Lumley is
looked upon as a Catholic, as he is, and they would not trust
him."

On February 4th he writes : " The earl of Arundel is
still arranging for his departure for Italy. He is going to
take the baths and has the Queen's permission, although
many think that when he is really about to leave the permission will be withdrawn. His son-in-law, Lord Lumley,
came to visit me (he who was to go to Scotland, a devout
Catholic and a worthy gentleman) and said that the Earl

offer them future remuneration and reward. Their importunity was such that Lumley, thinking perhaps that Suygo
had not pressed the matter sufficiently, sent me a note signed
with his own hand, saying as follows" (translated from the
Latin): " I beg your lordship that you will believe this our
friend, Juan Suygo, in these our businesses which I have
entrusted to him as thine own *Lumley*.

" Suygo dwelt upon the great expenditure that these
gentlemen had to keep up, and said that if I would advance
them a sum of money, the Duke, the Earl, and Lumley
would jointly bind themselves by ordinance to repay it, so
that I might be the more secure, and he begged me to send
him an answer in my own handwriting. In conformity with
the Duke's orders I answered as follows : ' Illustrious Lord,
I have faith in Juan Suygo in the name of your lordship
and promise liberal rewards for the work, but nothing can
be done till it is concluded.' "

Further on in the same letter he says : " Suygo, also, from
Lord Lumley has returned me the note I gave him, and has
received back his own from me. These gentlemen are much
grieved not to have received a sum of money at once, and
it seems to have cooled them somewhat, though I keep
them in hand with promises as best I can. This does not
satisfy them, however."

On May 23rd he writes: " The duke of Norfolk has not
hitherto shown himself a Catholic and seems to belong to
the Augustinian creed, but both Arundel and Lumley, the
brother-in-law of the Duke, believe that they will convert
him."

Later in June this year 6,000 crowns were sent by the
Duke of Alva to be given to Arundel, Lumley and Norfolk
to promote disaffection, but they were wasted, as the plot
failed through Leicester's treachery and Cecil's vigilance.
The Council wished to marry the Queen of Scots to the
Duke of Norfolk, but early in September Queen Elizabeth
vetoed this project. On September 27th the Duke of Norfolk
raised his standard, the result of which will be seen in the
next letters.

September 30th. " When the earls of Pembroke and

Arundel and Lord Lumley arrived at Windsor, they were very warmly welcomed by the Queen, but when they got to their lodgings they were ordered not to leave them without the Queen's permission. This has caused great consternation in the country, and everyone casts the blame on to Secretary Cecil, who conducts these affairs with great astuteness."

October 8th. "On the 30th ultimo I sent Medina, a Spaniard, to the duke of Alba with letters for your Majesty, advising fully that Arundel, Pembroke and Lumley were detained by the Queen at Windsor. They were judicially interrogated by Cecil and four other commissioners as to who had initiated the plan of marrying the queen of Scotland to the duke of Norfolk, and they replied jointly that it was the unanimous wish of all the Council. The interrogation was mostly directed to inculpate the queen of Scotland, but they all rightly exonerated her, although the commissioners showed great desire to blame her, and passionate words passed between the prisoners and them. In the meantime couriers and protests were being constantly despatched by the Queen to the duke of Norfolk urging him unceasingly to come into her presence. The Duke, either to avoid the first fury falling upon his own head, or with the idea that his friends were not yet ready, or else, as he himself says, to avert the evident peril of the queen of Scotland, who is in the hands of her enemies, or possibly confiding in the great promises made by Leicester, to the effect that if he would pacify the Queen by a show of obedience all his adversaries would promptly be overcome, and perhaps the road to his own marriage thrown open, has abandoned, for the present, his attempts at revolt, and returned with a few horse, and the gentlemen who accompanied him, to the house of Thomas Selliger three miles from the Court, where nearly all his servants took leave of him and where he is now detained. He has been interrogated like the others. The prisoners expect to be free shortly, and to take possession of the Court, although Cecil and the Lord Keeper, his brother-in-law, do not agree with the rest and want to send them to the Tower.

" The friends of the prisoners, who are the earls of North-umberland, Westmoreland, Cumberland, Derby, and many others, all Catholics, are much grieved at this cowardice, if such it can be called, of the duke of Norfolk, and they have sent Northumberland's servant, who spoke to me before on this matter, to say that they will by armed force release the Queen and take possession of the north country, restoring the Catholic religion in this country and effecting a general restitution of the goods of your Majesty's subjects within a year."

October 14th. " Having an opportunity by this ship to St. Jean de Luz I have despatched the present letter. They brought the duke of Norfolk to the Tower on the 11th inst. He was very foolish, they think here, to return to Court after having left it against the Queen's will. He never thought to come to his present pass, and upbraids himself for having believed the letters of Leicester and Cecil. The councillors are puzzled to know what to do with Arundel, Pembroke, and Lumley, who did no more than the rest of the Council in approving of the marriage of the queen of Scotland with an Englishman, and subsequently approving of Norfolk himself. They are afraid that if they let them go the disturbance will be all the greater."

October 23rd. " The duke of Norfolk is still in the Tower. The Earls of Arundel and Pembroke, Lord Lumley and Nicholas Throgmorton, are prisoners at the Court, or near to it, and the queen of Scotland is in the castle of Tutbury, guarded by the earls of Huntingdon and Shrewsbury.

" The earl of Northumberland's servant returned last night to assure me that, whenever your Majesty wished, they would release the queen of Scotland, would marry her to your Majesty's liking, and try to restore the Catholic religion in this country. They only want to be favoured by your Majesty."

Antonia de Guaras, who wrote the next letter to Albornoz, the secretary of the Duke of Alva, had been sent over by the Duke as one of the commissioners to settle the com-mercial quarrel between England and Spain. October 24th, 1569. " It is said the duke [of Norfolk] is so closely guarded that he is not allowed to leave the one room in which he is, and that he is only served by a single page in the Tower. His relatives and friends are greatly scandalised. It is believed for certain that they will take Lord Lumley to the Tower, and they have moved the earl of Arundel to another house, where he is guarded by a gentleman. Pembroke is in no more liberty than before."

On November 20th Guerau de Spes writes to the King: "Most of the pensioners left the palace to-night, and it is believed that they are going to join the revolted Catholics. The duke of Norfolk is guarded closely. The earl of Pembroke has given a thousand pounds to a favourite of the Queen, and left his two sons as hostages, and has therefore been set at liberty. He is now at his house, on the road to Wales, but Arundel and Lumley are guarded as before."

On December 26th, 1569, the King writes to Guerau de Spes: "On the 21st ultimo your letters of 27th and 30th September, 8th, 14th and 24th October, and 11th instant were received together. . . . I am much annoyed by the imprisonment of the duke of Norfolk, the earls of Arundel and Pembroke, and Lord Lumley, because as there are several of them and they will certainly be closely pressed, they will be sure to reveal the object that they had in view as to the marriage of the Queen of Scotland, and the whole business will fail, and even probably, their own safety be endangered."

On February 25th, 1569-70, Guerau de Spes writes to the King: "On the 21st instant I received your Majesty's letter of the 26th December, to which this is a reply. . . . The depositions and interrogatories administered to the duke of Norfolk, the earls of Arundel and Pembroke and Lumley will, I am informed by their agents, give but little proof of their intentions to the Council, as they were extremely cautious in the answers they gave."

On March 21st he writes: "Lord Lumley sends to say that if the English in Scotland can re-form the army they had and push on, friends will not be lacking here."

There is no notice anywhere of Lord Lumley's release

the Duke made all submission; but, as these last letters show, he was still unfaithful to his Queen, and at once joined in what is known as the Ridolfi Conspiracy. Roberto Ridolfi was a Florentine merchant, through whom a traitorous correspondence was carried on between the Duke, the Queen of Scots, the Pope, and the King of Spain; but in May Charles Baily, servant to the Bishop of Ross, who was always a partisan of Mary, was captured as he was coming from Ridolfi in Brussels with letters in cypher, among others two for Lumley and Norfolk addressed to 30 and 40. This is what is referred to in the following letters, all from Don Guerau de Spes to the King of Spain:

May 9th, 1571. ". . . In consequence of the capture of the Bishop of Ross's servant and the discovery of his cypher letters, they have put him to the torture, although lightly as yet. He is in the Tower, and the suspicions they have thus conceived have caused them to dismiss nearly all the queen of Scotland's servants, and she is strictly guarded, although, even in her guard, she has some good friends."

July 12th. "There is no doubt at all that Ridolfi's affair is serious, both on his own account and also because of the queen of Scots, the duke of Norfolk, earl of Arundel, and Lord Lumley, being concerned therein."

September 7th. ". . . A servant of mine has just come in saying that he has met the duke of Norfolk in the street being taken to the Tower with two or three gentlemen guarding him secretly."

September 29th. "Lord Lumley was sent to the Tower yesterday from Richmond, where the Court is, and the earl of Arundel was ordered to remain under arrest at Nonsuch. It is said that the same course will be taken with Lord Montague."

May 24th, 1572. "It is generally asserted that when Parliament closes the duke of Norfolk will be executed. The Bishop of Ross, the Queen of Scotland's ambassador, the earl of Southampton, son-in-law of Lord Montague, two sons of Lord Derby, and Lord Lumley, son-in-law of the earl of Arundel, are still in prison, the earl of Arundel himself being under arrest in his own house, and Lord Cobham under guard at Burleigh House. Thomas Cobham, brother of Lord Cobham, is in the Tower with thirty other gentlemen of high position, all of them for being concerned with the queen of Scots and the duke of Norfolk. The queen of Scots is being guarded very closely in a castle eighty miles from here by the Earl of Shrewsbury and Sadler of the Council."

The Duke of Norfolk was executed on June 2nd, but the others remained in captivity throughout the year.

On December 22nd Don Guzman writes : " The Earl of Arundel has been released, and, it is said, he will go to Court and fulfil his office as Lord Steward. There are good hopes, too, of his son-in-law, Lord Lumley, and of the Earl of Southampton." There are few letters extant written during 1573 and 1574, so that we have no means of learning how soon these hopes were fulfilled.

The Earl of Arundel was also the cause of the money difficulties into which Lord Lumley fell. Among the papers at Sandbeck are many referring to these matters. Thus on February 28th, 1554-5, an indenture was drawn up between "the right honorable Henry Erle of Arrundell lord stuard of our said sovereigne lord and lady the kyng and Quenis most honorable howsshold and lord president of their most honorable privy councell . . . on thon parte and thonorable John Lord Lumley on thother parte," by which Lord Lumley promises to suffer a recovery before Ascension Day of his lands in the " Mannors of Ile Bradbery Croke otherwise called Stokerle Croke Freresed otherwise called Frerehowsel Axwell howses otherwise called Axcheles Swallwells Ludworth Bradley Castell and the Mannors of little lumley gret Lumley Beautreby otherwise called Bitterby Stranton Seton otherwise called Seton Carrowe Bolom Heseldon Moreton and Howffeld." Lord Arundel's lands lay partly in Gloucestershire, and on October 14th, 1560, Lord Lumley let to Thos. Stoughton some in Woodchester, Gloucestershire, which had been conveyed to him by the Earl of Arundel on January 9th, 1559 ; and on October 16th in the same year Lord Arundel, Lord Lumley and Jane his wife, sold for £40 lands at Upton St. Leonard's, Gloucestershire. On August 16th, 1561, Lord Lumley let his manors of Seton, Stranton, Newborne, etc., etc., and Lumley Parke to Sir Thomas Pallmer for eight years in order to pay the Earl's debts, of which an account is inclosed in the deed:

" Debts of the right honourable the Earle of Arundells appointed to be payed yearely of the lord Lumleys lands demised by the Indenture annexed to this Schedule at the feasts of the birth of our lord god and the Natyvitie of Sainct John Baptist,

" First to Philipp Gunter of london upholster £800

" which is to be payed in eight yeares by £100 by the yeare.

" Item to William Albany of london merchaunte taylor the somme of £750

" which is to be payed in seven yeares and a half by £100 by the yeare.

" Item to Albert Demorary merchaunte £450

" which is to be payed in foure yeares and a half by one hundred pounds by the yeare."

These difficulties were increased by the "Florentines debt" of which the MS. books at Sandbeck belonging to this period are full. The following account of the debt is among the papers at the Record Office. It is docketed " 10th November 1570. The Erle of Arundel L. Lumley's case:

" The debte was £xi^{m}ccxlv. xvi^{s} viii^{d} and was owing to King Henry the VIIIth by the Florentynes to be paid by £v^{c} a yeare, wch remaineth unpaid sithenc the 37° of Henrye the VIIIth at wch time the debt began. The debt was such as Lodge and dyvers others refuced to compound for/ and offerid to the Florantynes and dyvers others, yeat non wold take it.

" My lorde and I did take it being in maner a desprat debte and paid therof in hande to hir M^{atie} £m and bonde landes for the paim^{t} of the residewe therof to be paid by £vii^{c}lxxi. xvii^{s} vi^{d} by the yeare, wch is a great and two great a paim^{t} considering this harde recoverye on comyng by that wch is thereof to be hade and recovered/

" My lorde is nowe also to sell lands for the paym^{t} of his debte and to settell the remaynder of his L. Lands in his

posterytie, wch to do he is greatly letted by reason sundrye
of his manors to the yearly valewe of £viii^c are tyede for the
paim^t thereof/ of wch dyvers of them were more convenient
to be soulde then those wch by reason of that incombranc he
shalbe enforcid to sell. Besides that these lands and bonds
therefrom depending as they doo men are lothe to deale wth
his L. to geve the somes of money he might otherwise make
of his Lands.

"Thenheritanc of that £viii^c a yeare also dependyth in
that eastat as it now standyth as my L. can in noe wyse
lymitt thenheritanc thereof according as he purposith till the
last money be paid wch is a great inconvenienc to his L. and
by that meanes shall desende to such as neither standith wth
the meaning of my lord nor of me namely to my colaterall
heyres.

"Itt may in respect of theis causes and of hir M^{aties} good
disposicion towards my lord and me to ease us both in this
case wth reson shall please hir M^{atie} by remitting of the
same, which shalbe acknowledged by us for a great rewarde
to us both and I for my p^t shalbe content to receave itt in
lewe of that honourable graunt y^t hit hath allready pleased
hir M^{atie} to graunt me at my Lorde of Leycesters desire
and yours for the fee simple of C marks land or otherwise at
hir M^{atis} good pleasure to remite such p^t thereof as shall
please hir M^{atie} & to take new assuranc competent for y^e
matter and to geve som reasonable tym for the paim^t of so
moch as hir M^{atie} shall not determyn to remitte."

Next year they were obliged to forfeit some of their land,
as they thought, unjustly. This will be seen by the following
paper, undated, but placed among those of 1571 :

" My Lord of Arundell. 1567 " (that being the first year
mentioned).

" My L. Lumley the xxth of Maie 1567 borowed of Alderman Jackman and Alderman Lambert the somme of £xiii^c
payable the xxth of Maie 1568. For wch his L. laide in gage
to the saide Aldermen the Mannors of Wonworth, Wollav-
yngton, Esthampnet, Bynderton and Erthham, beinge in the
hole of the yerely value of £lxvi. xvi^s xi$\frac{1}{2}$^{d} beinge late parcell
of the possessions of the right honorable Therle of Arrundell

the same money to be repaide the xxth of Maye 1568. upon payne of forfeyture of the saide Mannors./

"The xith daie of July followinge the saide Lord Lumley in like maner did borowe of the saide Aldermen £vi^c for which he did then in like maner delyver the Mannors of Northstoke and Southstoke beinge also sometyme parcell of the possessions of the Earle of Arrundell and of the yerely value of £xxxi. ii^s ii^d the same money repayable in the xth of July 1568 upon peyne of forfeyture./

"Afore the saide severall daies of payment Lambert dyed. Jackman survived and at the saide daies Jackman beinge paide his money and books drawen for the delyverie back of the lande agayne Jackman did furder agree to lend unto my L. Lumley agayne the saide severall sommes, the sayde £vi^c to be repayed the xvth of Marche in A° XI^{mo} of our now queen Elizabeth. And the saide £xiii^c to be repayed the xxth of April 1569 and to take for his assuraunce the lands wch he before had and his recompance for the forbearinge for that time beinge paide him/ And so was it concluded and agreed, and he was paide accordingly. And avoydinge of furder trouble and charge kept that lande makinge a newe defeisunce for the payment of the money at those daies wch defeisunce is extant/

"The daies come on and the saide Erle of Arrundell and L. Lumley sent commissioners into Sussex Hampshire and Wales to make money for his payment and others. Before whose returne the daies expyred and the saide Jackman nevertheles by entreatie of fryndes was contented to tarrye their retorne for his money and sone after their returne Thomas Stoughton one of the saide Commyssioners who brought the report of their doyngs, fell sick at Arrundell howse in London, to whome resorted the saide Jackman, and there on the behalfe of the saide Erle and Lorde Lumley the said Jackman agreed wth him to forbeare his monye till the ende of Michaelmas terme then next ensuynge, wherewth the saide Jackman departed from the saide Thomas Stoughton contented to forbeare till that tyme as afore, And within fewe daies after dyed./ And soone after that, the saide Erle and lorde Lumley were comytted to close and safe kepinge,

so as none could have accesse to them for conference touchinge their affares./

"In the meane tyme the saide Thomas Stoughton speak-
inge with somme of thexecutors they were contented the
money beinge paide to have taken it accordinge to the agre-
ment of the saide Jackman and to have done anything in
them was to doe for the restoringe the saide landes and
byndinge themselves to any inconvenyence./

"Memorandum to prove that Jackman never ment to
have the lande. He never entred all that tyme neither pri-
vately nor openly, he never toke any penye proffitt thereof,
wch he used not where be bought lande or landes forfeyted
that he ment to enioye./ It is also confessed by dyvers of
thexecutors that they think and dare take on them that he
never ment to have the lande./

"And so out of doubt will suche of his companye of the
Aldermen saie, that knewe his dealinge, It wilbe proved
that he saide dyvers tymes he wold none of their Lordships
landes nor no landes of that tenure./././

"It will also be proved that he saide what shall I doe w^{th}
this lande for I knowe if I shuld have it my L. will never
love me ne lett me have it wth their good will, it lyeth so
nere the Castell of Arrundell, therfore lett me have my
money wth good will, or some lande that I can agree for not
holden in Capite.

"Also it is to be remembred that if the said Lords had
ben determyned the said Jackman shuld have had those
landes, they wold not the first tyme have redemed them and
paied derely for them./././

"The saide Erle was holpen in this case folowinge in Kinge
Edwards tyme viz, being in the Tower and lande beinge
morgaged by him discended to one Infant by order from
the Kings privie Counsell the B. then beinge Chauncellor,
and Justice Mountague and Justice Hales and the Kings
Councell lerned appoynted to devise wth his L. Counsell for
his L. releif in that cause and it was don././

"It is to be considered that the saide Lords ment not to departe" (part) "wth this lande to Jackman at this price, for the
yerely value of the hole is £iiii^{xx}xvii xviii^s i½^d" (£97 18s. 1½d.)

"besides that there is a parke upon it not valued, worth
£xx per annum to be letten. Moreover it is of his owne
auncyent enherytunce not improved. And this money is
but xix yeares purchase and fortie pounds over.

" The saide Jackman was also never bounde to paie any
better price for it, if it were to him forfeyted/ wᶜʰ shuld
have bene if there had ben any meanynge he shuld have
had it."

The next paper, dated November 4th, 1574, is the
account of the Florentines' debt already referred to :

" The debte of the lord Lumley and howe it grewe to
kinge Henrie theight howe muche thereof is paid by his L.
howe muche is unpaid and what assuraunce the Quenes
Mᵃᵗⁱᵉ hath for the same.

" The state of the Cittie of Florence became bounden by
theire publike instrument bearinge date the last of August
1526 to pay to the kings Mᵃᵗⁱᵉ in london the somme of
£xiᵐccl of lawfull englishe money for the debt of John Cal-
vacaunt, Peter Frauncs de Barde Anthony Carsidonia and
other merchaunts of Florence in twentie and five yeres
next followinge which was due to the kings highnes by the
said marchaunts by theire obligacons but for what cause
those obligacons were taken this Remembrauncer cannot
presently finde   £xiᵐccl.
The said state off Florence by theire instrument publike
dated the eight of August 1545 became bound to the kings
maiestie to paie lx thowsand ducketts or Florencs in thertie
yeres next followinge which one Antonio Giudotto Cittizen
of Florence and his Father in lawe did owe to his highnes
and were not able to paie without the healpe of the said
state of Florence whereuppon the same state in consideracon
of xiiᵐviᶜlxvi ducketts and two third parts of a duckett paid
to theire use by the kinge became bounden to paie the same
lx thowsand ducketts as aforesaid which amounted in Cur-
raunte money of Englande to   £xvᵐ.
                    Sum totlie £xxviᵐccl.
                                                    whereof
There was paied and dischardged in the times of kinge

Henrie theight kinge Edward the sixte and Quene Marie the somme of £xiii^m ix^c.

And

so remained due to oure soveraigne ladie the Quenes Maiestie that nowe is the somme of £xii^m cccl.

which

were estalled unto the said L. Lumley by Indenture dated the first of June in the sixth year of our lady Queen Elizabeth to be paid viz at or before the feast of all saints 1564 £vii^c lxxi. xvii^s vi^d and so yerely untill the hole should be paid uppon thassuraunce hereafter menconed.

"According to which estallment there hath ben due to the Q. Matie before and at the feast of all saints 1573 the somme of £vii^m vii^c xviii. xv^s.

whereof

Paid by the Lorde Lumley £m.
And he is to be allowed for a pencon paid at Venice to Anthony Giudotto by kinge Edwards warraunte £mciiii. iii^s iiii^d.

So in solution and payment £mmciiii. iii^s iii^d.

And so

There remaineth due at daies past and yet unpaid by the L. Lumley the some of £v^m vi^c xiiii. xi^s viii^d

And that wilbe due at daies to come the some of £iiii^m vii^c xxx. viii^s iv^d

£x^m ccxlv. xvi^s viii^d (?)

And for the true payment hereof the right honourable Earle of Arrundell and the said L. Lumley acknoledged fynes and made assuraunce of lands of £viii^c by yere to the L. Treasourer Sir Richard Sackville and Sir Walter Myldmay knights and to their heires in this forme followinge viz. to thuse of the said L. Lumley and his heires untill suche time as he make defalte of paiement of any of the said sommes and if any suche defalt be made, Then the said L. Treasourer Sir Richard Sackville and Sir Walter Mildmay shalbe and stand seised thereof to theire owne uses to thintent they may receave and levie the proffitts thereof untill the said L. Lumley shall have paid all the money behind unpaid. And after the money so paid then to thuse of the said L. Lumley and his heirs as is afore said./

(Endorsed) " To the right honourable Mr. Walsingham one of her Ma^{ts} principall Secretaries and of hir Ma^{ts} most honourable privie Counsell."

Among the MS. books at Sandbeck are two giving an account of the Earl of Arundel's affairs. In 1574 the summary is as follows:

"Sum totall of the chardge" (rent and other receipts) " of the booke before apperinge is £3819.0.3¼. Sum totall of all the disburcements conteyned in the same, as before particulerly apperith is £3898.19.2½. And so layd oute more than the Chardge is £79.18.11¼."

In 1577 the deficit was £17 14s. 7½d. The Earl died on February 24th, 1580, having made his will on the previous December 30th, in which he appointed Lord Lumley his sole executor and residuary legatee, which, however, instead of at all improving his pecuniary embarrassments, only served to increase them, as the following paper will show :

" The Scute and Case of the L. Lumley and of the Lands of the Earle of Arrundell at the tyme of his Deathe.

" First all the Landes of the said Earle at the tyme of his death weare aboute the vallewe of nyneteen hundred Pounds by the Yeare/

"Whereof assured to my L. of Surrey lands to the value of seven hundred pounds by the yeare/

" And to her ^{matie} Lands to the vallue of £xxxii by the yeare.

"The Residue beinge of the vallue of twelve hundred pounds by the yeare is conveighed to the L. Lumley.

" The lands conveighed to my L. of Surrey for his porcion cometh to hym wthout burden or charge of paym^t of anny debts funeralles or other Legacies.

" The land conveighed to the L. Lumley standeth charged with the paym^t of xi thousand pounds to her ^{matie} for the florentines Debt.

" Also it appeared uppon the takinge upp of the Reckoninge of my L. of Arrundell his debts due to other persons

by my L. Chauncellor that now is and Mr. Solicitor that
now is that the same debt did amounte unto the sume of
xiii thousand pounds and more/ the wch sume is also to be
answered out of the L. Lumley's Porcion.

"Also it is well knowen that the L. Lumley hath departed
with £vi^c land of old Rent for other causes of his L.,
the wch land at this daie is worth £xii^c of yearly Rent
improved.

"It is well knowen that the £xii^c Land wch the L. Lumley
is to have is not farder to be improved other then by Dis-
parkinge of Parks.

"Addinge therunto the L. Lumley his spendinge of his
best yeares with the affection and love of the said Earle unto
his L. and so the consideracion of the £xii^c Land appeareth
wherby it is evident duringe the Q. ^{Maties} paym^{ts} wch will
continewe xiii yeares ther shall Rest unto the L. Lumley
not above £iiii^c by the yeare to lyve uppon and to answer
all the debts y^t are remayninge unpaid over and above the
Queens ^{Maties} Dewe.

"And hereunto is also to be added the charge of his L.
funeralls wch ought to be honorably donne wch wilbe to the
chardge of one thousand pounds at the lest, besides the
charge of the continuance of his L. house if any lye and
other Legacies.

"And farder is to be noted that the L. Lumley had never
any other advauncem^t or preferm^t in mariadge then this
before remembred. The L. Lumley his humble sute to her
^{Matie} is that itt woolde please her ^{Matie} to forbeare the halfe
yeres rent due at our lady daye next aswell of the lands
lyable to the paym^t of her ^{Matie} for the Florentines dett, as
also of the land allotted to the Erle of Surrey (which her
^{Matie} is to have for three yeres) wthout wch the sayde L.
Lumley shall have lyttel (or in effect nothinge) towards the
funeralls and to mayntenance of the house and kepyng of
the servaunts of the said Erle his father deceased or for the
payment of servants wags or legacies, according to his L.
laste will and testament.

"Also his L. farther petycion is that itt will please her
^{Matie} to make sum farther staye of her Highnes owne dett

afore sayde untyll other the detts of the saide Erle due to her Highnes poore subiects may be sattisfyed."

There is in the "Sussex Archaeological Collection," vol. xii., an account of the Earl's funeral, taken from the Dugdale MSS. in the Ashmolean Museum at Oxford, of which the following is a copy:

Ffirst, twoe conductors with black staves;
Then the LXVIII poore men in gownes ii and ii;
Then the Standard by Mr. Thomas Fewkner;
Then gents in blacke gownes ii & ii;

Then the Erle of Northumberland's gent;
Then Phillippe, Erle of Arundel, his gent;
Then the gent of the defunct;
Then the Councell learned in the Law;
Then Doctors of Physicke and other Doctors;
Then Chaplens.
Then the Constable of the Castle [Arundel];
Then the Steward, Treasurer & Comptroller;
Then the Buschop of Chichester
Then the Great Banner borne by Anthony Browne;
Then the Helmet & Crest;
Then the Sworde;
Then the Targe;
Then the Cote of Armes;
Then

Mr. Bellingham, Sir W. More, one banneroll,	Sir Thomas Palmer, Mr. Sheffield Assistants.
Mr. Willm Dawtrey, one banneroll	Mr. Pawlet,
Mr. A. Kemp. Sir R. Shelley one banneroll.	Mr. Anthony Browne, Son to the Viscount Montague
	Mr. Hy. Gorynge.

Philippe Earl of Arundel

Lord Lumley	Lord Buckurste
Lord La Warre	Sir Thos. Henage
Sir Thomas Palmer	Sir Thos. Browne

Then twoe Yoeman hushers;
Then all Yoemen in blacke;
Then the Mayor and Burgesses [of Arundel];
Then servants having no blacke.

Paid to heralds at the ffunerall, at the Castle Arundel, March 22nd, 1579-80,
    to Mr. Garter his fee and transportation,
Item, to Lancaster Herald, his fee and transportation from
    London to Arundel . . . . £6 13s. 4d.
Item, to Wyndsor Herauld for the same . . . . the same

Item, to Richmond Herauld for the same . . . . the same
Item, to Yorke Herauld for the same . . . . . the same
Item to the same Yorke Herauld for his coming before to
  prepare the hearse—
Item, for, and in consideration of the hearse, rayles, clothes, velvet pall,
  and all things in, and upon the same hearse, the some of

The omission of all the important sums paid is very disappointing.

CHAPTER VII

John, Lord Lumley's second wife, Elizabeth D'Arcy.—Letters from Lord Lumley to Mr. Hicks.—Death of Lord Lumley.—Portraits.—Learning of his first wife.—Death and will of his second wife.

LORD LUMLEY'S first wife died in 1577 and was buried at Cheam, where her husband erected a monument to her memory. In 1582 he married Elizabeth, sister to Thomas, Lord D'Arcy, and settled the Nonsuch estate on her by an Indenture of June 16th in that year; but this was later sold to the Queen, and in another Indenture of November 29th, 1594, the Manor of Stansted was settled on her instead. Lord Lumley, however, evidently stayed on for some time at Nonsuch as a tenant.

Unfortunately he was still corresponding with the friends of Mary, Queen of Scots, as can be seen by the two following letters, written by Thomas Morgan, one of the chief conspirators, to his mistress the Queen, from the Bastille:

"It may please yor M^{atie} perceaving the difficultie for the receyving of yor M^{aties} intelligence I thought good to putt my Lo: L: in remembrance of yor Ma^{ts} estate & my former familiarite wth him and so commended this packet unto his Care to make a conveyance to yor M^{atie} & w^t Care formed an Alphabet wth him to serve to intertayne good intelligence wth yor M^{atie} and wished him to send youre M^{atie} a copy of the same & encouraged him by all the meanes I could to this purpose for that he is hable & I hope willing to advance y^r Ma^{ty} Service wch I pray God may fall out to his glory & youre comfort, for the wch I shall alwaie pray in this captivitie of myne wch is all I can do for your M^{atie}. If the sayd Lo: make an intelligence wth yor M^{atie} I doubt not but your

Matie will so interteyne him by your Lres as he shalbe encouraged to serve your Matie. If he take the charge in hand
he wilbe hable to serve your Matie well and you shall fynd
him honorable & couragious, and his state is repayred since
the deathe of his father in lawe the old erle of Arrundell, If
he wryte to your Matie I pray you thank him for all his good
frendship towards me and lett him know that you be my
good & gracious lady & mistres wch is all the comfort that
I have in this Lyffe and indede comforteth me above all
worldly good as almightie God knoweth, to whose protection I commit your Matie/ Written in the place of my captivitie the XVth of December" (1585).

The second was written on October 5th, 1586: ". . .
And one point amongest many was y^t they shold by all
meanes labor to make your Hoste sure to your Matie & herein
I have delt wth my Lord Lumley verye earnestlye but I
have not yett receaved answer from him and others to
whome I wrote and if they resolve well yett the same may
be altered by my absence whereof God knoweth y^t I have
care as dutye doth binde me and the more for y^t I see the
decay in your service and y^t to be playne wth your Matie
men are drawne backe marvellowslye at home by the
tyrannye of the time and the hardenesse of Princes
abrode . . ."

On April 30th, 1597, an indenture was drawn up between
Lord Lumley and various parishioners of Chester-le-Street
witnessing: "That whereas the said Lord Lumley hath
caused to be erected within the parishe church of Chester
in the Streete aforesaid . . . two and twenty monuments or
thereabouts the which the said Lord Lumley earnestly de-
sireth may be preserved and kept and hopeth that there is
not any person of any godly or honest disposicon humor or
condicon that will offer to deface, distroye or take awaye
the same, Nowe this Indenture further witnesseth that the
said Lord Lumley for and in consideracon and to the intent
and purpose that the said two and twenty monuments or
thereabouts may be maynteyned preserved and kept safe
without spoyling or defacing And in consideracon that the
Clark of the said Church for the tyme being shalbe carefull

to sweepe and rubb the said monuments and to keepe the same faire and bewtifull and to thintent that the Vicar Curate or incombent of the said church for the time being shall call upon the said Clarcke for the performance and for the relief of the poore people of the said parishe hath given . . . unto the above one anuytie or yerely rent of 40 shillings . . . to be issewing owt of the mannor or lordshipp of great Lumley."

On June 1st of the same year Tobias (Matthew), Bishop of Durham, gave a licence to John, Lord Lumley, and Elizabeth his wife for liberty to grant to William Smithe and John Lambton "the Castle and park of Lumley, the manor of great Lumley, the fishery in the Weare and lands in Lumley, Great Lumley, Cold Hesilden, Chester in le Streete, Morton, Woostonhouse, Walridge, and Gateside alias Gateshead," but they were recovered on July 6th.

The following letter written "To my honourable good frend Sir Robert Cecyll Knight, chefe Secretory to her Maiestie" refers to Nonsuch : "Sir, I had well hoped my wyf shuld have delyvered unto yow my ryght hartyest thancks for yor frendlynes in my cause wh^{ch} I perseved by yor letter yow have used for me ; And being sory y^t it was her evell hapt to myss yow; I pray yow except" (accept) "them most frendly by this/ desyryng yor frendly remem-bringe to move my L. Tresorer for order of forberance of the rent for the tyme, The wch I desyer yow may be done as sone as convenyently yow may, I do here y^t ye do mete apon a comission this day, And therfor am the bolder to put yow now in mynd thereof./ So most hartely recommending yow to god, do leve farder to trouble yow/ this XVth No-vember 1599

"Your assured frend

"LUMLEY."

This request was evidently granted, as on December 22nd we have a note of a "Grant to Lord Lumley of the yearly rent of £222 reserved on his lease of the great park of Nonsuch during the remainder of his term of 21 years if he shall live so long."

It will be as well here to introduce two series of letters written by Lord Lumley. The first series is addressed to Mr., afterwards Sir Michael, Hicks (1543-1612), who was secretary to Lord Burghley, and also to his successor, Sir Robert Cecil. He is said in the "Dictionary of National Biography" to have "possessed much financial ability, and his personal friends sought his aid and counsel in their pecuniary difficulties," and this testimony is ably borne out in the tone of the following letters :

"Frend Hixe, yow shall perseve that I having hertofor made request to Mr. Secretory to accept Mr. Langley for his understuard of Edmonton, wch under his late good Mr., Mr Justis Otre dyd very well execut the same : do now fynd that Mr Secretory hath bestowed the same apon Mr Necton who is a man (as I take it) wyll wyllingly harken to eny reson from yow : wherefor yf I myght intreat yow for my sake to use some frendly means, that Mr. Necton may be compounded w^thall, so as Mr Lanley may styll wth Mr Secretory good favor contynew the place to his credit, having sundery years occupied the same : I shall thyncke my selfe much beholding unto yow therfor, And I am sur Mr Langley acknowledg yor kyndnes & frendship therin Thus yow see how bold I am wth yow, And therw^th byd yow most hartely far well, this 30 of Desember 1598

"yor assured frend
"LUMLEY.

"I doubt not but yor Gossipe wyll also thancke yow for eny favor yow shall show to this bearer."

The next is not in Lord Lumley's own handwriting, but is a copy made and inclosed by Mr. Langley :

"Good Mr. Hicks, I understande by Langley the bearer howe much for my sake he is beholdinge unto yow, I pray you still continew the same and both my self & yor Gossipp will take it verye kindlye att yor handes And I right frindlye to requite yor kindnes to you or anie of y^ors and therwith call Sr Geo: Frevill befo^r them, & sett downe, that the auncient Tenant may contynue wth possession, and Sr George to receyve such valewable consideration of money as ther Lo^p shall think fitting, wch will verie well content the petitioner, & tye him over to be thankfull, & make me in his behalf acknowledge the benefitt of yor kindnes, whereof not doubting, wth my best wishes unto you

From Nonsuch. June VIIth 1605

"yor assured Freinde

" LUMLEY."

There is a document of about the date 1601 docketed "A note of remembrance for the L. Lumley his debt to the Queen for which he offreth his house at Nonsuch." It is headed " The debte is about £11000 which is at £600 by yere And so riseth to XIX^{ten} yeres payment."

" If her M^{atie} be pleased to take my house at Nonesuch wch is more worth to be rated then will answere the same so shall her M^{atie} be paid in an instant, The memory of the Kinge her father continued, and for herselfe a place to withdrawe unto, and, during the time of her M^{aties} living there a savinge to her purse (as I have heard by her officers) nere a thowsand marks a moneth.

" Touching my parte of my land about y^t, I leave y^t to her M^{aties} own likinge to take or leave upon any reasonable recompence thought by my Lorde Threasurer or by any such as shall please her thereunto to appointe, But to pay her highnes out of my poore livinge £600 by yere, the sume not excedinge £8000 so shall her M^{atie} be 19 yeres in paiinge, I and my wief lefte in greate distres, the house enforced utterlie to decay, and so this burden to reste wholie upon me, the same growing by another man from whom I had reason to have expected a better fortune.

"This waie I have thought good to move, as well in payinge regard according to my dewtie to see her M^{atie} trulie satisfied of her dewe, as to covet to maintaine myself, to lyve in my elder daies in some reasonable sort to serve her highnes, as greatlie in troth I am bounde to doe.

" As touchinge the nature of the debtes and how the mass

thereof (being the Florentines debte,) was made by us from a doubtfull debte, somwhat I leave to yor owne good re-membraunce."

On June 21st, 1603, a warrant was drawn up to pay to Lord Lumley certain sums for keeping the house, park, etc., at Nonsuch; and on May 28th, 1605, a grant was made to Lord Lumley to preserve game and water-fowl within five miles round the manor of Nonsuch with assistance to William Richbell, keeper of the game there.

On September 21st in the latter year Ferdinando Malyn wrote the following letter to the Earl of Salisbury:

" Right Ho^{bl} Lord. Understanding that yor ho^r is a Com-missioner for the unparking againe of the old parke at Non-such where my dwelling is, and am tenant to halfe the sayd parke, I am bould to acquainte yor ho^r wth some hard measure like to be shewed unto me, hoping by yor ho^{rs} meanes onely to receive reliefe therein. I have of late bin so weakened by sicknes that I am not able to attend yor ho^r in person, as my desire is to doe, and therefore do humbly pray yor ho^r would vouchsafe to reade these few lines and my peticon hereinclosed, and to graunt your ho^{ll} direction and order therein unto this Bearer my sonne in law./ So it is my good Lord that about fower yeares sithence that I tooke in lease of the Lo. Lumley halfe the old parke at Nonesuch for divers yeares yet to come at the rente of £130 per annum, the same grownds being then rude and full of bushes and rootes, and without howses to dwell in, and hedges to keepe the same severall, And being perswaded by the unlikelyhod of unparking the same againe, seeing Nonesuch howse was of small receipt, and that there is a parke there already, did bestow at the least £300 in building howses and making the grownds fitt for tillage, whereby at this presente there may yearely arise uppon that old parke 1400 quarters of wheate and other graine: And now after all this costs, when as yet I have received small profeitt thereof I am lyke on the suddaine to be put from it wthout any recompence of my changes. His ^{Matie} (as it is reported) doth bestow a bountifull & gracious recompence unto the Lo. Lumley

" The third Recognizance was acknowledged 7th of April 11° Eliz: Wherin the Lo: Lumley and Thomas Staughton were bounde to Ridolphe in £4000, The condicon is to performe certaine Covenants of Indentures bearinge the same date. In wch Indentures is contayned, That wheras the Lo: Lumley did owe unto Ridolphe £1825 wch was agreed to be paid att fower paiments And that where for more securitie of Paimt the Lo: Lumley had delivered unto Ridolphe a certaine instrument of debte of 60000 ducketts made by Cosmo de Medices and the State of Florence unto Kinge H. the 8 to be paid by £500 yearlie paimts wherof £5300 was then unpaid and delivered alsoe an Assignment made from the late Queene Elizabethe unto the Lo: Lumley of that debte, and had alsoe made lrs [letters] of Procuracon unto Ridolphe for the receivinge of £3500 parcell of that £5500. The Lo: Lumley covenanted that yf he did make default of paiment of the £1825 That then Ridolphe might without interrupcon of the Lo: Lumley enioye the £3500 to himselfe without rendringe an account unto him for the same And that after suche default he would doe suche further act for the assureinge of that debt of £3500 unto Ridolphe as he should require And that he would doe noe acte wherby the debt due by the State of Florence or the assignment of the late Queene should be determined./

"This is the effect of theise 3 Recognizances: But whether the second were for paiment of parte of the first Some unpaid Or whether the last did include bothe the former in itt the Lo: Lumley remembrethe not/ Upon the laste Recognizance nothinge is due for that noe Counte was broken of the Lo: Lumleys parte.

" But Ridolphe hathe ever sithence detained the instrument of debte made by the state of Florence and the Lo. Lumley never had any parcell of the debte of £5500 the residue of the 60000 ducketts Soe as his losse by Ridolphe is more then his debte did any waie amount unto./

" After this it pleased the late Queene by her highnes Lrs Patts dated 10 Marcii in the 20th yeare of her Raigne to grant unto Willm Lane and Edward Lane (amonge other thinges) all suche somes specialties Recognizancs duties and all other debtes then pertayning unto her M^{atie} or wch shee ought to have by the Meanes of the Attaynder of any person beinge before the 10th of March then last past attainted of Highe treason and whereunto shee was not intituled by any Inquisicon found seisure, Certificatt or Retourne or act of Recorde then had comprehendinge that they were forfeyted but were concealed detayned and uniustlie witholden from the Queene.

" Wherin, Power is given to compound for any the said debtes and to release and discharge the debtor that the same release should be warrant to the Lo: Chauncelor to make any release or pardon of the same debte under the great Seale of England./

" There is alsoe in the same Pattent conteyned a Warrant to the Pattentees to make searche in her Ma^{ts.} Recordes for their further helpe and execucon of the Graunte./

" In the same Pattent itt is provided, and her Ma^{ts} pleasure is declared to be, that a third part of all that wch the Pattentees should gett, should be aunswered unto the Queene/

" That they shoulde not onelie make privie the Lo: Trer and Chaunceló^r of thexcheq^r of everie composicon that they should make, But alsoe that within six monethes next after the Pattent made they should become bounde before the Barons of thexchequer in suche Bondes and somes of money as the Lo: Trer and Chauncelor should thinke fitt wth Condicon for the paim^t to the Queene of a third parte of all, that should be received by them./

" The Pattentees demaunded theise debtes of the Lo: Lumley, whoe not doubtinge of any imperseison in this Pattent paid unto them a some of money and had therupon a Release from them under their Seales dated the 27th of May 21 Eliz:/

" The Lo: Lumley then conceivinge this discharge to be sufficient, sought for noe further discharge./

" Since wch tyme viz. in 35 Eliz: an office was founde That the Pattentees 14 or 15 yeares before the findeinge of that office had made certaine Composicons not acquaintinge the Lo: Trer or Chauncelor of thexcheq^r therwth, Wherby as is nowe said, their Patent is made voyde.

"Itt is alsoe nowe affirmed that Recognizances did not passe unto them by this Patent, because they are of Recorde, and cannot be tearmed concealed./

"And alsoe that the Pattentees became not bounde wthin six monethes to yeild unto her M^{atie} suche somes of money as they should receive, And therfore the Pattent is voyde, albeit the Lo: Tresorer and Chauncelor did never signifye in what somes they should become bounde./"

John, Lord Lumley, died on April 11th, 1609, and was buried at Cheam. In a newsletter written on April 21st a Mr. Dudley Carleton mentions: "My Lord Lumnie died the last weeke at Nonesuch and is like to be buried *in tenebris.*" They probably carried out his wish to be buried "with as little extraordinary charge as may be."

There are several portraits of him in Lumley Castle; two full-length pictures, one in full armour, and the other in his Chancellor's robes, prove him to have been a fine-looking, handsome man, his features showing decided power and intellect. There are also half-length pictures of himself and his first wife, Jane, already mentioned, who has regular features, and her expression does justice to the talents with which she was credited in contemporary biographies.

A paragraph in a newspaper a few years ago mentioned the sale, amongst other interesting works, of "Seven drawings in colours, with the arms emblazoned of the Funeral of Jane Arundel, first wife of John Baron Lumley, dated 1578. These drawings were 14 ft. 6 in. in length, and went for the sum of £100." They were bought by Mr. Nattali, though her Majesty wished to be their purchaser. The paragraph goes on to state, "This lady was greatly distinguished for her learning and talents." This opinion is amply borne out by a visit to the MS. Room of the British Museum, which contains four or five little volumes in which are bound up the exercises of the Earl of Arundel's daughters, Jane and her younger sister, Mary, who married the Duke of Norfolk. Those by Lady Lumley include the translations into Latin of the Orations of Isocrates to Nicocles, "The Tragedie of Euripides called Iphigeneia translated out of Greake

into Englisshe," etc., all written in a beautiful clear hand.
In one volume is an " Epistola ad dominum patrem" stat-
ing that, following the recommendation of Cicero, she is
devoting herself to the study of Greek literature. These
were all written after her marriage, as is seen by the inscriptions on the fly-leaf, one being "The doinge of la.
Lumley, the doughter of my L. Therle of Arundell," while
Lord Lumley has inscribed his name below. In fact husband and wife must have pursued their studies together, as
in the same collection of MSS. is a translation of Erasmus's
"Instructions of a Christian Prince," signed "Your lordshippes obedient sone, J. Lumley 1550." As has been seen,
his own father was executed in 1538, so this was evidently
addressed to his father-in-law, who has placed his name on
the first page. These volumes came to the British Museum
amongst the Royal MSS., having been handed down with
Lord Lumley's library.

Lord Lumley also gave a grant of books to Cambridge
University, as is seen by the following letter, taken from
Cole's MS. in the British Museum :

" To the righte worshipfull & my very loveinge Freendes
the Vicechauncellor the Non-Regentes and Regentes in
the University of Cambrige.

"Were I as able to declare my Love unto Lerninge, as
I am wyllinge to wytnes my affection to your Universitye,
you sholde bothe receave greater Monuments for common
Benefitt, & my best Furtheraunce for your honeste Studyes.
I have not bene inflexible to your Requeste, as your Sol-
licitors can reporte, nether wylbe unmyndefull of your
Petition, as the Evente shall prove. Yett lett not the Staye
of presente Perfourmaunce take awaye your right Judgement of my Intente. For my Purpose is, to confer [com-
pare ?] the Cataloge of your Bookes with myne, and the
Authors which I fynde duble and be wantynge in your
Librarye, I promyss shalbe yours. Whereto I wyll joyne
some certaine number of other Bookes, as an Increase of
my former Inclination and goodwyll towardes you. Thus
desyringe only your good Tolleration of some Tyme, and a

freendly Acceptance of your assured Freendes Disposition, I commytt you to God's good Favour.

"yours assuredly

" LUMLEY.

" From Nonesuche this XXIIIIth of Auguste 1587."

Lady Lumley had three children, Charles, Thomas and Mary, who all died in infancy. There is a touching reference to them in the panel in Lumley Castle put up by their father, recording the history of the family up to that time, and copied in the Red Book:

" This last John was happy with two wives, that is with Jane, elder daughter and coheiress of Henry, Earl of Arundel; and also with Elizabeth, daughter of John, Baron D'Arcy, a woman not only of an ancient pedigree and race, but, which is greatly to be praised, with the virtues of modesty, truth and conjugal love. Of the former of these marriages were born two sons, Charles and Thomas, and an only daughter, Maria, hardly indeed surviving, but in their infancy to our sorrow they were taken up above." They lie buried with their mother in the chancel of the Church of Cheam. One is constrained the more to admire the care for posterity displayed by Lord Lumley when his own hopes of giving an heir to the family were thus early blighted.

There is also at Lumley an undoubtedly genuine portrait of Elizabeth D'Arcy, Lord Lumley's second wife. She has also a look of refinement, and an intellectual, expressive countenance. This lady brought her lord no children, and thus in his old age he addressed himself to the task of discovering the most direct heir, as we have already seen. After doubtless much anxious thought, he fixed on Richard Lumley (eldest son and heir apparent of Roger Lumley, Esq., son of Anthony Lumley, brother to John, Lord Lumley, his grandfather), to whom he devised the principal part of his property, leaving his widow, Elizabeth, sole executrix.

With regard to the difficulties in his choice, we give the following story of the Lucky Leap for what it is worth. It is taken from Thomas Birch's collection of anecdotes in the

British Museum (5560), which, he says, are " Extracts from the Learned and Ingenious Dr Hen. Sampsons MS. Day-books." It is headed: "Another Instance of a Family coming to an estate & Honor."

" At Cotes-bridge near Loughborough in Leicestershire, some boys were leaping of [off] the bridge, amongst the rest was one *Lumley*, upon whose performance the boyes al cryed out Well leap'd Lumley: At the same time a Gent^n rideing by, whose name was Lumley, cald for the boy, ask'd him diligently about his name, made him spell it & write it, w^n he found it was the very same with his own, he took him home, bred him up carefully, made him his heir; & from him comes the present family of the *Lord Lumley*, made noble in the later end of K. Ch: 2^d and Earl of *Scar-brough* by K. Wilm 3^d.

" Note that the ancient family of the Lord Lumley was extinct in Q Eliz^s time vide Dugdales Baronage.

" From Mr. Crosse of Loughborough who saith it is a common tradition in ye town of Loughborow, of wch I may enquire more, vizt, w^n this happened."

Alas! if he did inquire more he made no further note thereof.

Amongst the numerous documents at Sandbeck is a copy of the Inquisition post mortem of John, Lord Lumley, containing mention of all his lands and possessions. Also an interesting indenture giving instructions for the proper education of Richard Lumley, then a minor, of which the following is an abbreviation:

" This indenture made the seaven and twentith day of February in the seaven and thirtieth yere of the reigne of our Soveraigne Lady Elizabeth [1594-5] by the grace of God Queene of England, Fraunce and Ireland, defend^r of the faith. . . . Betweene the right Honorable John Lumley knight lord Lumley on thone partie and Richard Lewkenor seriaunt at lawe and William Smyth of London Esquier on thother partie. Witnesseth that the said Lord Lumley for and in consideracon and to the speciall entent and purpose that the said Richard Lewkenor and William Smyth should have greate care and regard to the well and vertu us bringing upp and good educacon of Richard Lumley (sonne and heire apparaunt of Roger Lumley sonne of Anthony Lumley decessed second sonne of Richard Lord Lumley decessed father of John Lord Lumley decessed, father of George Lumley esquire decessed father of the above named John nowe Lord Lumley) during the mynoritie and nonage of the said Richard Lumley and untill the said Richard Lumley shall accomplishe his full age of one and twenty yeres, and for and towards the better mayntenance of him the said Richard Lumley during his mynoritie and nonage . . . hath bargained and sould unto the said Richard Lewkenor and William Smith all that his mannor or lordship of Lumley within the Bishoprick of Duresme and all that his parke and castle of Lumley . . . To have and to hould . . . unto the full end and tearme of fifteene yeres . . . yelding and Paying therefore yerelie during the said terme for and towardes the finding educacon and bringing upp of the said Richard Lumley the yerelie rent and somme of fiftie Pownds by yere . . . provided allwayes that if the said Richard Lumley shall happen to dye during the said terme or if the said Richard Lumley shall attayne or come to his full age of twenty and one yeres that then and from thenfurth this present lease bargaine and sale shall cease and be utterly void . . ."

Two incidents must not be omitted before taking leave of this last lord of the line of the old feudal barons.

When James I. was visiting the grand old pile towards the close of this worthy baron's life, the Bishop of Durham expatiated to the King on the pedigree of their noble host without sparing him a single ancestor, direct or collateral, from Liulph to Lord Lumley; till the King, wearied with the eternal blazon, interrupted him: "Oh mon, gang na further. I maun digest the knowledge I ha' this day gained, for I didna ken Adam's ither nam was Lumley." A room in the Castle still goes by the name of King James's room.

The second incident is given in the following extract from a newspaper. In 1586 Lord Lumley bought "the manor of Hert and the borough of Hertlepool" from George Clifford, third Earl of Cumberland, for £5,350.

LORD LUMLEY AND HARTLEPOOL PIER.

" Reading recently an old collection of voyages in search of the North-West Passage, I came across an unexpected item of local history. Captain Luke Fox, during his voyage in 1631, touched at Lumley's Inlet on the north of Hudson's Straits, and in his narrative quaintly says: ' It hath pleased God to send me thus happily to the land on the North side of Lumley's Inlet, so named after the Right Honourable the Lord Lumley, an especial furtherer to Davis in his voyages, as to many other lordly designs, as that never to be forgotten act of his, in building up the peere of that poor fisher-town and corporation of Hartlepoole in the Bishop-ricke of Durham, at his owne proper cost and charge, to the value of at least £2,000. At my first coming thither, I demanded at whose charge the said peere towne was builded. An old man answered: Marrye, at my good Lord Lumley's, whose soule was in Heaven before his bones were cold.'

" I have not a history of Hartlepool at hand, and cannot definitely fix the date of the building of the pier referred to by Fox. In 1493 a license was granted to the Mayor and burgesses for the building of a pier, and exactly a century later—in 1593—Queen Elizabeth granted a new charter to the burgesses and inhabitants at the request of John, Lord Lumley. The voyages to the North-West made by Master John Davis were in the years 1585, 1586, and 1587, and I infer from this that the Lord Lumley in question is the nobleman who obtained for Hartlepool its improved charter in 1593.

" J. L., F.R.G.S."

Lady Elizabeth Lumley survived her husband by some years, dying probably at the beginning of 1617, as in a news-letter of February in that year we find: "Lady Lumley dead and left most of her estate to her niece, Lady Darcy's daughter, Sir Thos. Savage's wife." The following letter from her was written on June 9th, 1611, and is endorsed:

" To the Right honarable my very good Lord therle of Sallesbory Lord tresorer of ingland:

"My Lord I have lately reseved letters out of Italy from my Lord my brother—in wch he remembers his love and sarves to your Lo: and hath sent unto your Lo a marble table w^t a head of Fardenando late duke of Tusken: & allthough he sayth it be not worthy of presenting to your Lo: yet he presumeth of your noble acseptans—it coming from one that supplyeth the meannes tharof w^t his affecsinat well wyshing to your Lo: who can never forget the many favors that himself & his frends have Reseved from your Lo: Sr Thomas Savage hath ordar from my brother to see them delyvered whar your Lo please to apoynt them: I wyll not troble your Lo ani further: that am fast bound unto you,

" ELIZABETH LUMLEY.

" This present Sunday."

These following extracts from a copy of her will bear out the account given in the newsletter:

" In the name of the Father of the sonne and of the holye ghost Amen. I Elizabeth Ladye Lumley late wyffe of the Right honorable John Lumley Knight Lord Lumley disceased, being in health and perfect memorye, for which I give Almightie god most humble and hartie thankes, doe make this my last wyll and Testament in manner and forme following. First I comend my soule to Almightie god my maker and redeemer, one hoping of my salvation, in the mercy and meritts of my Saviour Jesus Christ, and I bequeath my bodie to the Church of Cheyne in the County of Surrey to be buryed neare the bodye of my late deare husband, in the Tombe there prepared already for me and with as lyttle charge as conveniently may be done, And as concerning all my worldly good and chattells I wyll and bequeath as followeth. Whereas my late disceased husband dyd appoynt and lymitt that certaine assurances by him of dyvers mannors lands and tenements in the counties of Durham Northumberland York and Sussex and Sadbearge

and within the County of the Towne of Newcastle upon
Tyne should be tenure and did assure the same unto my
brother Thomas Lord Darcy of Chich and my friend Sir
James Crofts Knight for the tearme of twenty one yeres
after the death of the said Lord Lumley fully to be com-
pleate and ended one upon trust for my use; and to be disposed on as I shall think good to appoynt save £100 a
yeare towards the mayntenance of his kinsman Richard
Lumley now Sir Richard Lumley and others in the said
assurance mentioned, to whome the emedyate reversion
thereof from tyme to tyme shall come, during my Lease yf
he so longe doe lyve; now I doe appoynt by this my last
wyll and testament all the said mannors messuages lands
tenements and hereditaments lying and being wthin the
Counties of Sussex Yorke Durham Sadbearge Northumberland, and in the County of the Towne of Newcastle upon
Tyne unto my Executors during the resydue of such tearme
or estate thereof as shall be unexpyred at the tyme of my
death, to receyve the profitts thereof, and imploye them to
the performance of this my last wyll and testament and also
to the performance of what my Lord left in trust to me and
I to them, as well by wryting as by word of mouthe. And
whereas my Lord hath gyven to Sir Richard Lumley £100
a yeare during my tearme yf he so longe doe lyve, soe likewise out of my good affection to him at his marriage I did
gyve him £100 a yeare more during my Lease yf he soe
longe doe lyve, These £200 a yeare wch my Lord and I
have gyven him, I appoynt to be paid out of the Rents
yssues and profitts of those lands and tenements nearest
adioyning to Lumley Castle, wch lands are mentioned in his
wyves jointer to be paid half yearely at the Feast of St
Michaell Tharchangell and at the Feast of the Annuncia-
tion of our Blessede Lady by equall portions. And whereas
Sir Richard Lumley hath made a joynter to his wyffe of
Lumley Castle and Parke and the lands and tenements in
Great Lumley wth other lands and townes thereunto adioyning wth the Colemynes and the Mannor and Castle of
Wytton upon the water and dyvers other lands and tene-
ments in the Countie of Northumberland. . . . By this my

Last wyll and testament I doe devyse appoynt and declare
that within six monthes at the furthest after my discease
my brother the Lord Darcy and Sir Jas Crofts Knight or
such other for the tyme being as shall have interest, in the
said tearme and myne Executors or some of them shall
require of the said Sir Richard Lumley or his heyres or his
Lady to become bounde by obligation in the sum of £5000
starling wth condition not to disturbe or molest my Executors
in the Execution of this my last wyll and testament, nor
molest my tenaunts, or putt any of them out of there
farmes to whome by my wryting I have leased or graunted
or mentioned to have leased or graunted any part of the
premises for 21 years or lesse number of yeares, And yf
the said Sir Richard Lumley shall become bound as aforesaid, then I doe devise and bequeath the Castle and Parke
of Lumley wth all the mannors lands and tenements assuryd
by Sir Richard Lumley for his wyves joynter to the said
Sir Richard Lumley and his wyffe during my said tearme
wth the cole mynes about Lumley Castle and after to the
next heires maile lawfully begotten of the body of the said
Sir Richard Lumley . . . and then and in such case I give
and bequeath to the said Sir Richard Lumley and to those
that shall succeed him in the Castle of Lumley, all my
howshold stuffe with marbles and pictures as shall be in the
Castle of Lumley at the tyme of my death there to remaine
as Airelomes to that house so longe as they will endure.
And whereas Sir Geo. Shearly Knt did heretofore graunt
and assure to my late disceased husband the Lord Lumley
and his heyres a rent Charge out of certain lands upon
condition that upon payment of £500 to the said Lord
Lumley his Executors or administrators the same should
be voyde, and sithence the death of the said Lord Lumley
the said some of £500 hath bene paid to my hands . . . now
I doe wyll and appoynt that the profitt of that £500 shalbe
imployed to and for the mayntenaunce of Splandian Fludd
[Lloyd ?] my Lords neaphew during his lyfe to the value
of £40 a yeare. And after his death I wyll and bequeath
the like profitt that shall aryse of the s^{d} £500 to the mayntenance and bringing upp of my goddaughter Elizabeth

Floyde [Lloyd ?] the daughter of Henry Floyd my Lord's neaphew, and when she shalbe marryed I give her the s^d £500 charging my Executors to pay the same wthin six monethes after her marriage at the furthest. And yf my s^d goddaughter fortune to dye before her said marriage then I give and bequeath the s^d £500 to the right heires of Henry Floyd my Lords neiphew. Item I give and bequeath to Ann Lumley mother of the s^d Sir Richard Lumley £20 a yeare, and to her sonnes George and John and her daughter Elizabeth Lumley every one of them £15 a yeere yearely to be paid to them under my Lease half yearely out of the rent yssues and profitts of the mannors of Hart Hartnes and Hartlepoole, and the other lands and tenements next adioyning. . . . And whereas I have conveyed to my brother the Lord Darcy my howse neare the Towerhill in the parish of St Olyffes in Hartstreete London wth all ye tenements thereunto belonging for the tearme of his lyff excepting that tenement whereof the wedowe Thomas hath a lease paying out of these tenements £50 yearely unto my Executors. . . . I do by this my last wyll and testament confirme the s^d gift unto my brother . . . and after his discease . . . to his d^r my neace the Lady Elizabeth Savage. . . . And after the death of my s^d neace I give and bequeath my s^d house . . . to my neiphew John Savage eldest sonne of Sir Thos. Savage Knt. Item I give and bequeath to my brother the Lord Darcye my Ring wth one dyamond wch usually I doe weare upon my finger, And my best basen and ewer of sylver, and my best sylver salt, wth VI sylver plates answereable in work to the basen and ewer wth all the carpetts that I made myselfe, wth the Chaires and stooles of the same worke. And for such marbles and pictures as shalbe in my house at Towerhill at the tyme of my death wth all tables bedsteads and wooden stuff, my wyll is that the same shall remaine as Aireloomes to that house unto the heires thereof as long as they will endure. Item I give and bequeath to my neephew Sir Thos. Savage all my Armor with all that wch appertayneth thereunto wthin the Roome at Towerhill where it doth lye. Item I give to my neace the Lady Elizabeth Savage my Crosse of

Dyamonds. Item I give to my neace Manhood a gilt Basen and Ewer to the value of £50. Item I give to my neace the La: Trensheard a gilt Basen and Ewer to the valew of £50. Item I give and bequeath to my neace Jane Savage d^r of Sir Thos. Savage and to her sister Dorothea and to her sister Eliz. Savage £200 a yeere. Item I give and bequeath to my neiphew Thos Savage, seycond sonne of Sir Thos Savage the tenement near my house at Towerhill wthin the parish of St Olyffes now in the possession of the wedow Thomas with all stables barnes orchards gardens grounds thereunto belonging. . . . Item I give and bequeath to my neaphew Francis Savage and to my neiphew Jas Savage £200 a peece Item I give and bequeath to my good frend Sir Jas Crofts Knt 150 ozes of sylver plate Item I give to my frend Mrs Savige 60 ozs. of Sylver plate. Item I give to my nephew John Savage eldest s. of Sir Thos Savage my greene vellatt sparverye imbroidered wth purle and pipe. Item I gyve and bequeath to my neece the Ladye Trensheards eldest d^r a Ring wth a dyamond to the value of £30. Item I gyve and bequeath to Dumvell yf she be my woman at the tyme of my death £50 in moneye. Item I give and bequeath to John Lumley that was the Prince his servant £30 a yeare during my Lease out of the Rent of Downly Parke in Sussex. . . . Item I give and bequeath to Tonstall my servant £10 a yeare. . . . Item I give to the s^d Tonstall 40 oz of sylver plate. Item I give and bequeath to Xtopher Hopper £10 a yeare. . . . Item to the s^d Xtofer Hopper for his true and faithfull service to my Lord and me I give £5 a yeare more during his lyfe. Item I give and bequeath to my old servant Richard Beckinsall XL/s a yeare. . . . Item I give and bequeath to Anne Sowth yf she be my servant at the tyme of my death £20 in monye. Item I give and bequeath to Elizabeth Talbott yf she be my servant at the tyme of my death 20 nobles. Item I give and bequeath to Florence Easted yf she be my servant at the tyme of my death £5. Item I give to Tubman 20 nobles. Item I give to Hugh Worrell my Baker one yeares wages over and above his wages dew at the tyme etc. Item I give to Baker my Cator yf he be etc. one

yeares wages over and above etc. Item to Eaton and
Champion yf they be etc. I give to each of them 1 yeares
etc. To all other my howsehold servant I give £10 a piece
over and above their wages dew at my death. Item I give
to my faithfull servant that was, Thos Kymaston, now one
of his Mat^{ies} guard £50 . . . and to his sonne Richard K.
I give and bequeath £10. Item I give to the parish were
I shall dye for the poore £10. And to the poore of Cheyne
£10. Item I give and bequeath to my page Hallyman £5.
Item I give and bequeath £100 towards the setling of the
poore on work w^{th}in the Towne of Chich in Essex, desyring
my Executors, to take such course for the settling of the
same, as that it may not be deminished but imployed to
that use to the worlds end. . . . And what remaines of stuff
plate or debts dew unto me or any other goods or chattels
whatsoever is myne, I give it all to my deare neece the
Lady Elizabeth Savage wth gods blessing and myne upon
her and all hers. And I doe make my deare brother the
Lord Darcy, and my faithfull frend and neiphew Sir Thos
Savage the Executors of this my last wyll and testament.
And I intreate my Hon. frend and kinsman the Earle of
Suffolke Lord Treasurer of England to be the overseer of
this my last wyll and testament, and I bequeath unto his
Lo^{pp} £50 in gould. . . . And I desyre my Executors to preserve the woodes, and that no tymber be cutt downe at all
but for neadfull reparations; though it be in my power to
make my best profitt of it all. And my wyll is that Matthewes
and his sonne have the same charge of Stansted and of
those landes libertyes and woodes in Sussex during my
tearme which heretofore and now presently they have, carrying themselves as they ought to doe. And my wyll is that
my beloved neiphew Sir Thos Savage enioy his lodgings
in my house in Towerhill wch usually heretofore he hath
had, for two yeares or untill my wyll be performed w^{th}
egresse and regresse through the same during that tyme.
And for his lyfe tyme I give him the stable wch now he
possesseth wth egresse and regresse through my owne stable
for his Coatch. And yf any thing hereafter shall be sett
downe under my hand and seale and joyned to this my

last wyll and testament I desyre my Executor to see the same well and truly performed as my trust is in them. In witnesse hereof I sett to my hand and seale to every Leafe of this my last wyll and testament being in nomber 5 leaves the 6 day of November and in the fourthteenth yeare of our Soveraigne Lord King James his raigne in England 1616

" ELIZABETH LUMLEY."

" Witnesses of this my
" last wyll those whose
" names are hereunder wrytten.
" JOHN LUMLEY
" ANTHONY TONSTALL
" RICH. KYMASTON
" CHRISTOPHER HOPPER."

CHAPTER VIII

Captain John Lumley.—Richard, first Lord Viscount of Waterford.—His
difficulties in the Commonwealth.—His wife

ACCORDING to the most authentic accounts,
Richard Lumley was baptized at Chester-le-
Street in 1589. If he was baptized as an infant
he was only five or six when the deed already
given providing for his education was drawn
up, but in this case a letter written by a Richard Lumley
of Wintershill on October 12th, 1599, on money matters
must be from one of the younger branch of the family. His
father, Roger Lumley, was buried at Chester-le-Street. At
Lumley Castle is a portrait endorsed " Ralph Lumley 1567,"
which may represent this Roger.

Roger's wife's maiden name was Anne Kurstwich. He
left a large family, the youngest being born in 1599, just
ten years before the death of the last baron, so that Roger
must have been living when his cousin made provision for
his son's education. In one document family differences are
hinted at, and this may account for the action of Lord
Lumley with regard to Richard.

The youngest son, John, may have been " my loving
kinsman John Lumley," whom Richard, Lord Lumley, made
Master of St. Katherine's Hospital, Newcastle, in 1622.
He retained the post until his death in 1673. The following document from the Record Office also refers to him :

" May this VIIth 1639. One George Bland a prisoner in
the Kings bench, about three or foure monethes since upon
occasion of mentioning the Kings of England, Denmarke,
Sweden, France, and Spayne sayd y[t] four of these five were
knaves, wth other circumstances as hath bene more at large

declared in a certaine petition put upon the counsaile table by Capt James Sinclar forasmuch as he receaves a yearly pension from his Ma^{tye} of England & is a subject & servant to his M^{tye} of Denmarke. Since all this the above named Bland hath borne himselfe more and more insolently by undue practices; as (if leave be given to us who desire it) can evidently be proved. He hath procured one cap^t: Lumley the Ld Lumleyes brother to be bound to the peace for expressing some tokens of offence at the first hearing of those detestable speeches. Not content with this he often used vile words against the same gentleman further to provoke him."

In June the same year there is in a letter an incidental mention of "Capt John Lumley."

The barony expired with John, Lord Lumley. Richard was first knighted by James I. at Theobalds, July 19th, 1616 and he was created Lord Viscount Lumley of Waterford in Ireland on July 10th, 1628. There is a portrait at Lumley which is said to represent the Viscount by Kneller, being that of a cavalier in armour with love-locks and a lace collar.

There are several documents among the State Papers which refer to Lord Lumley. The first is interesting as giving us a picture of the narrowness of the streets and the absence of any pavement:

"John Mohun Esq., sonne & heire to the Lord Mohun examined by Me Sr Fran Windebank Knt principal Secretary of State etc. the 5 of July 1637.

"That upon Monday last the third of this present about tenne in the morning, he coming downe Snow Hill neere Holborne in the company of Cassius Borrowes Esq." (Borough) "sonne to Sr John Borrowes, Knt, King at Armes, & Obadiah Gossop clerke, chaplaine to the Lord Mohun, and having wth him two of his owne servants, crossed the streete to avoid a Cart, and a coach came sodainely upon him this Examinant, soe that the horses were upon him before he was aware of it, whereupon He strooke [struck] at the horses to keepe them back, with a Cane wch he had in his hand, wch the Coachman espying, lasht at him this examinant wth his whipp, and then the examinant strooke at the Coachman wth his Cane, and the Coachman lasht at him againe; then one of the Examinants servants named John Ennis a Dutchman, drew his sword and strooke at the Coachman, whereupon one that sate in the boote of the Coach drew his sword and strooke or thrust at the Examinant wch he boare off with his Cane as appeares by a Marke in the cane. And assoone as this Examinant was disingaged from the Coach he drew his sword and strooke at the Coach as it passed by, but knowes not that he hurt any man in the Coach and soe this examinant departed.

"(Signed) JOHN MOHUN."

"Cassius Burrowes" in his examination on the same day details the circumstances above mentioned with some additions. The coach was that of Lord Savagè, but they "knew not that it was his." Mohun struck the horses to avoid crushing against the houses. Ennis "drew his sword and strooke at the Coachman wth it thinking to have cutt the Reines, because he drove away so fast that he could have noe other satisfaction. . . . This Examinant seeing swords drawne of each party drew out his owne sword rather to defend himselfe then to offend others, and to avoid further mischiefe, but strooke not at the Coach nor knowes how my Lord Lumley became hurt, and assoone as my Lord Savage spake to this Examinant and named him, he retired, and caused Ennis and others to desist.

"(Signed) CASSIUS BOROUGH."

This would leave us rather puzzled as to Lord Lumley's part in the affair, were it not for a newsletter written by a C. Rossingham on July 13th, where we read: "Lord Mohun his son committed to the Fleet for drawing his sword on Ludgate Hill and hurting Lord Lumley, who sat quietly in his coach."

There are several letters from John Ashburnham of Westover to Nicholas, Clerk of the Council, about money matters between himself and Lord Lumley. In the first of these, dated October 15th, 1638, he says they are accorded, the composition being £1,800; but on January 28th in the following year he writes:

"In my iorney to Sussex I discovered the imperfect title my Lord Lumley hath made me of his Lease Lands of Bremers, butt deeply protesteth to make all good; and since there is noe way to doe it butt by taking in the Morgage, I have promised to lend him soe much mony as will disengage itt, with which I shall be furnished by the party that hath bought itt of me, who gives me £1400 for itt."

On February 18th he writes:

"My most deare freind.

"I am soe infinitly trobled at the receipt of my Lord Lumley his letter that I have almost lost all my patience, I am perswaded he doth absolutely intend to Compliment me out of this Lease lands: And though I am infinitly asshamed of the unfitting trobles I have given you, in regard of your many imployments yett I pray lett me entreat you, that you will take the pains to goe some morning to his Lodging with this letter; & desire him to promiss a certaine time of being in the cuntry, that I may meet him att his house, where I will provide soe much money as shall disingage the morgage, though itt be upon three or foure dayes warning, and will accept of reasonable security for itt, which you will perceave I offer to doe by my letter to him, and soe did before in my other, to which he answered nothing; when you have redd itt, I pray seale itt: I have likewise sent you his letter to me, by which I finde, he is glad of this occation of going into the North, to hinder the dispatch of my business with him. I pray urge the facility of the dispatch, since I will enable him to doe itt by furnishing him wherewith to disingage the morgage. Deer freinde pardon me for this perticuler importunity, for itt doth much concerne me: and I am loth to make a iorney to London expressly for itt: yett yf you finde him unwilling to satisfye me, & that his stay will be longe in London, I shall be forced to hunt him out there./ . . ."

A week later he writes: "I have receaved the Lord Lumley his letter, who is still upon such generall termes, that I feare he hath forgott that I cann quell his concupiscence yf he vexe my patience a little longer, I pray leave him nott till you have his more perticuler answeare."

Again on March 4th he writes: "The unworthy delayes of the Lord Lumley hath expressly dispatcht these, to entreat your furtherance in the business betwixt us; I confess the imployment will be troblesome to you divers wayes, both in calling you from your owne affaires, and in dealing with a person of soe much craft, and soe little honesty: yett since itt soe much concernes me, and that his stay in these parts is likely to be soe short, and that itt will be very inconvenient for me to come to Londonn, I earnestly desire your pardon, yf I yett sollicite you to take the paines to seeke him out with as much expedition as your occasions will give you leave; and to lett him know that I have sent my servant on purpose to receave his full resolution, which I have with much impatience expected theis tenn dayes, att the least; and nott doubting of his reall performances, I have hadd the mony ready this fortnight that I promised to lend him to disingage the Morgage, and in case he shold nott now finish with me, as he gave incouragement to beleeve he wold, the iniury he will doe me will be double. Yf you cann prevaile with him to sett a certaine day for his being in Sussex, I am confident I shall doe well enough, butt yf you finde him unwilling to doe that, then I feare he intends to steale into the North; and defraude me; of which yf you shall be perswaded then I pray press to him this faire end, that he give me his own Bonde of three thowsand pounds for the fullfilling & keeping of all the Covenants grants and agreements specified in one Indenture bearing date the six and twentith day of November in the fourteenth yeare of his Maiestyes raigne" (1638) "which he was to have donn at the ensealing of that Deed; and likewise his owne bond with some other sufficient surety of eighteene hundred pounds for the payment of eight hundred and sixty pounds with the consideration for six months, for which last bond, I will take of the Morgage."

It is to be feared that the debt was never paid, as nine years after (November 27th, 1648), among debts owing to him, there is " By Lord Lumley, £800."

The following order was made in consequence of the war with Scotland:

" Att the courte of Whitehall ye 27th of January 1638

Present

Lo: Ar: Bp of Cant.	Ea: of Dorset.
Lo: Keeper	Ea. of Salisbury
Lo: Trear. [Treasurer]	Ea: of Hollande
Lo: P. Seale	Lo: Cottington
Lo: D: of Lenox	Lo: Newburgh
Lo: Marq of Hamilton	Mr Trerer
Lo: H: Chamberlaine	Mr Comptroler
Ea: Marshall	Mr Vice Chamberlaine
Lo: Admirall	Mr sec: Cooke
Lo: Chamberlaine	Mr Sec: Windebanke

" This day was read at the boord his Matie sittinge in Councell the draught of the writt under written, when it was by his Mats expresse Commaund ordered that Mr Attorney Generall should be hereby required forthwth. to send writts accordingly to the Lord Will Howard, the Lo: Clifford, the Lo: Wharton, the Lo: Gray of Wake Sr Rich Lumly Kt Vis Count Waterford in Ireland whereof Mr Attorney is to take care not to faile."

The translation of the writ, which is in Latin, is to the following effect: " For certain causes touching the state and defence of our Kingdom of England, we have ordained that all Lords holding lands in Northumberland should dwell upon the said lands with their families, for defence of the same, and to resist the malice of our enemies and rebels, if they shall presume to enter therein. We command you, therefore, that all excuses set apart, you repair to your lands in the said county, so that you be there on the 1st March next at the latest, with your family and retainers, well arrayed and with competent arms, and that you continue there until you hear the contrary from us. In default whereof we shall take the said lands into our hands, and shall cause to be found out of the profits thereof persons sufficient for their safe custody."

This order was obeyed as far as Lord Lumley was concerned. As we have seen, for some time he had been living in Sussex, but he now returned to his ancestral home of Lumley Castle.

The next paper from the Record Office is of the same date: "Whereas wee are given to understand that some of the Coast of Flanders contrary to the Articles of peace betweene us & our good Brother the King of Spaine have lately taken at Sea Certaine Shipps & Vessells laden with Fish belonging unto our Right trustie & welbeloved Richard Lord Viscount Lumley, Henry Lord Maltravers and othere Adventurers in the Fishing Businesse of the Association of our Right trustie & Right welbeloved Cousen and Councellor Thomas Earle of Arrundell & Surry Earle Marshall of England, And have carryed them into Newporte, where they are still deteyned, and the Fishermen Imprisoned being Free Denizens, Which said Shipps and goods doe amount unto the value of Two Thousand five hundred pound, And have forborne to make Restitution thereof or Satisfaccon, notwithstanding the same hath bin demaunded, Wee doe therefore hereby will & require you to take soe many of the Shipps, & soe much of the goods belonging to any of those of Dunkerke, or any other place or parte of the Coast of Flaunders, and to send them safely unto some of our Ports there to be kept to the end that satisfaction may bee made unto the said Richard Lord Viscount Lumley, & the rest of the Adventurers in the said Shipps, And for soe doeing this shalbee yor Warrant Given at our Pallace of Whitehall this   day of March in the fourteenth yeare of our Raigne."

When the Civil War broke out, Lord Lumley showed his loyalty to the Sovereign to whom he had sworn fealty by taking up arms, and also made Lumley Castle into a garrison. He was a principal commander of the forces under Prince Rupert, and marched with him into the west of England,

and was at the siege of Bristol; and in the long correspondence between the Prince and Sir Thomas Fairfax as
to the terms of surrender of Bristol, Lord Lumley is mentioned as being present at a Council of War. The city
surrendered to the Parliamentary forces on September 10th,
1645.

During the Commonwealth, when so many fine castles
and noble churches were sacrificed to the zeal and bigotry
of the Covenanters and Roundheads, Lumley Castle remained unmolested. A quaint legend is attached to two
cannon balls preserved in the inner court of the castle. It
is said that Cromwell, struck with the appearance of the
castle, decided that it should not be bombarded, but caused
the two cannon balls to be thrown into the court as a me-
mento of his clemency, and a proof that, had he so willed,
he could have used the balls to more disastrous purpose.

Bolton Castle, mentioned above, suffered severely at the
hands of Cromwell, and was left an almost total ruin. Lady
Algitha Lumley, eldest sister of the present Earl of Scarbrough, is married to Lord Bolton, owner of Bolton Castle.

But although Viscount Lumleys castle escaped destruction, his estates suffered considerably, as will be seen by the
two following papers. The first, which refers to his wife as
much as himself, is a report of some of the doings of the
Committee for the Advance of Money:

" 15 May, 1644. RICHARD VISCOUNT LUMLEY, the Strand,
and FRANCES, VISCOUNTESS LUMLEY, Broad Street Ward.

" Lady Lumley assessed at £400.

" 1 July, 1644. Having paid in £200, respited for further
hearing.

" 15 July. To be discharged on her payment of £200
and £10 more, and to have the Public Faith for the £210.

" 8 Dec., 1644. Lord Lumley assessed at £1500.

" 21 May, 1645. Whereas rents in Houndsditch and elsewhere have been seized and sequestered as the estate of
Viscount Lumley for the nonpayment of his $\frac{1}{20}$, but they
appear to belong to his wife, formerly wife of Sir Wm.
Sandys, and are in trust for payment of her debts—order

that the sequestration be discharged, and the rents paid to those to whom they belong.

"11 Oct., 1648. Lord Lumley and his son to appear and pay their respective assessments for their $\frac{1}{20}$.

"9 Feb., 1649. Lord Lumley summoned to appear and pay his assessment, or sequestration will be issued against his estate.

"27 Feb. Ordered to bring, in a month, a particular of what he compounded for at Goldsmith's Hall.

"28 Dec., 1649. To be discharged on payment of £160, having paid £100 in co. Sussex, and £250 to Sir Wm. Waller."

The second paper, which will explain the last entry but one of the above, is an extract from the " Account of the Transactions of the Committee for Compounding," which sat at Goldsmith's Hall. The first step required of the delinquent on appearing before this Committee was the taking of the Covenant and of the Negative Oath, by which he bound himself never again to bear arms against the Parliament.

"17 Oct., 1645. RICHARD VISCOUNT LUMLEY and JOHN his son and Heir, Stanstead, Sussex.

"Note that John Lumley has taken the Negative Oath.

"24 Nov., 1645. Lord Lumley being at Bristol, too ill to travel, begs letters to the County Committees of Sussex, York, Durham, and Bristol, to certify the value of his estate, being desirous to take the benefit of the propositions. Promises to take the National Covenant and Negative Oath.

"5 March, 1646. The County Commissioners of Sussex to send up Lord Lumley's writings.

"August. Father and son both petition to compound. In Jan. 1644, they left Stanstead, in the Parliament's quarters, to join the King, but never bore arms, nor contributed in his service. Lord Lumley petitioned on Bristol articles before 1 December last, and has taken the National Covenant and Negative Oath. John Lumley came in on the sur-

There are two MS. books about the estates of Sir William Sandys, dated respectively 1532, when the annual profits amounted to £983 16s., and 1537, when they amounted to £1,022 3s. 2¾d.

Richard, Viscount Lumley, was buried in the vault at Cheam beside his kinsman, the last Baron, and was succeeded by his grandson Richard, his only son, John, having died in his father's lifetime. This John, as we have seen, had married Mary, daughter and one of the heirs of Sir Henry Compton of Brambletye in Sussex, Knight of the Bath (youngest son of Henry, Lord Compton, ancestor to the Earl of Northampton). He was buried in a family vault under the church of St. Martin-in-the-Fields, but the church was pulled down and entirely rebuilt in 1721, and all traces of the vault and monuments are lost, the only known mention of them being in a Harleian MS. in the British Museum, which among other monumental inscriptions gives the following:

Chancel
Within the Railes :—

Here lyeth Interred the Body of the
Honourable John Lumley, eldest son
to the Lord Viscount Rich. Lumley
of Stansted in Sussex. He was
buryed the tenth of October 1658.

On June 15th, 1658, there was issued a " Pass for John Lumley, eldest son of Viscount Lumley, with wife, two children, gentlewoman, maid and three men to France," but it is to be supposed that he returned soon.

John Lumley left besides his heir a son, Henry, and three daughters, Elizabeth, married to Richard Cotton of Watergate in the county of Sussex, Frances and Anne, who died unmarried. On June 29th, 1667, a warrant was issued to Sir Edward Walker, king at arms, to authorize Henry, Frances and Ann Lumley, and Elizabeth Lumley, now married to Richard Cotton, the children of the late John Lumley, son and heir to Richard, Viscount Lumley, to take precedence as children of a viscount as if their father had lived to succeed to the title.

CHAPTER IX

Richard, second Viscount Lumley of Waterford.—His connexion with the
Dutch War.—Made Lieut.-Colonel of the Horse Guards.—Adherence to
William III.—Created Viscount Lumley of Lumley Castle and Earl of
Scarborough.—Battle of the Boyne.—Letter from William III.—Death
of Lord Scarbrough.—Account of his brother, Sir Henry Lumley.

RICHARD, grandson of Richard, Viscount
Lumley of Waterford, greatly recommended
himself to the notice of Charles II. He seems
to have had unusual advantages of education
both at home and abroad, and to have been
distinguished amongst the most polite men of the age.

The first notice we have of him from the State Papers
is as follows :

"Charles by the grace of God King of England, Scotland, France and Ireland, Defender of the Faith etc. To
all Admiralls, Viceadmiralls, Captains of our Ships at Sea,
Governors, Commanders, Souldiers, Maiors, Sheriffs, Justices of the Peace, Bayliffs, Constables, Customers, Comp-
trollers, Searchers and others whom it may concerne, Greeting. Whereas of Our especial grace Wee have licensed &
by these presents do License Our R^t Tr: & Welb^d Cousin
Richard Viscount Lumley, together with his Mother, his
Brother, his two Sisters & Twelve Servants, & also Six
Geldings for their own use, to passe out of this Our Realme
into the parts beyond the Seas, there to remaine the space
of three yeares next after his departure out of this Our
Realme: Wee will & command you & every of you to suffer
him & them to passe by you out of this Our Realme with
threescore pounds in money, and his and their necessary
Carriages & Utensells as you tender Our pleasure : And
these Our Letters or the Duplicate of them shall be aswell

unto you as unto the said Lord Lumley sufficient Warrant & Discharge in that behalf. Provided always, that the said Lord Lumley do not haunt nor resort unto the Territories or Dominions of any foraine Prince or Potentate not being with Us in League or Amity, Nor yet willingly keep company wth any person or persons departed out of this Realme without Our License, or that contrary to the same do yet remaine on the other side of the Seas; And that he use not the company of any Jesuite or Seminary Priest or otherwise evill affected to Our State: Provided also that notwithstanding any thing in this Our License, whensoever it shall seem good unto Us; to recall the said Lord Lumley home againe before the end of the terme before limited, & shall signify the same unto him either by our own Letters or by the Letters of any four of our Privy Councell, by means of any Our Ambassadors, That then it shall not be lawfull for him to abide on the other side the Seas any longer time then the distance of his abode shall require & Our Laws do permit, And if he do not, without urgent and very necessary cause to the contrary returne in manner aforesaid, then Wee will this Our License to be taken as voyd & of none effect from the beginning, and to be interpreted and adiudged to all intents & purposes as though no such License had been given, but he departed without the same.

" Given at Our Court at Whitehall the 4th day of October, 1667, in the 19th year, of our Reigne

"By his Maties command

"W. M."

He seems to have travelled in state, as a Captain James Welsh in a letter writes:

"Rye, Octo^r 22th 1667.

"Yesterday came in to this harbor ye Kings pleasure boate (& allsoe ye Dukes) to carry over to France ye Duches of Richmond & ye Lady Lumley."

And four days later the same man writes: "Yesterday departed hence for France ye Ld Lumley wth his mother."

While he was away some of his woods were sold to the

Navy, as we learn by the following letters from a Captain
Anthony Deane of Portsmouth to the Navy Commisioners:

"Portsmouth, Decb. 21ˢᵗ 1669.

" Right Honᵇˡᵉ

" Heare is inclosed the Contract for the fowrteen
lardge Ellems which your honers ordered to be sent up,
And according as your honers disires I will use my utmost
Indeavors to incoreidge other Capmen to convert goods
for this service, that wee may not be so tyde unto master
Coale, And that wee may begin heare is inclosed a tender
of sixteen brave oakes which is fitt for gun decke beames
for the first rate ship now in hand, and will be dellivered
at emsworth to our hoys sides at 11ᵈhalfpeny a foot girt
measure, the advantage of which will bring it lese then
10d a foote, the which trees are now standing and wee
shall have the liberty to chuse in my lord lumblies woods
from whince the long beache planke comes, and if your
honors do refuse them, to be sure master Coalle will have
them next time he comes this way. . . ."

The tender mentioned above was drawn by Edward
Benson, probably Lord Lumley's representative, and is
dated December 16th. It is as follows :

" A tendʳ of provisions for supply of his Mᵃᵗʸᵉˢ stores att
Portsᵗʰ: viz: 16 oake trees of length & scantling fitt for
gun-deck beames for his Mᵃᵗⁱᵉˢ first Rate Ship now building Delivered at yᵉ waterside att emsworth by yᵉ 10ᵗʰ day
of Aprill next ensueing at 11½ᵈ per foᵗ girth measure, large
long 4 inch pla: 30 loads to meet att 32 foᵗ in length & 14
inch at yᵉ topp end; free of all charge to the King att
4 pound per load."

On January 15th Captain Deane writes: "According
unto your honours Desires I shall use all diligence for to
procure some knees if possible, for the new shipp at Chat-
ham, but I am doubtfull there can be noe thoughts of any
untill ye spring: for I am sure there is none at my Lord
Lumlies there being but seven trees felled besides beech ;
nor is ye tymber in beare forrest downe wᶜʰ is saide to be

bought by Mr. Clements of Southwicke." However, on March 8th he writes: " Mr. Binson hath promised to fell the sixteen long trees for our gun decke beames this weeke, yet not without greate perswations, he alleiadgeing the barke to [be] worth seaven pound, but at last brought him to be contented to take fifty shillings which I hope your honors will be pleased approve of. . . . Next Mr. Binson haveing heard the goods I lately contracted for is not yet payed, he seemes loath wee should convert the trees untill some further assurance of his mony, which I humbly pray your honors Incoridgement to give him Sattis-faction, for these sixteen trees being the verie choyce of my Lord lumblies woods, and a greate penyworth, he is the more stricter for his tearmes, for I assure your honors that wee did not ride lese than teen miles ere I made my choyce and these trees are the creame of those woods they being the best those parts affoards."

These ships were probably being prepared for the second Dutch War, an incidental notice of Lord Lumley's con-nexion with which is found in the following extract from a letter written on April 30th, 1672, by Colonel James Hamilton, Groom of the Bedchamber, to " Sr Joseph Williamson, one of the Clerks of his Maiestys most honor-able privie Councell," on the " Prince," one of the fleet under the Duke of York, which was hovering about at the mouth of the Thames :

" Last night I spoake with the master of a bylander that left Niewport on Friday hee could say nothing more of the dutch fleet then that it was generally sayd there that they would be out in a few days with 90 sayl of men of war.

" This morning arrived from London Sr Jeremy Smyth with stores of several kindes for the fleete.

" My Ld Mulgrave, my Ld Lumley and Mr Sidney are also arriv'd this morning."

Viscount Lumley was ready, like his warlike ancestors, to engage in any dangerous enterprise, and on June 12th, 1680, actually embarked at Portsmouth on an expedition intended against the Moors to raise the siege of Tangier, when the news came that there was a cessation of arms for four months.

The leader of the expedition was to have been Sheffield, Earl of Mulgrave, afterwards Duke of Buckinghamshire.

Viscount Lumley returned to Court, and was constituted Master of the Horse to Queen Catherine, the consort of Charles II.

In that station he so far commended himself that his Majesty, in consideration of his great merit and approved fidelity, and his descent from noble ancestors, ancient Barons of the Kingdom, advanced him to the state and degree of Baron of Lumley Castle in the County Palatine of Durham, and to the heirs male of his body, and in default of such issue, to Henry Lumley his brother, and the heirs male of his body, by letters patent bearing date May 3rd, 1681. But no Parliament sitting during the remainder of that reign, his lordship was not introduced till May 19th, 1685, when he was brought into the House of Peers between the Lord Colpeper and the Lord Baron of Weston, having received his writ of summons on February 14th preceding.

On the insurrection of the Duke of Monmouth in the West, he had the command of a regiment of horse, and was mainly instrumental in gaining the victory at Sedgmoor on July 6th, 1685; for the Duke of Monmouth, with the German Count who accompanied him, and the Lord Grey, were by his vigilance discovered, and surrendered themselves prisoners to his lordship.

Amongst various interesting documents the following letter was found amongst the Sandbeck papers. It is unsigned and is addressed to Sir Robert Thomson. A niece of Lord Scarbrough's, daughter to his sister Julia and Sir Christopher Conyers, Kt., married first Sir William Blackett, and secondly Sir William Thompson. Is it not possible that there may be a mistake in the Christian name, and that this letter is addressed to the second husband of Lady Blackett, trusting that through her interest it may be brought to Lord Lumley's notice, he being much in the King's confidence?

"Sr Think it not strange y^t I addrest myselfe to you for I hope under God you may be an instrument to prevent those dangers that hang over our heads and now ready to break forth into a Rebellion. S^r what I say I am able to make good, being privy to all their actions and may in time make myselfe knowne to his Màtye, S^r the association is carryed on with viger there being agents in every County in England, in some six, in some eight, and soe in all corporations many of which are now in London, There is twelve principally in England unto whome all intelligences come who sit most dayes and give orders, S^r in short the designe is to seize the King and Duke in London, they have a large declaration con " (hole) "streets, they take theire rise from King James " (the First) " how much in his dayes Popery was encouraged and priests and Jesuits suffered in England and though divers of them were seized and put in divers prisons they were released by the King's order, then they Rip up all King Charles's reigne, tell you of his ill usage of Parliaments, of his favoring of popery give you a list of all ye priests and Jesuits releast out of prison by his order wch was testifyed by divers witnesses examined in Parliament, of his usage in Parliament prorogueing and dissolving them when they once touch on grevances, of his usinge the five members and of his leaveing his Parliament which forct them to defend themselves against his Tyrany haveing raised ann Army to have destroyed us, which did consist most of papists and men debaucht and of lost fortunes, then they justifye the warr the murther of his Matye, of his breach of promise made at Breda and breach of covenant in Scotland, of all his miscarryages since his coming into England of ye affliction of gods people, of the persecution they sufer for theire conscience sakes of the likely hood of a popish succeser etc : and then invite all that love theire lives Libertys their wives and children to assist against tyrany, S^r tis too long to tell you halfe ye heads of it, but this I know that it will not be long before they break out into a Rebellion unless his Majesty secure his person better then of late he hath done ; I will give you noe further trouble not doubting but

you will discharge your trust and lett me desire your speed
in it for feare I will be to late, S^r I have noe other end in
itt then ye good of his Maty^e and Kingdom whome god
preserve.

"May the 30th 1683.

"Bee assured they will begin in London I know . . ."
(the rest is torn off).

It is endorsed in different writing:

"It was directed to Sir Robert Townser in Coventry
post p^d."

On February 7th, 1684, Lumley Park was mortgaged
for £2,000. When Viscount Lumley observed that King
James's design was to introduce Popery, and that our religion and laws were in danger of being subverted by the
arbitrary measures then taken, he forsook the Court, and
appeared on behalf of the seven bishops at their trial,
June 29th, 1688.

In 1687 the Prince of Orange had sent over Mynheer
Dykvelt to manage his affairs in England, and in Bishop
Burnet's interesting "History of His Own Time" we read
that Lord Lumley was among the chief nobility who
"met often at the Earl of Shrewsbury's. There they con-
certed matters and drew the declaration on which they
advised the Prince to engage." In the following year
Admiral Russel, afterwards Earl of Orford, returned from
Holland, where he had been consulting with the Prince,
and "communicated the matter, first to the Earl of Shrewsbury and then to the Lord Lumley, who was a late convert
from Popery and had stood out very firmly all this reign.
He was a man who laid his interest much to heart, and he
resolved to embark deep in this design." To the edition
of Burnet's "History" published in 1823 were added
"the cursory remarks of Swift," and to this passage we find
the following note, dictated of course by the writer's well-
known spitefulness and bigotry: "He was a knave and a
coward. S."

Burnet continues: "When matters were concluded on,
his Lordship with the Earls of Devonshire, Holderness

and Danby, undertook for the North, Lord Lumley by his interest and friends secured the important town of Newcastle which declared for the Prince soon after his landing."

An extract from one Jacob Rokeby to W. Gunston, Esq. (Duke of Leeds' Papers, 1688), is interesting :

" This day Lord Dunblane, Lord Danby, Lord Lumley and Sir H. Goodrick, seized the town [Newcastle], disarmed the soldiers, and took the governor, Sir John Rokeby, prisoner."

Another letter, dated December 13th, 1688, from one Sir Christopher (surname omitted), to D. Fleming, relates : " The town of Newcastle has refused the assistance offered by Lord Whittington from Berwick. On Wednesday Lord Lumley sent word he would be in the town that afternoon, but they answered having refused Lord Wittington, he need not fear they would accept Papist's assistance, that they would take care of their own town for the King, their religion, their laws and liberties, and that he need not trouble them." A decided snub for Lord Lumley !

But in spite of this Lord Lumley was instrumental, by his interest and arguments in the House of Peers, in gaining the vote that the throne was vacant, and also that the Prince and Princess of Orange should be declared King and Queen of England.

For which services, on February 14th, 1688-9, the day after their Majesties were proclaimed, he was sworn of the Privy Council, and declared one of the Gentlemen of the Bedchamber. He was also constituted Lieut.-Colonel of the First Troop of the King's Horse Guards. It is sometimes difficult to discover which of the official documents relating to military affairs belong to the Viscount, and which to his younger brother, Henry, of whom an account is given below. The following evidently belong to Lord Lumley :

" To Lt Coll Lumley, Warrant to apprehend Lieutenant Barnesley for dangerous, seditious, & treasonable practices, whereof he is accused & to bring him before me.

" SHREWSBURY.

" Whitehall 16 March 1688-9."

In order to carry out this duty, on the same day was issued a " Passe & Post-Warr^t to Lt Coll Lumley with 6 or 7 other officers to goe to Cambridge." They were evidently successful, as two days later John Fage, the Mayor of Cambridge, writes to the Earl of Shrewsbury as follows :

" Right Hono^{ble} May it please your Honor to understand that by vertue of your Honors warrant Mr. Peter Barnesley was yesterday brought before me by the honoble Leiutenant Collonell Lumley whereof Nathaniel Coe (whose letter was showne to me) had notice and he produced William Beale & Thomas Stevensen to give informatione against Mr. Barnesley which I tooke in writing upon their oathes & have sent true copies thereof inclosed unto you Lord^{pp} and have committed Mr. Barnesley to prison. . . ."

The next document quoted refers to Lord Lumley's promotion : "Our Will etc. Great Seal containing our grant of ye Dignity of a Visc^t of this Our Kingdome of England, unto Our R^t Tr: & Welb^d Cousin & Counc^r Richd Visct Lumley of o^r Kingdom of Ireland by ye name stile & title of Visc^t Lumley of Lumley
wth ye usuall Fee 50 marks Paiment to support ye dignity of a Visc^t payable at ye receipt of our Exchequer. . . . Given at Hampton Court 8th April 1689."

On April 10th a Warrant was drawn up giving to all those " to whom we have lately thought fitt to make severall grants of honor" the order of their "Rank and precedency"; and on the same day the Earl of Shrewsbury wrote from Whitehall to the Commissioners of the Great Seal as follows :

" The King intending my Lord Viscount Lumley should walk to morrow at the Solemnity of the Coronation in quality of a Viscount, has commanded me to acquaint your Lord^{ps} that He would therefore have you put his Patent for that Honour under the Great Seal to-night."

In April Mr. Charles Butler was constituted and appointed " to be Guidon and Major of Our First Troop of Our Horse Guards whereof Our right trusty and welbeloved Richard Viscount Lumley is Capt & Colonell." On April 25th was issued a " Passe to Lieut Coll. Lumley, Sir Rich: Bassett, Captain Crowther & six servants to go to Berwick."

On May 20th was issued the following Warrant: " To our Trusty & Welbeloved Cousin & Councellor Richard Viscount Lumley, Greeting. Whereas Wee are informed, y^t our Game of Hare Pheasant, Partridge, Heron, & other wild Fowle in & about our County of Sussex, is much destroyed by divers disorderly Persons wth Greyhounds, Mongrills, Setting Dogs, Guns, Tramells, Tunnells, Nétts, & other Engines contrary to ye Statutes of this our Realm in these Cases provided: For ye prevention hereof, & y^t our said game may be ye better preserved for our Royall disport and recreation at such time as wee shall resort unto those parts; Wee do hereby will & require you to have a speciall care y^t no person or persons do hereafter use any of ye said unlawfull means or Engines for ye destroying of Our said game within Our said County of Sussex; and if any person or Persons after ye signification of this our Pleasure, shall presume wth greyhounds, Mongrills Setting Dogs, Guns, Tramells, Tunnells, Nets & other Engines to hunt or kill Our said Game of Hare, Pheasant, Partridge, Heron, or other Wild Fowle within ye said County Wee doe hereby give full power & authority unto you, & to your Deputy or Deputies, to seize & take away all or any of ye said Greyhounds, Mongrills, Setting Dogs, Tramells, Tunnells, Guns, Nets or other Engines, & then to detain & certify unto Us or Our Privy Councill ye names of any person or persons so offending, to ye end further order may be taken for their punishment as shall be fitt in cases of such misdemeanor & Contempt: Willing & requiring all & singular Our officers Civill & Military whom it may Concerne to be aiding & assisting to you & to your Deputies herein. And for so doing this shall be to you and them a sufficient Warrant.

" Hampton Court 20th May 1689."

Lord Lumley evidently went north about this time, as on June 1st the Earl of Shrewsbury wrote him the following letter :

" Having rec^d the inclosed Information against Richard Carr and Henam within y^r Lieutenancy I thought it most adviceable to send it to your Lo^p who will [use] the best oppertunity passing neare to ye Place to enquire concerning this Person and whither it be fitt to secure him wch you have the same authority for that I have I make you no excuse for giving you this trouble knowing your care & concern for whatever relates to ye Kings Service.

" Now y^r L^p is upon entring into Northumberland I think it necessary to acquaint you further that by Letters from thence I am inform'd y^t some Officers of ye army have of late seized Horses belonging to Papists or those they took for such By what I understand there is occasion enough to putt the disaffected in those parts out of a Capassity as much as may bee of doing mischeif But ye late Act of Parliam^t hath provided y^t Horses & armes should be seized by ye Justices of ye Peace & ye Act for the Militia places that Trust in ye Dep^{ty} Lieuten^{ts} & I hope both are now appointed in that County & y^t it will be recomended to them by your Lo^p to be vigilant in their respective Stations y^t ye Officers seeing that work done in a regular way may not think it left to them to provide for ye publick safety by Extraordinary Methods."

Lord Lumley answered this letter from Penrith on June 17th : " Your Lo^{ps} with the enclosed enformation came to me at newcastle, I have toke care to have that matter examined, but had not time to doe it my self ; Carr that was enformed against being out of the towne when we passed through it ; the Commission of the Peace came downe while I was in the Countrie ; both that and the leiutennancie is now settled in the best hands I can find, though I wish the Countie afforded more choice, all the horsis belonging to papists were siesed before my comming by the officers of the army, and though it was irregular, it was soe absolutly necessary that it ought to be excused, there is a gentelman in northumberland called Charlton at whouse house most of the metings of papists have bin, it has bin the retreate for all those that came out of other places, Mr. Turner was siesed at his house, it wold be much for the kings service if he were sent for by a messenger, the enclosed which he writ to the late postmaster in newcastle will I suppose be sufficient ground for his being secured I having committed the party he writ to for spreading the late libells of which vast numbers have bin sent to all sorts of persons, Your Lo^{pp} has had an account of all the forces except Beamont Regiment of foot which is very good Langston^s of hors pretty good Lewsons of dragons good. Lord Hewets of hors very good, this day we shall turne oute soume officiers of which your Lo^{pp} shall have an account from

"my Lord

"Your L^{ps} most faithfull humble servant

"LUMLEY."

"The enclosed," which unfortunately is not now traceable, was on the 22nd forwarded to "Coll Williams or the Comander in cheif at New Castle" by the Earl, who says: "I send you here enclosed a Letter writt as it is said by one Mr. Charleton at whose house in Northumberland severall disaffected Persons are observed to meet; the Person to whom it is writt is already Com^{ted} by my Ld Lumley upon an other acc^t You are to apply to the next Justice of Peace for his assistance in examining ye said Charleton (when he is apprehended,) concerning the Contents of this Letter & I doubt not but there will be sufficient reason to secure him likewise at least to bind him over to answer this false & seditious news at the next Sessions. You will send Me a Coppy of his Examinations."

It would be interesting to learn whether this is the Charleton for the murder of whom one Greenway Field was condemned to death at the Old Bailey, and though appeals were made for a reprieve, the sentence was confirmed at Hampton Court on September 17th, 1689.

On July 8th Lord Lumley was made Custos Rotulorum of Northumberland. On August 27th the Earl of Monmouth, Lord Lumley, and T. Wharton reported on the Petition of Samuel Gibbs, Henry Rice, and others as follows: "Having examined the Petition of the sevll Persons . . . referred to us by your Maj^{ty} for making such provision for them in the Army as we should think they deserve they having attended your Maj^{ty} in your army from Holland Wee do find that they have been Tradesmen & dealers who left their respective trades & concerns to carry on your Maj^{tys} Service whereby they have been at great Charge & expence & there being no vacancy to receive them in your Ma^{tys} Army Wee do humbly offer if your Ma^{ty} shall so please that for their present support they may be admitted into such vacant Employments as are or may happen in your Ma^{tys} Customes or Excise as the respective Com^{rs} shall find them qualified for."

On January 16th, 1689-90, the Earl of Shrewsbury writes to Viscount Lumley as follows: "I here enclosed send your Lo^p some Papers lately put into my hands amongst which you will observe a List of severall Persons; purporting a Collection to be made of considerable Summs of mony for the use of the late King James, and seeing many of them are, as I am informed, within your Lo^{ps} Lieutenancy of Northumberland, I must recommend it to you, (as the only use that can be made of this dark discovery) to excite the Deputy Lieutenants and Justices of the Peace for that County, to have a watchfull Eye over all disaffected Persons, & particularly such of them as are mentioned in the List, to see if their future behavior will give further insight into this matter."

On February 15th a Warrant was issued for a Commission to Richard, Viscount Lumley, to be Lord Lieutenant of the county of Durham. There is an account of Proceedings at Whitehall on Februrary 21st, "Upon the petition of William, Innkeeper of the Crown Inn in Kensington Praying his Matie to order the paym^t of the money following due from some of his Maties Horse Guards.

Letters in Towne to the same effect, so that it seems necessary that something should be done to discountenance those
meetings of disaffected Persons & Papists & to quell the
minds of his Ma^{tys} peaceable Subjects who are cast into
apprehensions by them, & therefore I propose it to y^r Lo^{ps}
consideration whither it may not be fitt at this time to excite the Justices of the Peace & the Deputy Lieut^{ts} to looke
through the County again & to give order for disarming
the Papists & those that adhere to them & to secure such
horses as are forfeit'd by the late act & further to recommend it to some of those that are most active to have an
eye upon such as give these causes to suspect them & to
see that the Peace of the Kingdome be preserved I have
ordered the Express that came up from Berwicke to attend
you with these Letters who may give you further information in this matter & carry your Directions downe with him
into the Country."

This last is still addressed to " My Lord Lumley," though
he had just been raised to the Earldom, the original warrant
being as follows :

" Great Seale containing Our grant of ye dignity of an
Earle of this Our Kingdome of England unto our R^t Tr:
& Welb: Cous: & Counsell^r Richd Visc^t Lumley by ye name
Stile & Title of Earle of Chichester in this our King-
dome. . . . Given at Whitehall ye 3^d day of Aprill 1690."
Note at the side: "Memd^m this Warrant passed afterw^{ds}
wth this alteration, Instead of Earle of Chichester, Earle of
Scarborough."

There is no reason given why the title was altered, and
at that time the new Earl had no lands in Yorkshire,
whereas his family had for some time held considerable
estates, as has been seen, in Sussex. It will be noticed that
the name is spelt here Scarborough, but it very soon assumed its present form of Scarbrugh.

In a newsletter of May 13th, the Earl of Scarbrugh is
again called by his former title when it is recorded that
" Lord Marlbrough, Lumley & Mounser Overkirke has
each advanced £10,000 for ye paying of ye army."

Charles Butler, Esq., was, on the 18th day of December,

1690, appointed Cornett and Major of " Our First Troope of Our Horse Guards whereof Our Right Trusty & R^t Welbeloved Cousin and Counsellor Richard Earle of Scarborough is Captaine & Colonell," and on the 25th of the same month Frederick William, Count de Marton, was made " Guidon & Major" of the same regiment.

In this year Lord Scarbrough attended King William to Ireland, was at the battle of the Boyne, and afterwards waited on his Majesty at the great Congress of Princes at the Hague and came back with him to England.

It would not be out of place here to quote the lines on the battle of the Boyne written by the great-uncle of the present Earl of Scarbrough on his grandmother's side, Marcus Gervoise Beresford, first Lord Bishop of Kilmore, and later Lord Primate of All Ireland. It is perhaps needless to state that these lines were written when he was an undergraduate, in the fine frenzy of his hot Orange days. It was difficult in his latter years to get him even to own to them, though my mother, his favourite niece, could sometimes beguile him by misquoting a specially favourite line. Then with a twinkle in his bright blue eye, he would set her right, and once I heard him repeat the whole poem as here given :

THE BATTLE OF THE BOYNE

I

Woe worth the day when Ireland's Isle
To a Popish King did bow,
When Protestants without a cause
Were hanged to feed the crow,
When Popish Priests our pockets fleeced,
And made our blood to flow.

II

To take our lands and spoil our goods
They cruel laws did pass,
They took our churches from us,
In them they said their Mass;
They pinched our toes with wooden shoes,
And our money they made of brass.[1]

---

[1] A fact.—ED.

III

They trampled on our clergy,
And robbed them of their bread,
And priests came with their pixes
To tease our dying bed,
For a righteous cause there were no laws,
And freedom's soul was dead.

IV

That base apostate Fitton
Lord Chancellor they made,
And a Nugent too Chief Justice was,
Another Popish blade;
And Rice made three, that to the knee
In Protestant blood did wade.

V

Then loudly blew the shrilly fife,
And deeply rolled the drum,
And of ten thousand Orangemen
Not one of them was dumb;
With one accord they passed the word
"Now Orange William come."

VI

Our brave King William led them on
Across the rolling Boyne,
He formed his horsemen on the bank
That glorious day so fine,
And he charged their rank and he turned their flank
And he overthrew their line.

VII

King James cried out, "These Orangemen
I see are not in play;
Their arms are strong, their swords are long,
So we'd better run away;
So we'll say a Mass and we'll take a glass
And we'll fight another day."

VIII

You would have laughed had you been there
To see those heroes go;
Upon my word to see them run
It was a holy show;
To the mice and cats and the moles and rats
Their images they throw.

IX

The ground was strewed with scapulars
And relics lying there;
You would have thought of damaged goods
The Pope had held a fair;
There were Peter's toes and Bridget's nose
And Apollonia's hair;

X

The grinders of St. Dominic
That did his mutton chew,
St. Dunstan's tongs that pinched the snout
Of Satan black and blue,
And the holy thumb and the *Os sacrum*
Of St. Lorenzo too.

XI

Our fathers having won the day
Did then divide the spoil;
They burned some scores of wooden Saints
To make their kettles boil;
And they ate their lunch and they drank their punch
And rested from their toil.

XII

So here's to the glorious memory
Of William of Nassau,
Who saved us all from Popery,
Brass coin and Popish law,
From timber toes and wooden shoes
And thumping of our craw.

XIII

And here's to our noble forefathers,
Whose glorious courage broke
From off their own and children's neck
The cruel Popish yoke.
Their swords are rust and their bones are dust,
But we have their hearts of oak.

In January, 1690-1, the Earl of Scarbrough is named among those appointed as commissioners in the following commission, others being the Marquis of Carmarthen, the Earl of Marlborough, the Bishop of London, and several other earls and bishops :

"Whereas we are credibly informed that divers great abuses & irregularitys are committed in all or most of the

Hospitalls or Houses of Charity within this Kingdom, whereby great wrong is done to yᵉ Poor, and the charitable & pious Intentions of the Founders & of the Benefactors to the said Hospitalls are greatly perverted if not totally frustrated to the great Displeasure of Almighty God, and evill Exemple to others offending in the like kind. And We being resolved out of Our Religious & Pious Disposition to use the most effectuall means for yᵉ reforming and correcting of the said abuses and preventing the like in time to come, and reposing assured Trust & Confidence in your fidelities, circumspections and Judgement, Have thought fitt to Assigne & appoint you . . . to be our Commissioners. And we do by these Presents give unto you or any   or more of you full power and authority in Our Name, and as our Commissʳˢ to visit as well the severall Hospitalls hereafter particularly mentioned and expressed, that is to say : The Hospitall of St John the Baptist in or near Our Citty of Chester, the Hospitall of St Mary Magdalen in the Suburbs of Our Towne of Newcastle upon Tyne, the Hospitall of the Blessed Virgin Mary within Our said Towne of Newcastle upon Tyne, the Hospitall of St Sepulchre near Haw   within the Deanery of Holderness, the Hospitall at Ilford in Our County of Essex, the Hospitall of St Mary Magdalen within the Deanery of Colchester, the Hospitall of St Katherine neare Our Tower of London, the Hospitall of the blessed Virgin Mary at Nottingham, the Hospitall of Blythe in the Deanery of Bedford, the Hospitall of St Crosse neare Our Citty of Winchester, the Hospitall of St Mary Magdalen within the Deanery of Winton, and yᵉ Hospitall of St John at Litchfield . . . as also all & every other Hospitall or Hospitalls . . . within our said Kingdom of England Dominion of Wales & Towne of Berwick upon Tweed which are subject or Lyable to our Visitation.

"And we do further hereby give & grant unto you Our said commissioners or any or more of you full power & Authority from time to time to call send for, or cause to come before you . . . as well the Masters, Heads, Governors, Officers, & Ministers or any others of or belonging to the said Hospitalls ... to enquire discover examine or find out & inform yourselves of the Estate and Regiment of the said severall Hospitalls, and of the Masters Heads or Governors Officers Ministers poore People and others there abiding, and of the Disposition & Imployment of the Revenues given or purchased for the maintenance of the said severall Hospitalls, Houses Masters ... and of all Crimes, Defects, Excesses, Abuses, Corruptions, Offences & Enormitys as well in concealing abridgeing altering and diverting or misimploying of the said Hospitals or Houses, etc., etc."

Lord Scarbrough seems to have gone straight from the campaign in Ireland to that in Flanders, as the following extracts from the Domestic Papers refer some to the one and some to the other.

February 17th, 1690-1, in the " Memoriall to the Right Hono^{ble} Lords of the Com^{tee} for the affaires of Ireland," from the Commissioners of Transportation we have : " There are now nine ships that serve for the Transportation from Bristoll to Ireland, whereof six for horse cont. 770½ Tuns and will carry 230 horses, & three for Hay cont. 652½ Tuns and will carry 100 load of pressed Hay. Three of the Horse ships cont. 393½ Tuns are gone with 103 of Coll. Villers's Horse-Recruits for Corke, & one ship of 81 Tuns to Waterford to bring over 24 of the Earle of Scarborough's horses and his Groomes."

On May 4th, 1691, a commission was issued to " Edward Whitcomb Clerk to be Chaplain of ye first troop of Horse Guards commanded by Richard Earle of Scarborough whereof he is Capt & Colonell"; and on May 7th : " Sir Henry Goodrick Kn^t & Bart Lieut Gen^{ll} of our Ordnance" received a warrant to issue arms for the "granadiers" of the same troop. On July 23rd according to English calculation, August 3rd according to Flemish, in the order of the march in Flanders, the generals are said to be the " D. de Wirtemberg" and the " C. de Noyelles," while the first corps was commanded by the " Pr. de Sarbrugge, C. d'Athlone, Mr. D. Auerquerque, Mr. Macquay, Sr John Lanier, M^r la Forest, Mr de Zecylesteyn, and Ld Scar-

bourough." In August 10th-20th, Viscount Sidney, writing
to the Treasury from the camp at Court upon Heure, says :

" The Earl of Scarbrough having acquainted the King
that there is lately brought into the port of New Castle
being within his L^{ps} Vice Admiralty a French prize laden
with wines of the growth of that Country his L^p having
likewise desired his Maj^{tie} to grant him his Maj^{ties} Share
being a tenth part of the said Prize Wines if the King have
any share His Maj^{ty} has been pleased to condescend thereunto and accordingly has commanded me to signifie his
Pleasure to you Lpps to give orders that the said Earl of
Scarbrough have his Maj^{ties} share being a tenth part of the
said Prize Wines accordingly. There is likewise some
Brandy in the said vessel, whereof His Maj^{tie} has a like
share, which he has likewise granted to my Lard Scarbrough."

On September 5th a warrant was issued to Sir Henry
Goodrick, to cause " 20 carbines 8 pair of pistolls to be
issued for the use of Our first Troop of Guards commanded
by Our R^t trusty . . . Richard Earle of Scarborough, &
likewise 8 strapt Fuzees for the granadiers of the said
Troop, being in lieu of so many lost & broken in Our
Imediate Service in Our Kingdom of Ireland."

The Earl of Scarborough evidently remained on in
Flanders, but our knowledge of him for some years is very
scanty. The following Paper comes from the Treasury
Documents:

" The humble Petition of Richard Earl of Scarbrough

" Sheweth

" That King Charles ye 2nd by Letters Patents bearing
date ye 8th day of Febr. in ye 24th yeare of his Reign did
grant ye office of surveyor of ye Lesser Customes and of y^e
Subsidies of Tunnage & Poundage in ye Port of London
unto Geo. Porter Esqr for his life, and by ye same Letters
Patents did Grant ye same Office in Revercon to Sr John
Stapeley for his life : That his same Maj^{ty} by other Letters
Patents dat. 4th Decr in ye 26th yeare of his Reign did
Grant ye said Office to Richard Mountney William Water-

son and Philip Marsh in Revercon for and during yᵉ life of Sʳ Richard Fanshaw Barᵗ. That yᵉ said George Porter & Sʳ Richard Fanshaw are dead, so that yᵉ said Office is now in grant onely for yᵉ Life of yᵉ said Sir John Stapeley

"Your Petʳ doth humbly Beseech your Majᵗʸ out of your Royal grace and Bounty to grant yᵉ said Office in Revercon after yᵉ Life of yᵉ said Sʳ John Stapeley unto your Petʳ for yᵉ Lives of Richard and William two of your Petʳˢ sons."

This is, as is usual with petitions, undated, but on April 19th, 1695, George Bradley writes from St. James's to say: "The Earl of Scarbrough commands me to let you know yᵗ he will send you yᵉ names of three persons to whom he desires yᵉ grant may be made (to them and their Heires) during yᵉ Lives of Richard & William his sons, and yᵗ you would prepare yᵉ Warrant as soon as you have yᵉ names." This is minuted as granted.

The Earl was evidently at the Court of Flanders when the King wrote the following letter to the Lord Chancellor, which has recently been brought to light at Sandbeck, among others which prove how entirely the first Earl enjoyed King William's confidence:

"Loo, Aug. 15th, —98.

"I imparted to you before I left England that in France there was exprest to my Lord Portland some inclination to come to an agreement with me concerning the successing of the King of Spain, since which Count Tallard hath mentioned to me, and hath made proposalls, the particulars of which my Lord Portland will write to Vernon, to whom I have given orders not to communicate them to any other beside yourself, and to leave to your Judgment to whom else you would think proper to impart them, to the end I might know your opinions upon so important an affair and one which requires your greatest secrecy. If you think this negotiation should be carry'd on there's no time to be lost, and you must send me your full powers under your great seal, with the names in Blank, to treat with Count Tallard. I believe this may be done secretly, that none but you and Vernon, and those to whom you have communicated it, may have knowledge of it. Soe that the clarks who are to write the Warrant, and the full powers, may not know what it is. According to all intelligence the King of Spain cannot out-live the month of October, and the least accident may carry him off any day. I received yesterday your letter of the nineth. Since my Lord Wharton cannot at this time leave England I must think of some other to goe ambassador into Spain, if you can think of anyone proper let me know it, and be assured of my friendship.

" WM. R."

Lord Chancellor Somers in his reply urges the King to avoid if possible entailing any further wars on England. He warns him against trusting France, which country will naturally be very anxious to seize upon Spain. He apo-logizes for incoherence, as he is taking the waters at Tun-bridge Wells, which he says are known to discompose and disturb the brain. He concludes : " The Commission is wrote to Mr. Secretary and I have had it seal'd in such a manner that no creature has the least knowledge of the thing besides the persons already nam'd."

Under Queen Anne Lord Scarbrough retained his posts of Lieutenant-General of the Forces and Custos Rotulorum for the county of Northumberland, and Vice-Admiral of the Sea Coasts of Durham and Northumberland, and on June 24th, 1702, he was appointed Lord Lieutenant of the counties of Durham and Northumberland. He was also sworn of her Privy Council, and was constituted one of the Commissioners to treat of a union between the two King-doms of England and Scotland, and pursuant to that Act was sworn of the Privy Council, August 18th, 1708.

The only papers of note in this reign at present dis-covered are connected with the Earl's privilege of hunting in the Forest of Bere. The first is the following letter :

"Lumley, May 30th, 1704.

" S^r

" I have received yours and desire the favor of you, to returne my most humble thankes to my Lord Treasurer for his favor, in sending me Mr. Norton⁵ representation,

which I can assure his Lo^{pp} shall be answered to his satisfaction, I will attend him before the end of the next mounth,
& will make noe use of the warrant, till I know his Lo^{pp}
pleasure, and will be carfull of the representation til I deliver it to him, I am with a just sence of all your former
favors

" Your most humble sarvent

" SCARBROUGH."

This was directed: " For William Lowndes Esquire at
the cockpit neare Whitehall, London," he being the Secretary of the Lords of the Treasury. Mr. Norton, as the next
paper shows, was the Warden of Bere Forest. This is a
report dated March 28th, 1707, of Mr. Edward Wilcox,
" To the most Honble Sidney Earle of Godolphin Lord
High Treasurer of England," which begins thus :

" May itt please yor Lord^{pp}

" In obedience to yor Lordpps Comands I have considered Mr. Norton the Warden of Bier Forest his Letters
to yor Lordpp, together with his Reply to my Report about
that Forrest, in which he declares the Earle of Scarborough's
Grant for three Brace of Bucks yearly out of that Forrest
to be the Sole and onely Reason of his making his late
Proposall to yor Lordpp.

" 'Tis certaine that Grant whereby his Lordpp is im-
powered to hunt and kill the said Deer without asking y^e
Consent of ye Warden or acquainting him with itt, does in
some measure Eclipse the Power and Comand of the
Warden, which seems to be Greivous to him. And rather
than bare itt, Proposes to part with the Perpetuall Warden-
ship of the Forest, which is no doubt attended with pleasure,
Especially being so near to his Cheif seat, Provided he can
be well paid for itt . . ."

Finally, on July 1st, 1709, Richard Norton writes to
Mr. Taylor as follows : " Lord Scarborough's warrant I
have no coppy of here, but it is in effect that he is to have
3 brace of Bucks yearly during his life out of our forest.
the Warrant wch is in Mr. Lownds^s hands & wch he told me
he approved off, will not interfere wth the Lord Scarboroughs

warrant at all, as I can perceive, but this is purely for y^e
Queens service, & it is so necessary too, that I am very sure
her forest will be lost without it, & now Buck season is come
in & we shall loose ye benefit of ye warrant in a great
measure if it be not signed quickly; there is no doubt but
Lord Scarboroughs hunting dos a vast prejudice to the
forest, but till ye Queen is pleased to remedy that part
(which I have so often represented to my Lord Treasurer,)
her forest must suffer, but then I would have all other
hunting stoppt, if his must not that at least her Majestys
Deer may be preserved by all other means, that we can, I
could lett things go on at any rate, & not be found fault wth
by the borderers, because they would have their full pleasure at her Majesties cost; but since I have this office, I
will do my duty honestly, & represent what I know is for
ye Service, & if there is no support to be given to me in it,
I must be content if I can. I hope to get home on monday
next, for I can sacrifice my health no longer about it, I am
not able to do it, I wish I cou'd have ye warrant signed so
as to carry it with me, because this is ye very time to begin
ye cure; but I fear now I shall not have it but beg of you
S^r to lett ye gentleman I send wth this to have it as soon as
possible. I desire there may be no alteration made in it nor
any mention of Lord Scarborough for as wth submission I
think it wholly needless, so it would indeed be a strengthen-
ing of his warrant, & I hope yet ye Queen will be sensible
how unfair a thing his Lordsp desired of her, & how pre-
judiciall to her, & revoke it, or ty him up from hunting at
least, we would serve him with ye Deer & save them in other
people provided he might not hunt, but 'tis that destroys
our little forest, & drives our Deer to the Devil, whence
they scarce ever return again to us, but are waylaid & kill'd,
besides their being all surfeited wth being so driven in y^e
hot weather. I had much rather her Majesty would dis-
afforest us, than see her right & her Deer made use of onely
for the spoil & sport of her subjects, for it lessens ye Crown
too much in my poor opinion, & all I desire is to preserve
the prerogative, I do assure you, & think I am bound to
do it. and therefore give you & my self so much troble.

for I have not a farthing for my pains, but at constant expence."

The following letter, discovered in the British Museum, refers to Lord Scarborough's son, Richard, who succeeded him as second Earl, and was written to the Elector of Hanover, father of George I.:

"Your electorall Highnes will I hope pardon this liberty I take, by my secound son, whom having finnished his studies, I have ordered to begin his traveling, with paying his earliest respects & duty to your electorall Highnes, the favors I have formerly receaved from your Electorall Highness, oblidges me to make all my familie sensible of your greate goodnes, Mr. Smith Eldest son to the speaker of the house of Commons begins his travells with my son, in order to pay his respects and duty to your Electorall Highnes. May all prosperity attend your Electorall Highnes & Princely familie, which shall be the constant prayer of your Electorall Highnes

"most devoted, obedient, & most faithfull humble sarvant
"SCARBROUGH.
"July 22nd, 1706."

On the accession of George I., Lord Scarbrough was among those peers intrusted by his Majesty with the government of these kingdoms until his arrival. On March 9th, 1715-6, he was appointed Chancellor of the Duchy and County Palatine of Lancaster, which he resigned in May, 1717, and thereupon had the office of Vice-Treasurer, Receiver-General, and Paymaster of all his Majesty's revenues in the Kingdom of Ireland, with the power to act by sufficient deputies. And here, alas, we have a specimen of the maladministration of affairs in those days, for Lord Scarbrough accepted those lucrative posts, having no intention of crossing the sea even once; for he procured an Act of Parliament which passed the royal assent on July 6th, 1717, to enable him to take in England the usual oath to qualify himself for the said office. One would rather that the last public act of his life had been more in accordance

with the single-hearted service which his ancestors had
given to their sovereigns. It is from such glimpses as these
that one gets a fair insight into the wrongs of the sister
country in those days, and it makes one feel that Ireland
has much to forgive and to forget if there are ever to be
cordial relations between the Rose and the Shamrock.

Lord Scarbrough died on December 17th, 1721, and was
buried with his ancestors in the church of Chester-le-Street
in the bishopric of Durham. He married Frances, only
daughter and heir of Sir Henry Jones of Aston in the
County of Oxfordshire, and of his wife Frances, daughter
of Henry Belasis, eldest son of Thomas, Lord Viscount
Falconberg. She was one of the Ladies of the Bedchamber
to Queen Mary and to Queen Anne, and died in 1737.

The first Earl of Scarbrough left seven sons and four
daughters. There is at Sandbeck a full-length portrait of
him in armour, as also of his only brother, Henry Lumley,
who was a distinguished soldier, notably at the battle of
Landen, July 29th, 1693, when his regiment by the noble
stand they made saved his Majesty from being taken
prisoner.

As has been already said there are several notices of
Lieut.-Col. Lumley in the Record Office, which may refer
either to the Viscount or his brother; but several certainly
do, and others may, refer to the younger. Thus we have a
" Passe to Mr. Charles Copsey and Mr. Henry Lumley to
goe to Portsmouth & imbark on board ye Elizabeth. Whitehall 18th March 1688-9." Either this was on military service or he soon returned to his duties, as on June 1st the
Earl of Shrewsbury, besides the letter already quoted to
Lord Lumley, writes the following to " Colonel Lumley,"
by whom he must mean Henry, as he addresses him as
" Sir ":

" I have received your Letter of the 26th of the last
month. I am directed to acquaint you that the King is
very well satisfy'd with yor care in seizing Mr. Turner as
also with yor acc^t you give of yor Regim^t and his Ma^{ty} rather
beleives your rep^t of it then what hath been said to as-
perse it.

"You will give order for Mr. Turner being secured till his Ma^ty signifies his Pleasure concerning him."

On October 16th was issued a "Post Warr^t to Coll Henry Lumley with 5 horses to Pass from London to West Chester." On November 14th the Duke of Schomberg sends a letter from Luinegarve to King William by " Mons. Lomlay, Lieut. Collonel de Sr Jean Lannier." On December 1st was issued at Whitehall a " Comm^n to Henry Lumley Esq. to be a Col. of Horse and do give and grant you full Power and Authority to command and take yor Rank accordingly."

Then there is a gap for a few years until April 3rd, 1693, when Lord Ranelagh writes that he has "considered the Proposall of Francis Mollineux & Benjamin Tomlinson Wollen Drapers Concerning the Cloathing of the Regim^t of Horse Commanded by Coll. Lumley and do thereupon report to your Lord^sps as followeth

" The full Offreckonings of the said Regim^t from the first of Aprill 1692 (at which time they came under my care) to the last of December following amounts to   £3469. 17. 6.

" which is sufficient to answere the proposers demand, and the poundage and days pay for the Royall Hospital."

On December 11th, 1694 a Report was made by Charles Fox on a " Memoriall of Mr. Thos Freckleton, Agent to Brigad^r Lumleys Regim^t of Horse." On February 6th, 1695-6, the following letter was written by William Blathwayt to Mr. Lowndes :

" Brigadier Lumley having crav'd an allowance of £612. 8. 2¼ for Liverys for the Trumpeters and Kettle Drummers and for colours and Kettle Drum Banners for the Regim^t under his command I send you the enclosed Certificate that the same has been formerly paid, to be laid before the Lords Commiss^rs of the Treasury."

In 1701-2 there are three letters " For the Honble Major Gen^ll Lumley " about his soldiers. The first, written from Windsor by Chas. Potts, is dated February 12th : "S^r, I received the 8th Instant a letter signed by your self Coll

GENERAL SIR HENRY LUMLEY, BROTHER OF
FIRST EARL

G. KNELLER

Lumley

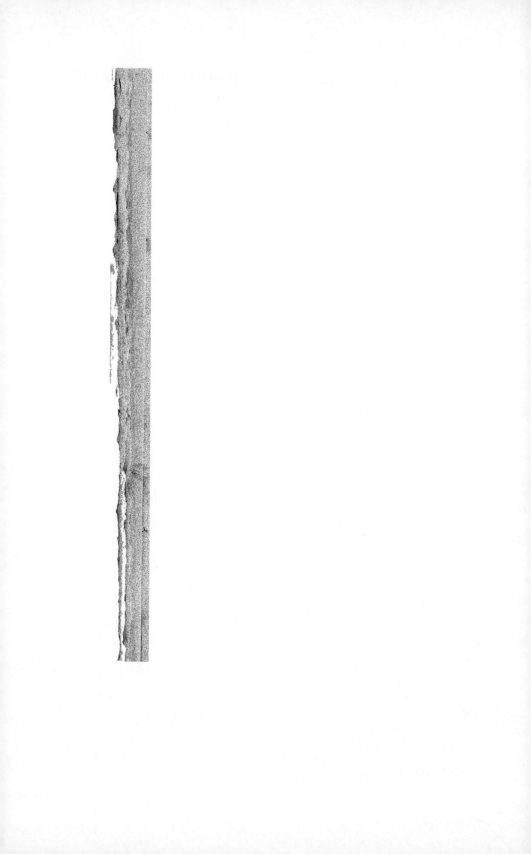

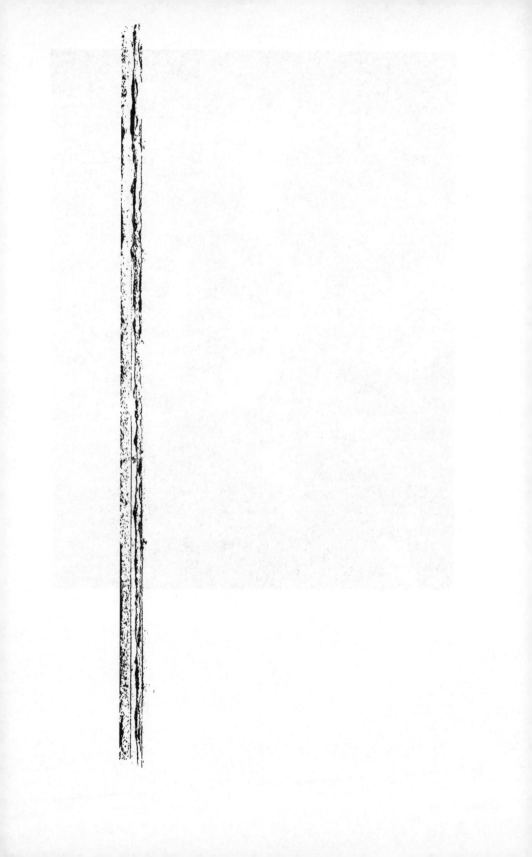

Whithers & Coll Wood signefieing your desire to have me view and report to you the condicon of the Invalids in this Garrison of their being capacitated to be received into Pention; wherein I complyed and finde very litle cause to Complaine as to this Company there being Scarse one but what have bin wounded in the service of the crowne I have alsoe incerted some that are Sick and on furloe. I have nothing to ade but to assure you that I shall at all times be readie to receive your Comands and testifie my self yor humble Servt."

The second, dated February 19th, was written by Rich. Hindmarsh from Walsend: "S^r, As soon as I received yo^{rs}, pursuant to yor orders therein expressed, I made a review of the company of invaleedes att Tynemouth Castle, and upon a serious Examination of their present state and condition and strict Inspection into their severall quallifications I doe think them truely quallified, and noe other then invaleedes, for many of them are very aged, severall have been in the service 30: 25: and 20 yeares, most of them are disabled by woundes or Bodily Infirmities soe that I cannot say there are above 4 or 5 fitt to doe his Majesty any Service abroad. . . ."

The third was written from Chester, February 25th, by Major Tho. Hand: "In obedience to yor Hon^{rs} Letters of the 7th Instant I have caused the company of Invalid Soldiers here und^r the Commande of Captn Twiddall to be called together (which had been done sooner had my health permitted) and with the assistance of an Expert surgeon I have examined every one of them particularly with respect to the qualifications menconed in yor Letter except some few which the Captn says are sick or out upon furlough. But affirms they are dewely qualifyed and except the persons in the Inclosed List who the Captn says do reside altogether at London. And I doe hereby certifye to yor Hono^r that I conceive all the said persons whom I view'd to be duely qualifyed as superannuated or Invalid soldiers except these 7 vizt Christopher Fouracres, John Whitehead, James Roberts, Richard Asmond, James Bullen, John Eaton and John Jackson whereof the four first seem very

fitt for Land Service save only that Asmond complaines of
some weakness in his eyes, Bullen says he has ben above
twenty years in ye Service but he is but ab^t 40 years old
and seems to be perfectly cured of his wounds, the two last,
Eaton and Jackson say they are not able to endure long
marches but are very fitt and willing to serve in her Ma^{tys}
fleet."

The next paper refers to horses "lost in Holland in y^e
last Campagne": "Henry Lumley Major Genl & Colonel
of her Majestys Regim^t of Horse Certifyeth for the Losses
of the Severall Regim^{ts} undermentioned wch appears by the
Certificates of an Officer belonging to each Regim^t.

	Lost at sea	By Canonading etc. at Charter-hous	On party	Total
Major-Gen. Lumley's Regim^t	11	19	6	36
The Earle of Arran	11		1	12
Bridag^r Woods	3	5	2	10
Major Gen. Wyndham . . .	6	5		11
Duke Schomberg	19	6	9	34
	50	35	18	103

"Dec^{br} 4 1702. I do hereby certify according to the Certificates given mee there appears to be lost as above one
hundred and three horses

"(Signed) HENRY LUMLEY."

This was forwarded on January. 6th, 1702-3, to Mr.
Lowndes by "Ad. Cardonel," who says: "I am likewise
comanded by my Lord Duke" (of Marlborough) "to trans-
mitt to you the enclosed Certificate from Major General
Lumley of the Loss of Horses in Holland. His Grace
having recomended itt to my Lord Treasurer, that some
provision be made for answering the Loss of the 53 horses
under the Two last heads, at £15 each Horse."

After several documents as to the clothing of the Lieut-
tenant-General Lumley's men in 1706 and 1707, we have
on March 7th, 1711-12, a letter from Robert Peter to James
Taylor, Esq., saying, "The Coats wastcoats and Banners
being all ready to be putt on board in the River Thames

on monday next pursuant to her Majesties Commands but before I can deliver the same I must desire you to acquaint mee who must be my Paymaster. Generall Lumley at parting hence acquainted me, That Mr. Benson ye Chancellor of the Exchequer had promised him that the money should be payd to you in a very few dayes. and unless you make me due payment according to the Generalls directions it will be impossible for me to deliver them and a very great Losse if I am not payd the same speedily being nine parts in tenn out of pocket for the gold lace which cannot be bought without ready money. I pray youre Answeare by too morrow morneing."

Unfortunately his Petition was not granted, and on December 2nd, 1714, John Remy de Montigney made oath "that in the Month of February 1711 One Stephen de la Cruize on the part of Robert Peter Cloathier applyd to him the said John Remy de Montigney to borrow of him Seaven Thousand five hundred pounds South Sea Stock on the creditt of Two Cloathing Assignments One dated ye 10th Jan. 1711 for the offreckonings of Gen^{ll} Lumley's Regiment amounting to Five thousand five hundred and ninety two pounds two shillings & 2^d the other for the Offreckonings of Coll. Kerrs Regiment Dated the 17th January 1711 amounting to Three thousand five hundred and twenty six pounds Tenn shill & 5$\frac{1}{2}$^{d}."

Of this he had only received at various times sums amounting to £2,371 8s. 8d. In a further paper relating to the same matters we read that "This Purchase was made above Two Years before Mr. Peters became a Bankrupt."

Finally on February 18th, 1714-5, the Commissioners for Duties upon Hides wrote to the Lord of the Treasury that, having considered the Report of the Attorney and Solicitor-General, they directed the money to be paid.

The remainder of Henry Lumley's life can best be related by quoting the marble monument in the parish church at Sawbridgeworth in the county of Hertford, in the vault under which he lies buried:

"Here lieth the honourable Henry Lumley, Esq., only

brother to Richard Earl of Scarbrough, who was in every battle, and at every siege, as colonel, lieutenant colonel, or general of the horse, with King William or the Duke of Marlborough, in twenty campaigns in Ireland, Flanders and Germany, where he was honoured, esteemed, and beloved by our own armies, by our allies, and even by the enemies, for his singular politeness and humanity, as well as for all his military virtues and capacity.

" He sat long in Parliament, always zealous for the honour of the Crown, and for the good of his Country, and knew no party but that of truth, justice and honour.

" He died Governor of the Isle of Jersey, the 18th of October, 1722, in the sixty third year of his age."

The present Archbishop of Canterbury, when Bishop of Winchester, gave to the Earl of Scarbrough papers signed by Henry Lumley, presenting various persons to livings in the Island of Jersey.

We have next a pathetic little touch of domestic joy and sorrow in this active stirring life, for following the record of these events are the following lines :

" Here also lieth Mrs. Francis Lumley, his only dear and beloved child, of great beauty and greater hopes ; who died October 13th 1719, the sixth of her age : sometime the joy, then the anguish of her fond parents.

" Here lieth also Dame Anne Lumley, daughter of Sir William Wiseman, of Canfield, Essex, who set up this monument 1723 in memory of the best of husbands, and her dear child near whom she was deposited anno 1736."

She died on March 4th of that year. Her mother was Arabella, sister and heiress to George Hewitt, Viscount Hewitt of Gowran in Ireland. This monument does not mention General Lumley's first wife, who was Elizabeth, daughter of — Lincoln, Esq., by whom he had no children.

CHAPTER X

F the first Lord Scarbrough's seven sons, the eldest, Henry, Lord Viscount Lumley, died unmarried in 1710, during his father's lifetime, of smallpox, the scourge of that age, and was buried near his grandfather, the Hon. John Lumley, in the Church of St. Martin-in-the-Fields.

The second, Richard, succeeded his father as second Earl of Scarbrough in 1721.

The third, William, was brought up in the sea service, and was killed in an engagement in the Mediterranean on April 9th, 1709.

The fourth, Thomas, succeeded his brother Richard as the third Earl of Scarbrough in 1739-40. He was born in 1690.

The fifth, Charles, was made Groom of the Bedchamber to his Majesty George I. on December 22nd, 1726, and died August 11th, 1727, being then Member for Chichester.

The sixth, John, was one of the Grooms of the Bedchamber to Frederick, Prince of Wales, Member of Parliament for Arundel in Sussex, and he was also appointed Colonel of a company of Grenadiers in the Coldstreams Regiment of Footguards on February 1st, 1731-2. He departed this life October, 1738, and was buried in the vault of St. Martin-in-the-Fields.

The youngest, James, succeeded his brother Charles as Member for Chichester, and later his brother John in his two posts of Groom of the Bedchamber to the Prince of

Wales and Member for Arundel. Also in May, 1734, he was constituted "Avener" (in feudal law an officer of the king's table whose duty it was to provide oats) and Clerk Marshal of his Majesty's Horse, and was appointed, with Colonel Henry Berkeley, Commissioner for executing the office of Master of the Horse.

There are several letters from him among the "Letters to the Duke of Newcastle" in the British Museum, which are chiefly remarkable for their bad writing, spelling and grammar. The first, dated "October ye 21, 1740," acknowledges a letter from the Duke and says he is "ready to think and hope I have your Graces friendship which no body can Esteem more & am allways ready to Oblidge your Grace in every thing that is in my power."

On May 31st, 1741, he writes: "I should with a great deal of pleasure been at the meeting with the rest of the gentlemen to appoint a proper person to represent the County but hopes your Grace will excuse my personall appearence having something of my own affares prevented my coming down but the person that I hear will be proposed I shall use my utmost endeavour to support, I desire your Grace will pay my compliments to the Duke of Richmond Dorset and Ld Willmington." On August 7th he writes from Tunbridge Wells to let the Duke know "that lieutenant Colonell Beckwith of Colonell Handysites Regiment which is one of the seven encamped here is dead. Major Montague is the eldest majer of these regiments. I beg the favour you will get this commission for him." This was evidently granted, as on the 20th he writes to say: "I think my self extreamly obliged to you and return you thanks for the favour you have done." On November 14th he "should not have given you this trouble but not having the honour to be acquainted with my Ld Lincoln tis to recommend George Pate who was butler to my Late Brother [the second Earl] to be butler to his Ldship he served my Brother a great many years and is a very honest sober man." On August 15th, 1753, he writes: "I received the favour of your graces letter and will be sure to be at Lewis on the Sunday night and at the meeting a Wednesday and

will do my self the honour to dine a thursday at Ayland
with your grace. I had a great deal of company dined with
me yesterday, they was all a saying they intended to go to
the assizes at Lewis." The last two refer to a matter which
appears again in the letters of Thomas, third Earl. "Mr.
Lumleys compliments to the Duke of Newcastle, begs leave
to remind him of his promise to speak to the Bishop of
Durham to desire a prebendary of a living for Mr. Hammore
when a vacancy Happens. 18 of March 1760." "June ye
23 1760. My Lord. I have received a letter from Lord
Scarbrough to inform me that a prebendary at Durham is
vacant by the death of Dr. Chapman, and that he desires I
would wait on your Grace to desire you would speak to the
bishop of Durham in favour of mr. Hammore to succeed
him in doing of which we shall esteem it as a singular
favour." He died unmarried in 1766.

Of the four daughters, the eldest, Lady Mary, was married
to George Montagu, first Earl of Halifax, and died on September 10th, 1726.

Lady Barbara was married to the Honourable Charles
Leigh, of Leighton Beaudesert, brother to Lord Leigh.
She left no children and died on January 4th, 1755.

Lady Anne was, like her mother, one of the Ladies of the
Bedchamber, and on December 30th, 1729, an order was
issued from the Lords of the Treasury, endorsing a warrant
from the Duke of Grafton to the Master of the Great Wardrobe, dated November 24th, for the provision and delivery
to Grey Maynard, Esq., Yeoman of his Majesty's Removing Wardrobe, of the following particulars for his Majesty's
service at Kensington, viz., four window curtains for Lady
Anne Lumley. She was married on February 15th, 1738,
to Frederick Frankland, Esq., M.P. for the borough of
Thirsk, and in the marriage settlement, found among the
Lumley papers at Sandbeck, her fortune is stated to be
£9,000. But the marriage must have been a very unhappy
one, as there has also been found a deed of separation between them, executed in the July of the same year. Lady
Anne died on February 17th, 1739-40.

Lady Henrietta died unmarried on November 6th, 1747.

There are at Lumley portraits of several of these children; a beautiful one of Richard and Thomas together as
children (the lace on their dresses is now in the possession
of Lady Scarbrough), as well as several of Richard as
second Earl in Court dress; also a later one of Thomas,
and small oval pictures of John and James, and one of
Lady Henrietta or Harriet, who must have been very
pretty. Lastly, there is one of Lady Halifax in the style
of Lely.

Richard, second Earl of Scarbrough, was elected one of
the members for East Grinstead to the Parliament called in
1708; and for the borough of Arundel in two other Parliaments, whereof the last was sitting on the demise of the
Queen. On the accession of her successor, he was appointed
one of the Gentlemen of the Bedchamber to H.R.H. the
Prince of Wales, and soon after was constituted Master of
the Horse, and was also Captain and Colonel of the first
troop of Grenadier Guards. On March 10th, 1714-5, he
was summoned by writ to the House of Peers. He succeeded in the year 1721 to his father's titles and honours
as Lord Lieutenant and Custos Rotulorum of the county of
Northumberland, and to the same position in the town and
county of Newcastle-upon-Tyne. On May 2nd, 1721, he stood
proxy for Ernest, Duke of York, at the baptism of William
Augustus, afterwards the Duke of Cumberland, who is
notorious for leading the English forces against the High-
landers at the battle of Culloden, and to whom the nine
of diamonds owed its sobriquet of the " Curse of Scotland,"
the duke having written the order which led to such a
disastrous result upon it.

Lord Scarbrough was constituted Colonel of the 2nd
Regiment of Footguards, June 22nd, 1722. On June 9th,
1724, his lordship was elected one of the Knights Companion
of the most noble Order of the Garter, and was installed at
Windsor on July 28th following. On the accession of
George II. he was, on June 15th, 1727, constituted Master
of the Horse to his Majesty, and sworn one of the Privy
Council, and retained his honourable posts in Northumberland and Durham.

HON. RICHARD AND HON. THOMAS LUMLEY, SONS OF FIRST EARL OF SCARBROUGH C 1695

Sandbeck Park (?

? Jnl önght —but ? to' v

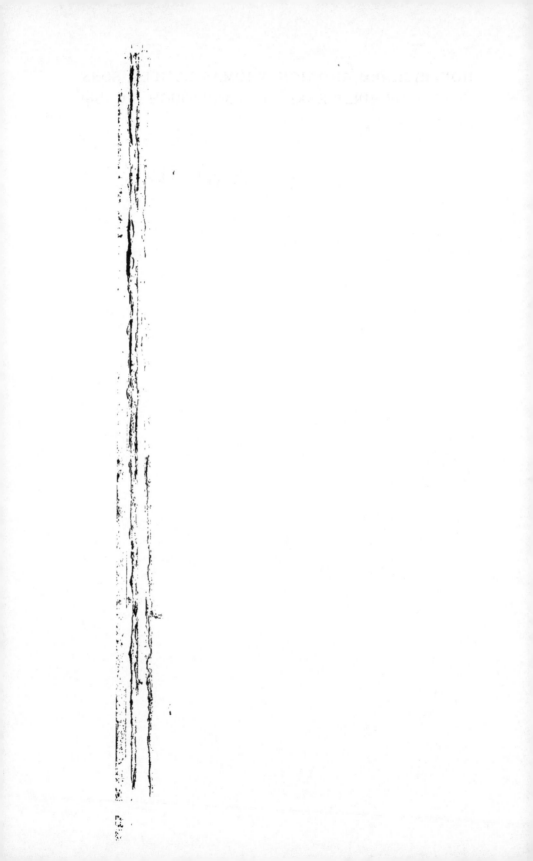

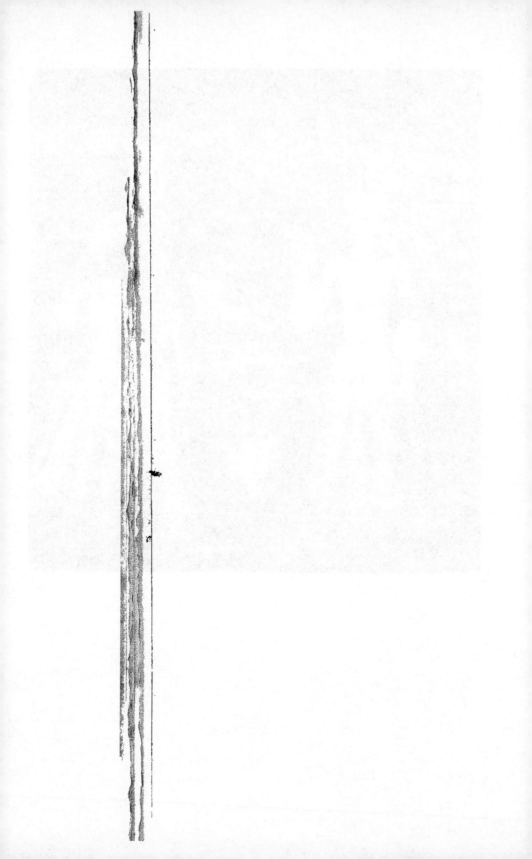

We obtain most of our information of this period of his life through the various biographies of his intimate friend, Philip Dormer Stanhope, fourth Earl of Chesterfield. Thus in Dr. Maty's Memoir of the life of Lord Chesterfield prefixed to his edition of his Miscellaneous Works, published in 1777, we have the following reference to Lord Scarbrough's duties: " Lord Scarborough seemed to have been distinguished more early. He was immediately appointed master of the horse and made a Member of privy council, into which lord Chesterfield was not admitted till six months afterwards" (p. 46).

In Croker's edition of John, Lord Hervey's " Memoirs of the Reign of George II." (vol. i., p. 98), the following contrast is drawn between the two friends : " If anybody had a friendship for Lord Chesterfield it was Lord Scarborough, yet it was impossible to see a stronger contrast of character in any two men, who neither wanted understanding, but the sort of understanding each possessed was almost as different as sense and nonsense : Lord Scarborough always searching after truth, loving it, and adhering to it; whereas Lord Chesterfield looked on nothing in that light—he never considered what was true or false, but related everything in which he had no interest just as his imagination suggested it would tell best. . . . Lord Scarborough had understanding with judgment and without wit; Lord Chesterfield a speculative head, with wit and without judgment. Lord Scarborough had honour and principle ; Lord Chesterfield neither; the one valued them wherever he saw them ; the other despised reality and believed those who seemed to have most, had generally only the appearance, especially if they had sense. . . . Nor were the tempers of these men more alike than their understanding and principles ; Lord Scarborough being generally splenetic and absent; Lord Chesterfield always cheerful and present; everybody liked the character of the one without being very solicitous for his company ; and everbody was solicitous for the company of the other, without liking his character. In short, Lord Scarborough was an honest, prudent man, capable of being a good friend; and Lord Chesterfield a dishonest, irresolute, imprudent creature, capable only of being a disagreeable enemy."

There are several entries in the Treasury Papers about the money transactions connected with Lord Scarbrough's duties. Thus on September 18th, 1727, there is a letter from "the Earl of Scarborough, Master of the Horse," to the Lords of the Treasury, asking for £3,000 to be issued to him at the Receipt of the Exchequer upon an unsatisfied order for £10,000 for the stables. Again, on December 11th he asks for a further sum of £3,000, which was paid to him on December 12th. Altogether the charge for the year ending June 30th, 1728, was £10,000, for which he received a discharge of £10,046 1s. 7½d. ; for the year following the charge was £12,500, and the discharge £11,452 11s. 11¼d.

There are several warrants as to the King's stud, of which this is the first: "Whereas it is our Royal Will and Pleasure to order direct and appoint that the Management of our Studd be under your care as Master of our Horse from the first day of Oct. 1728 and that the Expense of maintaining our said Studd shall be defrayed by you for the year commencing the said 1st day of October out of such our treasure as shall from time to time be imprested to you at the Receipt of our Exchequer for the extraordinary Expenses of our Stables our further Will and Pleasure is that you pay or cause to be paid as part of the expenses of the Studd for the said year the severall allowances following amounting to £258 8s. 2d.

	£	s.	d.
To the grooms at £36 each	72	0	0
To four Helpers at £30	120	0	0
To the Farrier	20	0	0
To the Bittmaker	10	0	0
For the maintenance of two horses for the attendance in the Studd at £18 4. 1. each	36	8	2
	258	8	2

"which the said officers and servants are to obey and observe such rules and directions as you shall from time to time give them for their conduct and behaviour in their several stations; And our further Will and Pleasure is that

you do make or cause to be made a contract or contracts
for the purveyance of provisions for our said Studd, and
also a contract or contracts for the Farrage and Medicines
of our Studd for the said year, and that you cause Quarterly
Bills to be made out of the Quantity of Provisions delivered
by the Purveyor for the Maintenance of our said Studd with
the amount thereof in money and also Quarterly Bills for
the Farrage and Medicines of our said Studd and likewise
that you cause Quarterly Bills to be made out of the sadlers
goods and contingent Expenses that you shall see necessary
or allow and provide for the use and Benefit of our said
Studd and the Receipts and Acquittances of the said Officers
and servants for the sums they shall severally and respectively receive and the Receipts and Acquittances upon the
severall Bills which you shall pay for the Maintenance,
keeping, and providing necessaries for our said Studd in
pursuance hereof shall be as well to you for payment as to
the Auditors of our Imprest and all others concerned in
passing and allowing thereof from time to time in a distinct
head upon your account of the Extraordinary Expenses of
our Stables a sufficient Warrant: And our further Will and
Pleasure is that our Studd shall have free Liberty to graze
in the proper seasons in our severall Parks as they have
been accustomed to do for which you are to give orders
from time to time in writing to be delivered to the Rangers
or Keepers of our said parks by the persons whom you
shall order to carry any part of our said Studd to graze.
And whereas our household Physitian, Apothecary and
Surgeon have been accustomed to have care of the servants
when sick or hurt by any accident whilst the servant was
on the Establishment of our Stables, our Will and Pleasure
is that the Servants of our Studd when sick or hurt by any
accident shall be under the care of our said Physitian,
Apothecary or Surgeon as they have been heretofore, Although our Studd is now placed on the Extraordinary Expenses of our Stables. And lastly our Will and Pleasure
is that as soon as may be after the 30th day of September
next you shall lay before us a specifick account of the
whole years expense in pursuance of the appointment to

x

the intent that we may give such Directions for the maintenance of the Studd thenceforward as we shall judge best
for our Service and for so doing this shall be your Warrant.
Given at our Court of St. James's this 5th March, 1728-9,
in the second year of our Reign."

On May 9th, 1729, Lord Scarbrough wrote the following
letter to the Lords of the Treasury:

" My lords. I desire your Lordships will please to direct
the sum of £2500 to be issued to me at the Receipt of His
Majesty's Exchequer upon the unsatisfied order in my name
for £5000 for defraying Extraordinary Expenses of His
Majesty's Stables.

" I am, my lords, your Lordships most
" obedient humble servant
" SCARBOROUGH."

This was issued on September 18th. Among the Treasury Papers are a series of documents of 1728 which one
Jezreel Jones sent in to the Lords of the Treasury as to the
expenses he incurred in the service of Abdiah Haman,
cousin to the Emperor of Morocco, and Cossum Hoja, the
Tripoli Ambassador. Among these is the following, dated
November 16th, 1728 :

" To the Right Honourable the Earl of Scarbrough,
petition for payment of £36. Jezreel Jones his account for
the Tripoly Ambassador, since his Audience at Windsor,
being for coaches with six and four and two horses from the
fourteenth of September, 1728, to the fourteenth of Nov.
following, viz, for coach and horses for two days with six
horses and for the rest of the time with two horses for one
month from Sep. 14 to Oct. 14 at £4. 10. 0. a week ; £18.
To ditto from the fourteenth Oct. to the fifteenth Nov.
following including coach and six three times and coach and
four twice in that time and the rest of the time with two
horses and attendance at £4. 10. 0. a week ; £18.
" Total £36. 0. 0."

On April 23rd, 1730, an order was issued by the Lords
of the Treasury for the execution of a warrant dated Feb-

ruary 14th, 1728-9, from the Duke of Grafton to the Duke of Montagu for the delivery of eighteen colours for his Majesty's Coldstream Regiment of Foot Guards under the Earl of Scarbrough, he having announced that his regiment has had no colours for several years past and is in great want of them. "Mem. This warrant will amount unto £162. or thereabouts."

Lord Scarbrough at this time was living at Stanstead, as we learn from the following letter written by Pope to his friend Mr. Caryll from Twickenham on February 3rd, 1728-9: "Then I assure you I had a merit you do not know of, for I did my utmost to make you in my way home, and had accomplished it, had not my Lord Scarborough's design of going then tò Sussex been put off. *Note.* The estate of Stanstead which adjoins Ladyholt (where Mr. Caryll lived) belonged to the Earl of Scarborough" (Elwin's edition of Pope's Works, vol. vi., p. 301).

Lord Scarbrough was interested in the famous Excise Bill introduced by Sir Robert Walpole in 1733. The following extract is taken from Lord Hervey's "Memoirs of George II.," vol. i., p. 187:

"On the Monday morning (9th April) before that Wednesday that was appointed for the second reading of the Bill, Lord Scarbrough came to Sir Robert Walpole, to let him know that he found the clamour so hot and so general, that it was his opinion the Administration ought to yield to it; that, for his own part, how right soever he might think this scheme in an abstracted light, yet, considering the turn it had taken, he was determined not to contribute to cram it down the people's throats; and came to tell Sir Robert that, if it should be forced through the House of Commons, and brought into the House of Lords, he would oppose it there. He said, by the best information he could get, the dislike of this scheme was almost as universal among the soldiery as the populace, and that the military part of the commonalty were as much prejudiced against it as the mercantile people. The soldiers, he said, had got a notion that it would raise the price of tobacco, and upon this notion were so universally set against the scheme, that they cursed the Administration and the Parliament, murmured treason even under the walls of the palace, and were almost as ripe for mutiny as the nation for rebellion.

"Sir Robert Walpole heard him with a great deal of temper and patience, and at last said, 'My dear Lord, you have too much honesty to suspect, and consequently to see, how little there is in some who bring you these tales, or get them conveyed to you, and are, without knowing it, influenced by men who are as much inferior to you in understanding as in integrity. We both understand one another, and whatsoever may be the fate of this Bill, I have nothing but this to desire of you—as I am your friend, and wish to have you continue mine—when those who have kindled this flame and fomented these discontents till they have brought things, as you say, even at the door of the palace, to the brink of rebellion—when they shall receive their reward for that conduct—do not you make their cause your own, or sacrifice your interest to those who have throughout this whole proceeding had no regard to yours, or to anything but the gratification of their own capricious resentment.'

"Lord Hervey came into the room just as Sir Robert Walpole had pronounced these words, and soon after Lord Scarbrough took his leave. Sir Robert immediately told Lord Hervey what had passed, who said he was not so much surprised as Sir Robert seemed to be : 'for you know, Sir, I long ago told you Lord Chesterfield governed him as absolutely as he does any of his younger brothers : and though you may think Lord Scarbrough loves you personally, which was the security you told me you depended upon for his never undertaking or joining in anything against your interest, yet I own I see very little difference between that attachmennt not existing at all or existing in a degree inferior to the influence of those who wished to prevent its operating.' . . . Had Lord Scarbrough, from apprehension only, said this in private to Sir Robert Walpole, it would have left people some room to excuse his conduct, and think his proceeding fair and honourable ; but before he made this declaration to Sir Robert Walpole he had already told his opinion and the resolution to several people who had circulated the news of this considerable deserter through all the town. He certainly ought not, after the part he had acted, to have opened his lips on this subject to any one but Sir Robert; for, as he had been so warm a promoter of this scheme, and, till three days before it was laid aside, on all occasions asserting the propriety of it, most people were of opinion his defection proceeded from the increased number of objectors to the Bill and not from the discovery of any new objections.

"This evening (9th April) Sir Robert Walpole saw the King in the Queen's apartment, just before the Drawing-room, and the final resolution was then taken to drop the Bill; but, as there was a petition to come from the City of London against it the next day, it was resolved that the Bill should not be dropped till that petition was rejected, lest it should be thought to be done by the weight and power of the city. . . ."

That evening Lord Hervey in a conversation with the King said to him: "It is reported, Sir, by the enemies to this Bill, that several of the Cabinet Council and several of your Majesty's domestic servants have asked audiences to let your Majesty know that they will not positively vote for the Bill; and the comment that is made on this report is, that if those who have the honour to serve your Majesty in such near and high stations did not know this declaration would not be displeasing to you, they would certainly not have ventured, so explicitly at least, to have made it." On being pressed by the King for names he said, "that the two that people talked most of at present, as they were reckoned the last that had absolutely declared themselves, were Lord Clinton (a Lord of the Bedchamber) and Lord Scarborough (Master of the Horse). The King replied with great warmth, It is a lie; those rascals in the Opposition are the greatest liars that ever spoke. Clinton has been with me, but Scarborough never had mentioned the Excise to me at all, and for these last 5 or 6 days he has kept out of my way. I have not so much as seen him, nor have any of my servants dared to tell me they would do what I would have them."

Sir Robert, as may be remembered, withdrew the Bill, but never forgave those who had opposed him. The following account of how it brought Lord Chesterfield into disgrace, is taken from the Earl of Carnarvon's edition of Lord Chesterfield's Letters, published in 1890 (p. xix):

"On 11th April, the Government abandoned the Excise Bill; and on the 13th, Lord Chesterfield was visited with the Royal displeasure for his opposition to the Bill. That day as he was coming from the House of Lords in the company of his intimate friend Lord Scarborough, and was walking up the great stairs at S. James', he was stopped by a servant of the Duke of Grafton, who said that the Duke had that morning been at Lord Chesterfield's house desiring to see him on a matter of importance. Lord Chesterfield, as his chariot was not ready, was taken home by his friend and immediately followed by the Duke of Grafton, who informed him that he came by the King's command to require the surrender of his white staff."

In the same year, according to Lord Hervey (vol. i., p. 222), "as there had been a strong party made against the ministry in the House of Lords, in case the Excise Bill had come there, those who had been at the trouble of working this defection, since they were disappointed of showing their strength, and the good effects of their cabals on that occasion, began to look out for some other point to squabble upon.

" An inquiry into the state of the South Sea Company was the subject chosen, and the reason of its being chosen was Lord Scarborough's having declared the last year that as there were great murmurs in the world against those who had been concerned in the management of the great moneyed companies, and doubts arising in the minds of the proprietors with regard to the value of their property there; that in order to ease those doubts, to quiet their clamours and let people know what they had to depend upon, whenever a scrutiny of these matters should be proposed by Parliament, he should be strenuously for it, and if any fraud was proved on those who had been intrusted with the management of any of these companies, that no one should go farther than he would towards the punishment of such delinquents and procuring such satisfaction to those who had been defrauded.

" This declaration was casually and digressively thrown out by Lord Scarborough, when the affair of the Charitable Corporation was under consideration the year before : but it was too explicit not to pin him down when anything of this nature should be proposed, to be for it."

This question was debated in the House of Lords on May 24th, from which time the opposing Lords grew weaker and weaker till they did not dare to stand a division, and the Ministers were defeated.

There are several letters from Lord Scarbrough among the Newcastle Papers. The first belongs to the previous year, but as there is in it no reference to matters already noticed, it seems better to put them in here all together. _ It is unfortunately impossible to discover who the " noble spirit" was :

" MY LORD

" The hopes I had of seeing your Grace at London, by this time, made me deferr returning my thanks to you for yr great goodness in writing to me, & it is now so late, that I have nothing to depend upon for yr forgiveness, but the kindness you have gave me so many marks of : I congratulate yr grace upon the good situation of the Kings affairs, & I am most exceedingly glad to see y^t noble spirit y^t has plagued for so many years all Europe, is at last employed in another quarter of the world : I beg yr grace to believe that I am wth the greatest respect & affection my dear Lord

" yr most faithful humble servant

" SCARBROUGH.

"Lumley Castle July 21st."

There is an interval of a year before the next letter, and then follow four written within a month, the first being dated :

"Lumley Castle, July 24th 1733.

" I received yr graces kind letter too late on Sunday to answer it by that post : I do beg that you will be persuaded that, tho' I wish it had not happen'd, I don't in the least take ill yr having shown my letter to the Queen, for I am very sure it proceeded from y^t friendship & warmth of heart towards me, wch I have received so many proofs of, & wch I shall ever value, as the greatest honour & happyness: I can't sufficiently express the sense I have of their Majesties great goodness to me, & if you shall judge it proper, I wish yr grace would say for me something to them on this occasion; I flatter my self y^t neither their Majesties nor yr grace will think I did wrong in accepting the freedom after the Mayors explanations & instances to me, & indeed I must have disobliged the whole town of Newcastle if I had persisted in refusing & tho' I had much rather have offended them, than done w^t I thought undutyfull to the King, or wrong to my friends, yet when y^t was to be avoided consistently wth those higher considerations, I thought it in many respects the most prudent part: none of the people at Newcastle to this hour know anything of this transaction but the Mayor and the Town Clerk: I wish you a great deal of pleasure in Sussex, & beg you to believe that I am &c."

The next letter refers to the troubles in Poland. On February 1st King Augustus II. died, and Stanislaus, who had already been King from 1702 to 1709, returned. He was chosen King on September 12th, but his election was opposed by Austria and Russia, and finally Augustus III., son of the last sovereign, was crowned on January 17th, 1734.

"Lumley Castle, July 27th 1733.

" I return you my humble thanks for yr letter of the 21st, & the account you are so kind to give me of our foreign affairs: notwithstanding all appearances I cannot think the world mad enough to go to warr about a King of Poland, nor the Poles mad enough to make a choice wch they apprehend will draw a Muscovite army into their Country & they have a plain & unexceptionable expedient to stop the mouths of all the world by chusing any Pole except Stanislaus: I am afraid I shan't have the pleasure of seeing yr grace so soon as I expected, for since I am two hundred miles from London, I would willingly make an end of the business I have to do here; & wch is really of great consequence to me: I am &c."

The Prince of Orange landed in England on November 7th, but in consequence of his ill-health, his marriage with the Princess Royal was postponed until February 14th, 1734.

"Lumley Castle, August 10th 1733.

"Having business here of consequence, I shou'd be very glad to stay to finish it, & therefore I beg your grace will be so good to let me know when it is likely the Prince of Orange will be over, for I had much rather leave my affairs unsettled, than be absent upon that occasion: In the course of seventeen years service about his Majesty I have been so very little absent, that possibly the King may think my staying from Court so long now a neglect of my duty, therefore I must entreat yr grace to take an opportunity to say something by way of excuse for me: I am &c."

"Lumley Castle, August 21st 1733.

"My being away from home when yr graces kind letter of the 14th came here, has hindered my answering & returning you thanks for it so soon as I should have done: I am very much obliged to you for being so good to excuse my absence to their Majesties whose great goodness to me I have the most dutyfull sense of: I was extreamly surprized to hear of Mr. Fullers standing for the County; as there can be no chance for his succeeding, it must proceed from an agreement among the Tories to oppose everywhere: I shan't trouble yr grace wth any account of the Elections in these parts, because I take for granted Mr. Pelham will have acquainted you with w^t I wrote to him a few days agoe: I am very glad the Duke of Somerset has declared for you, not y^t you will want his assistance, but it gives me hopes y^t he won't be for Fenwick in Northumberland tho' the Tories flatter themselves y^t they shall have his interest there.

"I thank yr grace for the account you are so kind to give me of our foreign affairs & I beg you to believe me," etc.

Lord Scarbrough must have returned to town soon after the last, and we have not another letter from him till the following May. It will be remembered that at at this time Arundel and Chichester were represented by his brothers, John and James.

"Stansted May 6th, 1734.

" Major Battine is this moment come hither to let me know that he has heard that Mr. Yates's friends have sent into the Country to desire the freeholders would not vote for Mr. Pelham & Butler unless the Mayor of Chichester returns Yates wch at present there are difficulties about. I thought it proper to give yr grace immediate notice of this, that you may consider what is proper to be done : The part of the Country that Battine heard this is stirr'd in, is in the Manhood & away towards Arundel : yr grace will be the best judge whether it would not be proper for you or Mr. Pelham to write to Yates or to Sr John Miller : for fear the Duke of Richmond should not have heard of this, I will write to him as soon as I have sent away young Blaxton with this letter : in case you should think proper to send anybody over to Chichester, Wednesday is a market day : Everything in this part is as well as we could expect : Pray give my service to Mr. Pelham, & believe me," etc.

"London, June 6th 1734.

" Mr. John Bristow brother in law to my Lord Hobart is married to a French protestant, & is now in France with her : She was formerly taken away from her relations, put into a Convent from whence she made her escape & has been naturalized in England : my lady Suffolk desired me yesterday to give yr grace this account, & she desires you will mention this affair to my Lord Waldegrave, & recommend the lady to his protection if it should be any way necessary for her safety."

"Lumley Castle, Sept. 15 1734.

" Having seen in all the publick papers that there was immediately an addition to be made of troops & companies to the regiments now on foot, I beg the favour of your grace to let me know whether it be true or not : Sir William Middleton has desired me to inform him, having a brother in the service whom he would endeavour to get some advancement for, if the report be true : If it be any way improper to have it known, I beg you will not satisfy my curiosity, tho' I am very sure I could trust Sir William : I was in hopes to have had the pleasure to see yr grace by this time, but I have been detained here by some business yt I fear I shall not get done till the middle of next month."

In the struggle between France and Spain on the one side and Austria on the other, Marshal Broglio was surprised on the banks of the Secchia in Italy on September 15th, which is doubtless what is referred to in the last of these letters.

"Lumley Castle, Sept. 27th 1734.

" I am extreamly obliged to your grace for yr very kind letter, tho' I am heartily concern'd at the news you send me in it ; the infatuation yt has seized the Germans in Italy is astonishing, for this is the second disgrace they have mett wth by fighting upon ground where they could not use their horse, who could be of no service in attacking intrenchments ; but however I flatter my self, yt their loss is greatly magnified by the French from whom the account comes ; I return your grace many thanks for yr goodness in relation to Sir William Middleton, & I really think such a favour as he desires could not be more properly plac't, Sir William is as worthy honest a man as ever was born, very zealous for the King, & the administration, & I dare say, would not take an employment himself if one was offer'd him : These surmises " (?) " of the French, & the indolence of the Dutch put England into such a situation yt great difficulty must attend any part we can take, & it is certainly much easier to foresee the dangers than to find a remedy for them ; if France & Spain cou'd be divided all is sett to rights at once, you know my thoughts upon yt matter ; I hope you have had better weather for hunting yn we have had here or else yr sport has not been very good, but bad as the roads are I intend to wade thro' them about the middle of next month borough, as well as by the dukes of Argyle and Bedford, he could not succeed in his endeavours, and this disappointment proved a fatal omen of what was to happen during the remainder of the session.

" Lord Scarborough's conduct, in this as well as in all other debates, cannot but inspire us with the most exalted ideas of his candor, delicacy and moderation. Strongly attached by principle to the government, and by inclination to the king, he supported the ministry a long time against the efforts of those he was most intimately connected with, and lived for many years upon the best terms both with Sir Robert Walpole and with Lord Chesterfield. (*Note*—As Sir Robert's and lord Chesterfield's houses were situated opposite to each other in St. James's Square, lord Scarborough was often seen going directly from the friend to the minister; and such was the opinion entertained by both of his integrity, that he never met on this account with the least controul or censure from either.) Forced at last by conviction to deviate from his former course, and to express his disapprobation of the late public measures, he did it with a becoming frankness and generosity, wishing earnestly to reconcile both parties at this interesting period and to unite them against the common enemies of their country. This attempt, however, was ill received ; heads of parties seldom allow a latitude of thinking, and in affairs of state, still more than in matters of religion, intolerance is by every side disavowed, but too constantly practised by all.

" Unfortunately a nobleman equally beloved by the nation and by his friends could not long resist the struggle between his former engagements and his present feelings. A turn to melancholy, which shewed itself in his countenance, joined to an ill state of health (*Note*—He had two shocks of apoplexy or palsy, which, in the opinion of lord Chesterfield, considerably affected his body and his mind), hurried him to an act of violence upon himself. The morning of the day on which he accomplished this resolution, he paid a long visit to lord Chesterfield, and opened himself to him with great earnestness on many subjects. As he appeared somewhat discomposed, his friend pressed him in vain to stay

and dine with him; which he refused, but most tenderly
embraced him at parting. It happened in the course of the
conversation that something was spoken of which related to
Sir William Temple's negociations, when the two friends
not agreeing about the circumstances, lord Chesterfield,
whose memory was at all times remarkably good, referred
lord Scarborough to the page of Sir William's memoirs
where the matter was mentioned. After his lordship's death,
(*Note*—His body found surrounded with several books,
which he had brought into the room, and piled about him,
with the pistol in his mouth,) the book was found open at that
very page. Thus he seems in his last moments to have been
still attentive to his friend, and desirous that he should know
he was so. This fatal catastrophe was universally lamented,
tenderly censured, and entirely excused by those who considered the unaccountable effects of natural evils upon the
human mind. But what must lord Chesterfield's situation
have been upon his being informed of this unfortunate
event? His excellent lady does not even now without the
greatest emotion speak of the manner in which his lordship,
on her return home at night, acquainted her with his loss
of that amiable nobleman; and he ever after lamented that
he did not detain him at his house, saying he might perhaps
have been saved, if he had not been left to himself that day.
(*Note*—I have sufficient authority to contradict the reports
that were spread about the cause of this fatal resolution.
The friend who knew him best, considered it merely as the
effect of some distemper. Suicide never had an advocate in
lord Chesterfield, but he was temperate in his censures, and
ready to make allowances for it.)"

Dr. Maty has take the kinder way to consider the tragedy,
but it is to be feared that the reports may have been cor-
rect. Both sides of the question are given in Elwin's edition
of Pope's works.

In "1740, a Poem" (line 78), Pope says:

Brave S . . . . w lov'd thee and was ly'd to death; '

and Croker's note on this gives the more charitable version
of the reason for his act: "Richard Lumley, Lord Scar-

George I., Queen Caroline, Walpole, Pulteney, Hardwicke, Fox, and Pitt. These were reprinted in the Annual Register for 1777, with the exception of the first two, and then was added a Life of Lord Scarbrough by the same author, which is headed by the following preface: "The following Character appears to have been drawn in the Year 1759, nineteen Years after Lord Scarborough's Death. It is more finished than any of those which we have already exhibited, and furnishes convincing proof of the noble Author's Discernment and Observation."

We give this "Character," as showing to the credit of both these friends: "In drawing the character of Lord Scarborough, I will be strictly upon my guard against the partiality of that intimate and unreserved friendship, in which we lived for more than twenty years; to which friendship, as well as to the public notoriety of it, I owe much more than my pride will let my gratitude own. If this may be suspected to have biassed my judgment, it must at the same time be allowed to have informed it; for the most secret movements of his soul, were, without disguise, communicated to me only. However, I will rather lower than heighten the colouring; I will mark the shades, and draw a credible rather than an exact likeness.

"He had a very good person, rather above the middle size; a handsome face, and, when he was chearful, the most engaging countenance imaginable; when grave, which he was oftenest, the most respectable one: he had in the highest degree the air, manners, and address of a man of quality; politeness with ease, and dignity without pride.

"Bred in camps and courts, it cannot be supposed he was untainted with the fashionable vices of those warm climates; but, if I may be allowed the expression, he dignified them, instead of their degrading him into any mean or indecent action. He had a good degree of classical, and a great one of modern knowledge, with a just, and at the same time a delicate taste.

"In his common expences he was liberal within bounds, but in his charities and bounties, he had none. I have known them put him to some present inconveniences.

-RICHARD, SECOND EARL OF SCARBROUGH

G. KNELLER

not even hear of an injustice or a baseness without a sudden indignation ; nor of the misfortunes or miseries of a fellow-creature, without melting into softness, and endeavouring to relieve them.

" This part of his character was so universally known that our best and most satyrical English poet says :

> ‘When I confess there is who feels for fame,
> And melts to goodness, Scarb'rough need I name?’[1]

He had not the least pride of birth and rank; that common narrow notion of little minds, that wretched mistaken succedaneum of merit : but he was jealous to anxiety of his character, as all men are who deserve a good one. And such was his diffidence upon that subject, that he never could be persuaded that mankind really thought of him as they did. For surely never man had a higher reputation, and never man enjoyed a more universal esteem ; even knaves respected him, and fools thought they loved him. If he had any enemies (for I protest I never knew one) they could only be such as were weary of always hearing of Aristides the Just.

"He was too subject to sudden gusts of passion, but they never hurried him into any illiberal or indecent expression or action ; so invincibly habitual to him were good nature and good manners. But if ever any word happened to fall from him in warmth, which upon subsequent reflection he himself thought too strong, he was never easy till he had made more than sufficient atonement for it.

"He had a most unfortunate, I will call it a most fatal kind of melancholy in his nature, which often made him both absent and silent in company, but never morose or sour. At other times he was a cheerful and agreeable companion; but, conscious that he was not always so, he avoided company too much, and was too often alone, giving way to a train of gloomy reflections.

" His constitution, which was never robust, broke rapidly at the latter end of his life. He had two severe strokes of

---

[1] Pope's "Epilogue to the Satires," Dial ii., line 64.

apoplexy or palsy, which considerably affected his body and his mind.

" I desire that this may not be looked upon as a full and finished character, writ for the sake of writing it ; but as my solemn deposit of the truth to the best of my knowledge. I owed this small tribute of justice, such as it is, to the memory of the best man I ever knew, and of the dearest friend I ever had."

One account of Lord Scarbrough, attributed to T. Constantine Phipps, the author of a malicious apology, 1748, describes him as the very reverse of the character of him given by the friend of more than twenty years' standing. In that friend's hands we are surely justified in leaving him, while his portraits certainly contradict the verbal portrait of him attributed to E. W. Montagu, who says, " he was a thick vulgar-looking man," though, he is fain to admit, " not destitute of a certain intellectual development."

In a quaint old MS. book by one Thomas Macdonald, in the possession of Lord Scarbrough at Sandheck, there is the argument of a proposed play, entitled " The Court Secret, A melancholy truth, translated from the original Arabic, by an adept in ye oriental tongues—Remember that a prince's secrets are balm if concealed, but poison if discovered—Chester-le-Street. 1742."

Dramatis Personae.

Sultan	The King.
Sultana	The Queen.
Achmet	Lord Scarborough.
Behemoth or Vizier	Sir Robert Walpole.
Osmyn ye Aga	Duke of Argyle.
Ibrahim	Mrs. Hardy.
Fatima	Duchess of Manchester.

Then comes the description of the characters and the plot of the play, which may be briefly summed up as follows :

Achmet is a true and faithful friend of the Sultan, and in opposition to Behemoth or the Vizier. Achmet persuades the King that Osmyn ye Aga is a fit and proper person to be intrusted with an important mission. To this the Sultan agrees, but charges Achmet to guard the secret of his intention from everyone, which Achmet promises faithfully to do.

But the wicked Vizier has spies everywhere. Achmet is madly in love with Fatima, who has won his affections during the lifetime of her husband. She is now a widow, and is shortly to be married to Achmet. Ibrahim, a creature of the Vizier, is sent to Fatima to induce her by taunts to worm out of him the secret which Achmet is known to possess. This course is adopted after the Sultana has failed to extract the secret from the Sultan, for the Vizier was troubled by no scruples as to what tools he employed to gain his ends, and had considerable power over the Sultana, who was at times able to serve him with the Sultan.

After strong resistance Achmet yields to the wiles of Fatima and reveals the secret. The price is that the following day is fixed for their nuptials. Meanwhile Fatima, inflated with pride at her victory, betrays the secret to Ibrahim, who soon makes it known to the Vizier. The Vizier repairs to the Sultan and taxes him with his intentions, telling him brutally how he has obtained the information. The Sultan sends for Achmet, and more in sorrow than in anger tells him that Behemoth has informed him of his own intentions, and that Achmet must consequently have revealed the sacred secret. The Sultan goes on to say that he has such trust in him that only his own mouth shall condemn him. Achmet realizes Fatima's treachery and faints away. When he recovers from his swoon he confesses his weakness to the Sultan, who forgives him while telling him that they must part to meet no more. But he would still prove his trust in him by fulfilling his promise with regard to the employment of Aga Osmyn, from whom he would also conceal the weakness of Achmet in suffering so sacred a trust to be cajoled out of him. The Sultan parts from his trusted servant with these words: " Adieu, Achmet; we have both of us lost a friend which neither can ever regain."

Achmet leaves the Sultan's presence in a state of mind more easily imagined than described. All his joy in his approaching marriage is changed to misery. The sense of shame and degradation are intolerable. How heavy they proved the fatal result shows.

Meanwhile Fatima prepares for her wedding with a heart full of pride and exultation. Nothing is wanting to her triumph except the presence of the bridegroom. Why does he tarry? Suddenly footsteps are heard, but instead of the beloved form, a messenger appears with a note. The bride-elect trembles, turns pale, and after reading the missive faints away. The female friends try in vain to restore her, while the other guests with irresistible curiosity peruse the lines which have power to effect so sudden and so sad a change.

The play was never written, but this argument confirms what has already been quoted as the probable cause of the sad tragedy.

There are several portraits of Lord Scarbrough. The following extract is taken from Lord Carnarvon's Memoir, which has been already mentioned :

" There is a touching testimony to this intimacy" (between Lords Scarbrough and Chesterfield) " at Bretby in the pencil drawing of the two Earls. It was executed apparently in accordance with Lord Chesterfield's written instructions nearly three years after the unfortunate end of Lord Scarborough, and the motto, altered from Virgil's line, shows the lasting regret which still animated the survivor. . . . The sketch . . . is by T. Worlidge and inside the frame is a slip of paper in Lord Chesterfield's handwriting —perhaps an instruction to the artist—in the following words:—The Earl of Scarborough sitting on one side of a Table towards the end of it, and Lord Chesterfield on the other. Two or three books scatter'd upon the Table. These words written over the Earl of Scarborough's chair, *Avulso deficit alter.*" (The other was missing, having been torn away.). " The date of the drawing is 1743, and looking to that date and the fact that the motto is placed over Lord Scarborough's head, it is clear that it was intended to record their long friendship, and his unfortunate death.

" Upon another portrait of Lord Scarborough, still at Bretby, the Horatian motto is written:

'Incorrupta fides nudaque veritas;
Quando ullum invenient parem ?'

(Uncorrupt faith and undisguised truth; when will they ever find his equal ?)

"On those walls the old picture had hung for many years, its place unnoticed and its traditions forgotten, till in the sunshine of a bright autumn day, I discovered the two lines which time and dust had almost effaced, and the recollection of Lord Hervey's description of the intimacy of the two political friends came into my mind with a certain sense of pathos for the generations that had for ever passed away, with their hopes and schemes and aspirations" (pp. l and lxxix).

There is a full-length portrait of this Earl in Court dress, wearing the George and the Order of the Garter, at Lumley Castle. Another, evidently a replica, is on the staircase at Sandbeck, and a half-length portrait is over the chimney-piece in the dining-room. There are coloured prints reproduced from the half-length picture, and others uncoloured, one of them probably taken from the above described pencil drawing at Bretby.

A will in Lord Scarbrough's own handwriting has come to light amongst the documents at Sandbeck. It is headed, "I Richard, Earl of Scarborough, do make this my last will and testament." It is very brief and simple. It makes provision for Richard and Mary Williamson, who, he considered, had claims upon him, assigning to each the yearly sum of £500. The will also desires that all the servants who shall be in his employment at the time of his death shall receive one year's wages. He leaves annuities to his sisters, Lady Anne Frankland and Lady Henrietta Lumley. To his brother, Sir Thomas Saunderson, he leaves his estates, and he appoints his brother, James Lumley, his executor. He also leaves £100 a year to his good friend, Mr. Cleland, commonly called Major Cleland, and to his wife. He wishes to be buried with as little expense as possible in the church of the parish where he shall die. It is dated the 18th of January, 1739-40.

This will makes it very difficult to understand what we have quoted from Horace Walpole's letter on page 167.

CHAPTER XI

Thomas, third Earl of Scarbrough.—His money difficulties.—Letters from
his widow to the Duke of Newcastle.

RICHARD, second Earl of Scarbrough, was
succeeded by his brother Thomas Lumley-
Saunderson, who had assumed the latter name
on the death of James Saunderson, Earl of
Castleton, to whose estates he succeeded on
May 24th, 1723, by the will of the said Earl of Castleton;
and thus he was independent of the Lumley possessions and
might have been richer than his elder brother, if he had not
squandered his money. The connexion of the Lumleys and
Saundersons will be explained by the accompanying extract
from Hunter's "History of Doncaster": "The Earl of
Castleton gave Sandbeck and the other Estates to Mr. Lumley who was at the time of the Earl's death Envoy to Portugal. This gentleman did not descend of the blood of the
Saundersons, but was related to the Earl through his mother,
who was a Bellasis, sister to the Earl of Falconberg. Another
sister married Sir Henry Jones, of Aston in Oxfordshire,
and had an only daughter and heir, married to Richard,
the first Earl of Scarborough, the mother of Mr. Lumley.
He was enjoined to take the name of Saunderson, which he
did, and in 1725 was installed a Knight Companion of the
Order of the Bath. In 1739, by the death of his elder brother
without issue he became Earl of Scarborough" (vol. i.,
p. 274).

The pedigree on page 180 has been drawn up to explain
these notes.

In 1724 Thomas Lumley-Saunderson, having taken possession of his new estates, returned to his duties in Portugal,

SAUNDERSON CONNEXION.

HENRY BELASIS.

THOMAS, VISCOUNT FALCONBERG. = MILDRED SAUNDERSON.

GRACE. = GEORGE, 4TH VISCOUNT CASTLETON, 3rd son of Nicholas, 2nd Viscount, died 1640, succeeded his brother Nicholas, 3rd Viscount, in 1655, died at Sandbeck, May 27, 1714. = SARAH. = 1. SIR JOHN WRAY, of Glentworth, 3rd Bart.

FRANCES. = SIR HENRY JONES, of Aston in Oxfordshire.

Two sons, died s. p.

NICHOLAS, died before his father. = ELIZABETH, dau. of Sir John Wray.

HENRY, died an infant, 1655.

GEORGE.

CHARLES, d. 1694.

SAMUEL.

JAMES, 5TH VISCOUNT CASTLETON, created Earl of Castleton 1720, died without issue, May 24, 1723.

FRANCES, d. 1737. = SIR RICHARD LUMLEY, 1ST EARL OF SCARBROUGH, died 1721.

HENRY, VISCOUNT LUMLEY, M.P. for Arundel, died 1710.

RICHARD, 2ND LORD SCARBROUGH, succeeded his father 1721, died 1739, unmarried.

THOMAS LUMLEY-SAUNDERSON, succeeded to the estates of the Viscount Castleton in 1723. Became 3rd Earl of Scarbrough 1739-40.

where he celebrated the birthday of the Prince of Wales, afterwards George II., and distinguished himself as he had done before by the sumptuous manner in which he did honour to his nation. This is shown by the following extract from " The British Gazette," No. 6324, namely: "That he entertained the foreign Ministers, nobility of Portugal and other persons of distinction at dinner. In the evening there was a concert of vocal and instrumental music, at which were a great appearance of ladies, who were afterwards conducted to a fine collation, followed with a ball that held till morning. The whole entertainment passed with a magnificence suitable to the occasion."

This style of expenditure gives a clue to the difficulties in which Sir Thomas Lumley-Saunderson found himself involved. Thus to a deed drawn up on August 12th, 1724, to arrange for the payment of his debts is appended the following :

" The Schedule of the debts of the said Thomas Saunderson referred to by the above written Deed :

To the Rt Hono^{ble} Rich, Earl of Scarborough, principal money		£10,459
To Coll Blaithwaite	Do	430
To Mrs Catherine Cotton	Do	350
To Coll John Campbell	Do	200
To Mr Peter Campbell	Do	200
To Mr Buckmaster	Do	150
To Mrs Mary Morey	Do	850
To Mrs Johanna Roth	Do	458
To Mrs Richard Keech	Do	804
To Mrs Gilberta Talbott	Do	2226
To Mr Ralph Harrison	Do	2939
To Mr Erasmus Philips	Do	4872
		23,938 "

There are several bonds, among others two dated February 11th, 1735, in which Sir Thomas Saunderson, of Henrietta Street, declares himself bound to Philip Vincent, of Bury Street, for the sums of £1,500 and £2,100.

In May, 1738, he was appointed Treasurer of the Household to Frederick, Prince of Wales, and a great many documents referring to his duties as such are among the Sandbeck papers. One dated May 27th, 1738, gives him a Commission on the Fees and Poundage of 12*d.* in the £1 with a minimum sum of £1,000, which was increased on October 29th, 1742, to a minimum of £1,600.

As was said in the last chapter, he was very disappointed at the terms of his brother's will, having evidently hoped for a much larger sum of money. In 1742 he further increased his difficulties by large investments in the South Sea Bubble and other speculations.

There is one letter from the third Lord Scarbrough among the Newcastle Papers, which refers to the Battle of Dettingen :

" MY LORD DUKE

" I am ordered by the Prince to desire your Grace will please to send the two inclosed letters one to the King the other to the Duke by the messenger you send.

" Give me leave to congratulate your grace upon the late event, & to assure you I have the honour to be with great respect

" Your Grace⁵

" most obedient

" Humble Servant,

" SCARBROUGH.

"Clifden June 24th 1743."

Of the last ten years of his life we know nothing, except a few hints which we get in the following letters of his widow. He had married Frances, second daughter of George Hamilton, Earl of Orkney, by whom he had two sons and three daughters. His elder son, Richard, succeeded him on his death in 1752. The younger, George, died unmarried on December 11th, 1732. Of his daughters the eldest, Frances, married Peter, Lord Ludlow of Ireland. The other two, Anne and Harriet, died unmarried.

There are nineteen letters between Lady Scarbrough and the Duke among the Newcastle Papers, all of them concerning " my son Ludlow," as she calls her son-in-law. They are here given in full, as they yield an insight into

?, a sister, 3rd Earl.

COUNTESS OF SCARBROUGH, WIFE OF THIRD
EARL *No*
SIR PETER LELY *7 studio*

4th wife 4th earl

Lady Scarbrough's character, and also into the ways and customs of the time.

"MY LORD.

"I return your Grace many thanks for the favour of your most obliging and satisfactory answere to my letter, which gives me great pleasure, but am still happier, that your Grace thinks it won't be very long, before my wishes are accomplished. I hope yr Grace will excuse this trouble, to assure you, that I shall allways retain a gratefull Sence of this obligation and am with the greatest Regard
      "My Lord Your Graces
            "Most obliged and
                  "Obedient Servant
                        "F. SCARBROUGH.

"Midgham June yᵉ 29ᵗʰ 1754."

Endorsed: "Hopes it won't be long before some Irish Peers are created."

"MY LORD. I am very sorry to trouble your Grace again about my son Ludlows being made a Viscount of Ireland, as I thought it entirely settled with the Duke of Dorset, as by yr grace letter to me you express'd it was to my satisfaction; tho the Duke of Dorset at first objected to it; but upon my speaking to him about it, I find he does not seem to understand it so, which I think proper to acquaint yʳ Grace with not doubting but you will remove the Duke of Dorsets objections, and confirm your promise to me, of his being made a Viscount; as I never asked, or should have thought of his being a Baron of Ireland, for many reasons; as yr grace may believe from what I first mentioned to you, of Lord Castletons Pearage that was promised to my Lord. besides this being the first favour asked by, or for, any of my Family. And I think I have now a stronger Plea for his not being disapointed, he having been engage for this twelve-month past, in a strong and most expensive opposition for his Borough of Navan against the Country Party; which obliged him to go to Ireland last July, where he had repeated Elections, for four Burgesses, and the Portrif twice who is the returning officer, and on which the Election depended; all which he has hitherto succeeded in, against a subscription Purse of the whole opposite Party, Lord Kildare (tho' doubly related to him) at the Head of it. they have also put it into the King's Bench as a false return, so he has not only the expence of the Election, but also a Law suit, neither of which Expences can cease, till the Member is chose, which your grace knows can't be till the Lord Lieu[t] is in Ireland, and which would not have been worth his while to have been at any trouble, or Expense about, but for his Majestys Service, as he never proposed being chose there himself, and could have been brought in at two other Boroughs, without a sixpence expence, had he liked it; besides its having prevented [*sic*] being in Parliament here, which he would have been had he been made a Peer, as soon as I had reason to hope for; but could not accept it without the loss of the Borough, which had I had an opportunity, I should have explain'd to your Grace before, but hope I have said enough to confirm your promise which will much oblige My Lord your Grace[s]," etc.

"March y[e] 12th 1755."

The Duke's reply is given as copied into the volume of papers, except that the numerous capitals and stops are omitted, as being probably the peculiarity not of the writer but of the copyist:

"Newcastle House March 18th 1755.

"MADAM. I had sooner return'd your Ladyship my thanks for the Honor of your letter, had it not been necessary for me to speak to the Duke of Dorset upon the contents of it. I find there has been a rule for some time, to make no Peers in Ireland Viscounts at first, which rule has been constantly adher'd to, ever since it was made; and particularly in the case of my Lord Milton, the Duke of Dorset's own son-in-law; and therefore my Lord Dorset cannot break in to it. This being the state of the case, I hope your Ladyship will excuse my not being able to obey your commands, who am with the greatest respect,

"Your Ladyship's

"most obedient

"humble servant

"HOLLES NEWCASTLE.

"Lady Scarborough."

"MY LORD DUKE. I received the honour of your graces letter, with equal Vexation and surprise; as I was in great hopes, yr grace would have removed the Duke of Dorsets objections, instead of complying with them; as his Grace might have made Lord Milton a Viscount now, or an Earl of Ireland if he pleased, and as the request of one family could be no rule to that of another, I flattered my self I might with great reason ask & expect this favour, & I hoped I was sure of it, from your graces former obliging letter. Lord Galway was made a Viscount at first, & the Duke of Dorset told me the last Sunday sennight that there could be no rule against making a Viscount; for his Majesty could if he pleased make an Earl at once, so can be only his Graces rule on this occasion, and your grace I cant doubt has some very sufficient reason to acquiesce to the Duke of Dorsets rule, in preference to yr graces former ententions, which I cant possibly judg of. but I do assure yr grace, I had much rather had my son Ludlow made a Knight of the Bath, then only a Baron of Ireland, and which by Inclination I should now decline his Acceptance of, but for his having assur'd his friends in Ireland who press'd him to stand for Member at Navan, that he had very sufficient reason why he could not, and I should be very sorry to see any of my children act Inconsistent with honour, and themselves; so must submit to what your Grace pleases. but hope after the New Lord Leut is made, who cant make any objections, and for a Word speaking will do as you desire, that yr Grace will then make my son Ludlow a Viscount according to your promise.

"After all the professions of friendship of the Duke of Dorset to my son Ludlow, & that he would be glad to serve proved their zeal & attachment, at so great an Expence as he was at by yr Graces desire, for yᵉ Navan Election which cost above six thousand pounds; all which sum he might have been Re-imbursed by the opposite Party if he would have given it up; which yʳ grace may well remember you insisted he should not; which I hope may plead some merit, so beg yᵉ favour of an Answer if yʳ grace will get him made an Earl, in these next promotions of yᵉ Irish Peers, as I know it is absolutely in yʳ Power to get done if you please; which would infinitely oblige me.

"March yᵉ 16ᵗʰ 1759."

"Newcastle House March 17ᵗʰ 1759.

"MADAM. I have again spoke to the Duke of Bedford upon your Ladyship's application, for the promotion of my Lord Ludlow to an Earldom. His Grace apprehends that the doing it at present just before the Meeting of the Irish Peers may be attended with Inconveniences. But I have reason to hope that your Ladyship's Wishes may be complied with, after the Session of Parliament in Ireland is over. This is all I can do, & I flatter Myself that your Ladyship will see, that I am desirous to obey your Commands as far as is in my Power.

"I am &c.

"HOLLES NEWCASTLE.

"Countess of Scarborough."

"MY LORD DUKE. I return your Grace many thanks, for the Honour of yr obliging letter, but was in hopes my request might be comply'd with now, & am still, as yr grace flatters me that you wish to oblige Me; for I cant apprehend how any Inconveniency can Atend Lord Ludlows being made an Earl now, more then Lord Bracos being made one before ye Meeting of the Irish Parliament and hope & believe yᵉ Duke of Bedford would agree to it, if yr Grace will be so good to desire it may be so; the manner of confering a favour doubles the obligation and as my health is much impair'd I cant be sure of seeing my wishes comply'd with, if postponed till after ye next Sessions of Parliament in Ireland. So hope yr Grace will be so good

to me, to let Lord Ludlows Patent for an Earldom be made
when Lord Brecos is. I shall be most extreamly mortify'd
if it is not: and this will prove yr Graces ententions to
oblige me, as yr Grace is so good to say you are desierous
of doing, and I am sensible it is entierly in y^r Power, or I
should not ask & so hope you will comply with my Request
with these next promotions in ye Irish Peers, which will be
acknowledged with great gratitude by me, who am," etc.

"Monday morning March ye 19th 1759."

"Newcastle House, March 20th 1759.

"MADAM. I am extremely sorry that your Ladyship
should think, that it was either proper or practicable for
me to do more than I have done: The Lord Lieutenant
must be judge of the Promotions to be made in Ireland.
The case of my Lord Bracoe is quite different. He is not
an Irishman, has no interest there; never was nor ever will
be in Ireland as I apprehend; and therefore his Promotion
is very indifferent to the Peers of Ireland. The inconvenience that my Lord Lieutenant apprehends is, that the promotion of a Peer of Ireland to an Earldom, would create
great uneasiness just before the Session of Parliament begins, amongst those Peers who are older and desire the
same thing; and for that reason the Duke of Bedford proposed that it might be postponed till after the Session. In
these circumstances I would submit it, whether it would be
proper for me to press my Lord Lieutenant further upon
point of time only, when he is so good at my request as to
be willing to do it after the very next Session of Parliament,
& when His Grace apprehends difficulties, & inconveniences to the affairs there if it is done before."

"MY LORD DUKE. I am most extreamly sorry to find by
your Graces letter of the 20th that your Grace would post-
pone the making Lord Ludlow an Earl, to the Duke of
Bedfords return from Ireland, for give me leave to say I
cant foresee any more Unneasiness nor believe his Grace
wont find any from the Peers of Ireland, in Lord Ludlows
being made now, then Lord Braco, as he will not now be

"Decr 5th 1767.

"The Duke of Newcastle sends his Compliments to my Lady Scarborough and has the Pleasure to acquaint Her Ladyship that he had this day a letter from my Lord Rockingham, by which he is informed that my Lord Carysford declines standing for the County of Huntingdon; & that the Duke of Manchester recommends my Lord Ludlow to succeed him; and that my Lord Sandwich says he cannot fail.

"The Duke of Newcastle flatters himself that he may be of some use to my Lord Ludlow upon this occasion, and begs my Lady Scarborough will be assured that he will exert himself to the utmost of his power.

"The Duke of Newcastle is more happy at this event as it would have been impossible to him to have obey'd Lady Scarborough's Commands contained in her Ladyship's Letter."

"Dow^r Lady Scarborough presents her comp^{ts} to the Duke of Newcastle and is extreamly glad to hear His Grace is so much better, and returns him many thanks for his obliging Answere, & further protection he is so good to promise Lord Ludlow; from Whome she has received y^e same account, and was just going to communicate to His Grace when His servant came."

"Decr y^e 5th 1767."

Unfortunately the date of Lady Scarbrough's death is unknown.

CHAPTER XII

Richard, fourth Earl of Scarbrough.—Marriage with Barbara Savile.—
Rufford Abbey.—Sir George and Gertrude Savile.|

RICHARD succeeded his father as fourth Earl of Scarbrough in 1752. On Tuesday, December 26th of the same year, he married Barbara, sister of Sir George Savile, the eighth and last Baronet of Rufford Abbey in Nottinghamshire. The marriage took place in the private chapel attached to the house.

The first visit of the present chronicler of the Lumley history was paid to Rufford in May and June, 1896. Her host, Lord Savile, a member of the Lumley family, put at her disposal all the available documents, as well as numerous letters, from which it was easy to gather a consecutive account, and even in imagination to people the rooms with the ancestors of a hundred years ago.

Some brief description of the place as it was and as it is may add interest to the narrative. As its name denotes, a religious house once occupied either the site or the neighbourhood of the present pile. A nephew of William the Conqueror, one Gislebert de Gaunt, became the possessor of the Manor of Rufford, then called Rainford from its proximity to the River Rain.

His grandson, Gilbert, Earl of Lincoln in right of his wife, after enjoying somewhat unrestful possession during the troublous reign of Stephen, made legacy to a colony of Cistercian monks from Rivaulx of his lands of Rainford, now Rufford, A.D. 1148. Copies of this deed of gift are amongst the papers at Rufford.

Here in due time arose the fair and famous Abbey of St. Mary, of which not one stone remains to mark the spot, save a slab recording the death of a holy brother of the order, which is now let into the floor of the chapel, attached to the present mansion. The inscription is as follows, translated from the original Latin: " Here lies Brother Robert de Markham, a monk of this house, whose soul we pray the Lord that it may rest in peace. He died 16th of the calends of Ap. in the year of our Lord 1309."

The oldest part of Rufford Abbey, the crypt and what were probably cloisters, form at this time the servants' hall, cellars and offices. The eldest son of the Marquis of Halifax had rooms in this part, which still go by the name of Lord Eland's rooms. An unroofed corridor connecting the various rooms is striking and picturesque, and on a fine day offers a tempting subject for a most characteristic sketch. Above this are the men-servants' quarters, and their rooms may have served the monks for cells, as there is little doubt that this part dates back to the reigns of Stephen and Henry II. Additions have been made to the house at various periods. The result is a picturesque whole, of which Louisa, Marchioness of Waterford, wrote in great admiration, when she described this house " of the many gables."

It is probable that the original dwelling-house of the monks was left standing when the adjacent abbey was so ruthlessly destroyed, and that it was occupied for twenty-one years by Sir John Markham, being granted to him after the explusion of the monks by Henry VIII. for the yearly payment of £22 8s.

Afterwards the King gave the abbey and lands to George, fourth Earl of Shrewsbury and Waterford, in consideration of the prompt measures he took for the suppression of the rebellion in the north, known as the Pilgrimage of Grace. It will be remembered that a Lord Lumley took part in the same rebellion, but obtained forgiveness by his ready submission. It is interesting to trace in these different centuries the simultaneous condition of members of the Lumley and Savile family, destined later to be so closely united. When Ralph, first Baron Lumley, was summoned to the Upper

House by writ in 1384 under Richard II., a Sir John Savile was sheriff of the neighbouring county of Yorkshire. This worthy knight was great-great-grandson of John Savile of Savile Hall, County York, in the time of Henry III.

In what is now called the Brick Hall there is a beautiful carved oak cradle, to which is appended the following account:

" HISTORY OF THE CARVED OAK CRADLE AT RUFFORD ABBEY.

" The old carved oak cradle has been in my family for generations, it was sold in 1730 with the fittings, wainscotting and furniture of Howley Hall, Batley, Yorkshire, by order of the Earl of Cardigan, who had by marriage succeeded to the estate which originally belonged to Sir John Savile, afterwards Baron Savile of Pontefract. It is said to be the identical cradle of Thomas Savile, first and last Earl of Sussex, date 1590, and son of the above named Sir John Savile, ancestor of the present Earl of Scarborough's family.

" The old cradle was shown at the Leeds Exhibition in 1835, when my father refused fifty guineas for it. Howley Hall was destroyed by being blown up by gunpowder on the false representation of Christopher Hodson, the steward to the Earl of Cardigan.

" (Signed)   E. F. HEMINGWAY.

"Sutton Valence,
  " 25/3/90."

A narrow and very ancient oak table in the Hall is supposed to have been used in the days of the monks. The chapel in its present state was fitted up in the time of Charles II.

A three-light window commemorates the following events:

" George, Sixth Earl of Shrewsbury, married: first, Lady Gertrude Manners, daughter of Thomas, First Earl of Rutland ; secondly, Elizabeth, daughter of John Hardwick of Hardwick, Esq." N.B.—This lady is better known as Bess of Hardwick.

In the centre light we find the marriage of her daughter thus recorded :

" Charles Stuart, Earl of Lennox, married in this chapel, 1574, Elizabeth Cavendish, step-daughter of George, Sixth Earl of Shrewsbury." The unfortunate Arabella Stuart was the offspring of this marriage.

The third and last light contains this record:

" Richard, Fourth Earl of Scarbrough, married in this chapel, December 26th, 1752, Barbara, second daughter of Sir George Savile and younger sister and co-heir of Sir George Savile, eighth and last Baronet."

Rufford came into the possession of the Saviles by the marriage of Lady Mary Talbot with Sir George Savile of Barrowby in Lincolnshire, first Baronet, and it was by the marriage of the sister of Sir George Savile, eighth Baronet, to Richard, fourth Earl of Scarbrough, with which this chapter commences, that it passed to the Lumley family.

The dining-room, library, and hall, with its minstrels' gallery, the tapestried bedrooms, and the long passages remain much as they were when Barbara, Lady Scarbrough, and her large family were the welcome and constant guests of Sir George Savile. Modern and commodious additions have been made by the present Lord Savile, who converted some disused rooms into a picture gallery, opening out of the library. He also made a very handsome staircase, which greatly improves the house.

In Julia Cartwright's " Sacharissa " are to be found many interesting allusions to Rufford. Dorothy, the daughter of the noble Earl of Sunderland and the beauteous Sacharissa, married Sir George Savile, fourth Baronet, the distinguished statesman, better known as the first Marquis of Halifax.

It is plain that his happiest days were spent when still Sir George, with his fair young wife, in his beloved home at Rufford in the heart of Sherwood Forest. All through his life he loved the leafy shades and clear waters of his Nottinghamshire home, where the Saviles had always lived since their ancestral home at Thornhill in Yorkshire had been burnt to the ground in the Civil Wars by order of the last Baronet, who could not bear to see his house garrisoned by rebel forces. After the death of his first wife, Sir George married Gertrude Pierrepoint, but this did not interfere with the friendship between himself and Sacharissa, which was maintained through her life.

His eldest son, George, died young; the second, Henry, Lord Eland, died without children; so that he was succeeded by the third son, William, who became the second Marquis of Halifax. (See the pedigree on page 200.)

The devotion of Lord Halifax, and indeed of every member of his family, to Rufford, where Lady Sunderland spent many happy and peaceful years, is much dwelt upon in "Sacharissa." But time will not permit of further lingering amongst those fascinating records. All who have not done so should read the book, and live again with those celebrated people who have left such a worthy mark upon their times. Tudor and Stuart sovereigns have been honoured guests at Rufford, and doubtless enjoyed the peace and quiet of its sylvan glades.

All the sons of the second Marquis of Halifax died before him, and the Rufford property and Baronet's title reverted to the family of the first Baronet, by his second wife, Elizabeth, daughter of Edward Ayscough. They had among others two sons, John and Henry. The elder of these, Sir John Savile, knighted in 1627, died in 1660, and was succeeded by his eldest son, Thomas, who on his death in 1677 left all the Lupset estates to his sister Anne, thus disinheriting his brother John, who, however, succeeded to the Rufford estates and baronetcy as sixth Baronet in 1700. He died unmarried in 1704 and was succeeded by George, son of the Rev. John Savile, Rector of Thornhill (son of the above-named Henry), by his second wife, Barbara, daughter of Thomas Innison of Newcastle. They had also two daughters; the elder, Anne, married first Sir Nicholas Cole of Brauncepeth, and secondly a Belgian, Baron Dognyes, who seems to have been held cheaply by his wife's family; and Mrs. Savile in her will (see the Rufford Papers) made strict provision that he was to derive no benefit from her legacies to

1. The Lady Mary Talbot, dau. of Geo., Earl of Shrewsbury, d. Feb. 169⁴⁄₅ = SIR GEORGE SAVILE, of Lupset, Thornhill, and Wakefield, Knt. 37 Eliz., Bart. June 9, 1611; d. Nov. 12, 1622, aet. 72. = 2. Eliz., dau. of Edw. Ayscough, of South Kelsey, d. Jan. 25, 162⅝

Other:

rge Savile, of Thornhill, d. Aug. 24, 1614.

Henry Savile, of Bowling, b. Dec. 7, 1599; d. April 2, 1666.

Barbara, dau. o Thos. It nison, c Newcastle

Sir John Savile, of Lupset, Knt. 1627, d. May 5, 1660. = 2. Ann, dau. of Sir John Soame, d. 1651.

Rev. John Savile, Rector of Thornhill, d. 1700. = 2. Barbara, dau. o Thos. It nison, c Newcastle

RGE SAVILE, 2nd Bart., b. 1612, d. 19, t.17.

SIR WILLIAM SAVILE, 3rd Bart., b. 1612, d. Feb. 15, 164¾. = Anne, d. of Thos. Lord Coventry, d. 1662.

Geo. Savile, d. unm.

Henry Savile, d. unm.

Others.

Thos. Savile, d. 1677.

JOHN, b. 165?, disinherited by brother, succeeded to baronetcy (6th Bart.) and Rufford 1700, d. unm. 1704.

Anne, b. 1636, succeeded her brother.

.1636. SIR GEORGE SAVILE, 4th Bart., 1st Marquis of Halifax, b. Nov. 11, 1633; d. April 15, 1695; bur. at Westminster Abbey. = 1. Dorothy, dau. of Henry, 1st Earl of Sunderland, and Sacharissa, d. Dec. 16, 1670. = 2. Gertrude, dau. of William Pierrepoint, m. Nov. 1672, d. 1727.

Gertrud

SIR GEORGE SAVILE, bap. Feb. 10, 167⅞, 7th Bart., m. 1722, bur. Sept. 25, 1743. = Margaret Pratt.

Anne, m. 1st, Sir Nich. Cole; 2nd, Baron Dognyes.

Others, d. s. p.

WILLIAM, 5th Bart., 2nd Marquis of Halifax, b. 1665, d. Aug. 31, 1700.

Henry, Lord Eland, d. s. p.

d.

Sons all died

SIR GEORGE SAVILE, 8th and last Bart., b. 1726, d. 1784, aet. 57, unmarried.

Arabella, m. 1744 to John Thornhagh Hewet.

Barbara, m. 175 to Rich., 4th Ea of Scarbrough, July 22, 1797.

his wife, which in case of her predeceasing him were to revert to Mistress Gertrude Savile, her second daughter. The Baron, however, died before his wife ; and it appears from letters relating to the event that, had she borne him a son, he would have inherited considerable wealth. As, however, the Baron died childless this devolved upon his brother, one Baron de Courriere, who also died without issue. There is at Rufford a letter from this brother in German character in a mixed lingo of German-French, which seems to be a sort of defence or plea of justification. There is also a letter to the widow from his sister, la Vicomtesse de Nieuport.

The younger daughter, Gertrude, referred to above, never married. Her diary and letters supply us with a great deal of the information contained in this and the following chapters.

The letter which follows, written by one Tom Ogle to his aunt, Mrs. Savile, gives a description of her son's bride-elect:

"She is a Miss Pratt, daughter of the Receiver-General of Ireland. Her mother was Miss Brooke, sister of Sir James Brooke, and to Mrs. Piggott.[1] Also a near relation to Mrs. Bethell and Lord Cadogan. She said she formerly knew you. Sir George has this day been to see them, has free access, well approved of. She, as we understand, may be a fortune from 10 to £60,000 as her Parents please. Under 20 years old, and handsome. He desires your consideration of this affair and that both my mother if she be

[1] In the old burial ground of St. George's, Hanover Square, there still exists, though much worn away, the following inscription on an ancient tombstone to the mother of this Lady Savile : "Honoretta Pratt wife of the Rt Hon. John Pratt, Treasurer of Ireland, daughter of Sir John Brooke of York, Bart. She died 20th Sep. 1769." On the other side : "This worthy woman believing that the vapours arising from graves in churchyards of populous cities may prove harmful to the inhabitants, and resolving to extend to future times as far as she was able that charity and benevolence which distinguished her through life, ordered that her body should be burnt, in hope that others would follow the example. A thing too hastily condemned by those who did not enquire her motive." This monument was renewed by her kinsman in 1818. She was an early advocate of cremation ! She must have lived to a great age, as her eldest great-grand-daughter was born in 1749.

with you and you may consult, and recollect what you can of them and advise him. He likewise desires from the receipt of this you may keep yourself in readiness to come up to town upon any summons from him, doing it with all secrecy, Save from my mother whose advice he desires with yours. That likewise you will lay out to be in readiness his books with the Papers, the Rent from London, also the spaterdashes with the silver Buckles which hang in his cloathes press, also the embroidered waist-coat and breeches.

"'Tis very late. Sir George's and my humble service to Lady Cole, duty to yourself and Mother

"Your most obedient nephew

"TOM OGLE.

"Bath Dec. 22 1722."

Sir George and Miss Pratt were married early in 1722, and had three children, George, Arabella and Barbara.

In a letter written by Sir George to his mother from Rufford on October 22nd, 1726, occurs the earliest allusion to the great Sir George to be found among the Rufford papers:

"MADAM

"It is so long since I heard any thing of you and my sisters y^t I grow very uneasy. We wean'd our boy last Monday. He took it ill for a day or two, but is now, God be thank'd very well, and ye girl too, who improves in talking, good humour and a pretty air as well as in growth."

He goes on to complain of his mother's long silence. There were evidently some more or less serious differences of opinion in the family circle, and the sisters seem to have somewhat kept mother and son apart.

Later we have a letter from Sir George Savile to his sister Gertrude, describing his elder children, Arabella and George. After expressing great affection for his sister and asking to see her verses, he says: "Miss Baby is her Aunt's Humble Servant. I desire you to accept a double portion of my thanks for myself and her, till she is more sensible of the value of your favour and can take upon her ye obligation to return it in kind."

Sir George speaks of his spinet, which "stands sullen and seal'd up" in Gertrude's absence. Then he goes on about the precious son.

"My mother commands me in hers of the 25th to give some acc. of ye children. The animal somebody beginning to open ye buds of Risibility, which ye learned say is ye Criterion of Rationality; and accordingly takes much cognisance of ye Phœnomena (that is Fiddle Faddle) of this world specially (like his cotemporarys in this habitation) if they shine much. It is probable if he had a state of Pre-existence that he has formerly been a bird, but by his frequent attempts to fly it seems he is not yet sensible y^t he has lost his wings, nor materially considered how much of gravitating matter he has lately acquired, by which I find people of his age are valued, as well as mutton etc.: and a considerable portion of which lodging about his cheeks makes him bear the Port, especially in his sedentary moments of ye crest of his coat (the owl) or a justice of ye Peace. He and his sister are very great together. She is very much taken up in her care of him as being sensible he is but a child, tho' she has many avocations, a considerable one of which is to dress her Papa's head every day, which tho' she does it with much pains and delicacy, like her sex, gives me ye air of those matronly ladys under ye displeasure of ye Reformers of Drury Lane etc., but that is none of her fault: thus it may be truly said I have lived to dote and become literally a Baby of which I thank her she seems as fond as of her other . . .

"Your ever affte humble Servant

"G. Savile.

"Mar. 29th 1727."

The following letter from Mrs. Savile is endorsed by Sir George: "Part of a letter from my mother dated Mar. 5th 1730, and answered Ap. 9. This letter being most of it repetition and not necessary to be kept most of it was burnt." It was addressed to her elder daughter, then married to the Belgian Baron, the person slightingly alluded to in the letter:

"He" (presumably Sir George Savile) "gives his affec.

A little faded piece of paper that had fitted into a watch-case contains the following inscription :

> Her love and care who set my feet to run
> Require my love and duty to be done.

Above this is an hour-glass, and below the initials "G. S." To this is pinned another paper, on which is written : " My kind son's writing for my watch, grown dim, get him to make it clearer." On another piece of paper in very faded ink are the following lines :

> Madam, give leave I may depend
> Soe by your side to my Live's end
> Alike in welfare or distress
> Your most obedient son G. S.

On her death, Sir George Savile wrote a letter full of kind sympathy to his sisters, the Baroness Dognyes and Mistress Gertrude Savile, which makes it difficult to understand Gertrude's bitterness against her brother. He concludes with this practical remark:

" Pray leave sufficient margin to y^r letters and sett not y^r seal on ye writing."

Paper and postage had to be considered in those days. Mrs. Savile, writing to her elder daughter, when Lady Cole, asks her to consider whether she can safely send letters to her without cover. Anyhow, Mrs. Savile will do so to Lady Cole to save postage.

There are pictures at Rufford of Mrs. Savile and her two daughters; that of Mrs. Savile decidedly handsome. The two daughters have clever, hard faces, and a certain proportion of good looks.

Sir George Savile's marriage, that seemed to give such fair promise, turned out unhappily. He had been deceived about Miss Pratt's fortune, in the first place ; and the result of differences of opinion on this and other matters ended in an effort on the part of Sir George to dissolve his marriage.

Mistress Savile thus alludes to this and other matters in her diary:

" The cause between Sir George and Lady Savile tryed,

given against Sir George, May 18th, 1740." On the same day Aunt Gertrude "had her last apple pie baked and ate her last walnuts."

"May 27th 1742—Cause between Sir George and Lady Savile heard again but remained as it was in Lady Savile's favour."

"Sir George Savile seventh baronet dyed Sep. Buried at Thornhill Sep. 17th 1743."

"Dec. 1743. The new Sir George and his sisters came to town to his house in Leicester Square."

"Feb. 14th 1743-4. Miss Baby Savile came to be with me on acc. of Mr. Thornagh [her brother-in-law] having yᵉ small pox, and her good brother Sir George being almost always with him. A great favour."

It is thus evident that, though Lady Savile gained her cause against Sir George, she did not retain the custody of her children.

In May, 1744, the diary remarks: "Lady Savile married to Captain Wallis."

One wonders if he was the cause of the dissensions. Her third and last husband was a Doctor Morton, who did not find favour in her children's eyes.

In the same month and year Gertrude records the death of Sarah, Duchess of Marlborough: "the Great Duke's widow dyed aged 84. The richest subject in Europe."

Sir George was brought up at home by his tutor, and went to Cambridge, where he distinguished himself.

In March, 1745, the diary tells us, "Dear Sir George went out of town to Cambridge. 17th of June same year Mrs. Thornagh's child dyed."

"July 24, 1746. Mrs. Thornagh's daughter born. Sir George went out of town to Cambridge June 3rd 1747."

"Lady Harriot Lumley died Nov. 10th 1747."

"July 1st 1749. Grand Show at Cambridge. Duke of Newcastle's installation as Chancellor. Sir George with several more made Doctor of Law."

In March, 1750, Gertrude mentions the great earthquake. It was on this occasion that the chimneys at Rufford came down from the shock. Sir George's guardian was Mr.

Mitchell, who was at one time chaplain of Rufford. He was transferred to the living of Eakring, and he seems to have enjoyed Mrs. Gertrude's confidence and approval, with, however, one notable exception. He thought no opinion of any value compared with his own, a common failing from which Mistress Gertrude herself could scarcely claim exemption.

CHAPTER XIII

The Savile Family.—Marriage of Arabella to John Thornhagh Hewet.—
Gertrude Savile's Diary.—Education of " Miss Bab."

HE interesting collection of letters of the Right Hon. Francis Foljambe of Osberton throws considerable light on this period, and the diary continues to fill in details full of interest to all concerned.

There was a pleasant coterie within easy reach of Rufford. Dukes, earls and squires were on the most intimate terms, being each others' obedient servants and most affectionate friends. In the heart of the most characteristic and truly English sylvan scenery, with beautiful and romantic Sherwood Forest close at hand, it is natural that human nature should seem at its best. Time softens certain asperities and smooths over inevitable differences of opinion, and though Mistress Gertrude Savile did not approve of her elder niece's marriage to Mr. Thornhagh, he was liked and trusted by other members of the family, and seems to have been the pivot round whom the correspondence turned.

Mistress Gertrude shall now describe this marriage, which took place eight years before that of Lady Scarbrough, at this period called Miss Bab by her Aunt Gertrude. Mr. Thornhagh assumed the name of Hewett or Hewet, when he inherited Shireoaks for his life only, from his godfather, Sir Thomas Hewet, who disinherited his only daughter, tradition says, in consequence of her marriage with a gipsy or fortune-teller.

On Mr. Thornhagh Hewet's death the property reverted to a distant relative of Sir Thomas Hewet's. It afterwards passed by purchase to the Duke of Norfolk, whose Worksop Manor estate it adjoined, and with that estate in 1838 was purchased by the Duke of Newcastle.

"Account of Miss Savile's Marriage to Thornhagh,
afterwards Hewet. a.d. 1744. (London.)

"On ye 23rd July 1744, Miss Savile, my niece, was marry'd to Mr. Thornhay, at St Ann's Church. The same morn: they with Sir George and Miss Bab went to Shire-oaks, which Sir T. Hewett left for ye youngest son of old Mr. Thornhay, with all his estate, real and personal, after Lady Hewett's death, upon condition of changing his name; but ye son being since dead, ye present will have it, and must I suppose change his name to Hewett upon my Lady's death, at present she has given up ye house, &c., and has an annuity for her life from Mr. Thornhay. This match has been in hand ever since my Brother's death; it has been delay'd first by his having ye small-pox in which he was in great danger, and is much pitted—also by an Act of Parliament which was necessary for his making settlements from something in his Father's will, wch was made some years before his death too much in favour of his youngest son,—also by Lawyers; but for a month or six weeks, it was expected every day, and none, not ye guardians, or the nearest relatives knew what occasioned ye delay. There never was any but a stolen wedding carry'd on in ye private secret manner to ye last—neither Guardians or hers or his relations except Sr George, being acquented wth any thing about it, wch was I think very wrong and very imprudent in Miss Savile and particularly ungrateful to his Mother who was extreem fond of her, and gave her some months ago her Familie Pearl Necklace valued at £1000—so far was ye secret carry'd, y^t tho' Mrs. Thornhay comes to Town in Winter I believe upon ye account as well as ye marrige of one of her daughters to one Mr. Ward (a very good match and a pretty gentleman) she went out of Town, a fortnight since, without knowing ye time of ye Wedding, to her great consern I doubt—even Mrs. Newton in y^e

house with ye Bride knew not ye time till it was over. I
had no reason therefore to take it ill, nay I believe I was
let into more y^n anybody, for Sunday ye night before, she,
Sir George, Mr. Thornhay and Miss Bab, came to take
leave of me. She told me they went next morn: and w^{hn} I
asked if ye wedding was not to be first, she owned it was,
wch was a great deal from her. There was not any woman
at ye wedding (which I believe was very particular and very
wrong) only Sr George besides ye bride and bridegroom.
A week ago she let me see her cloaths—wch I think too
fine for a private gentlewoman—A Princess could not have
richer, and there was abundance of them. I hear Mrs.
Newton told somebody they cost £700. She let me see her
necklace also, and told me Mrs. Thornhay's presents, w^{ch}
were a cross, earings, strap for ye stays and a Girdle Buckle.
It is certainly a love match on both sides (tho' it was very
equal too in circumstances) for all her discretion wch in
everything but ye secrecy about the wedding (wch I think
not at all so) has been very great, espeshily since her
Father's death; I say for all her discretion and ye extraordinary closeness of her temper (wch she has too much
communicated to her Brother) her fondness of Mr. Thornhay was very visible even in company—his also seemed to
be very great of her also—but Sr George's Friendship to
him was wonderful, tho' it proceeds from ye goodness, y^e
honesty and sincerity of his own heart and temper, I doubt
it shows a foible in him y^t he is easily gain'd and will be
too easily persuaded. I doubt there is another strange and
sad proof of it, in his keeping Grancy and Mignon contrary
to every body's advice and opinion, Mr. Mitchell's particularly. Miss Bab I understand is to be with her sister hence-
forth."

It is possible to form a very fair estimate of the characters
thus introduced, through their own letters and the records
of their shrewd if sometimes harsh relative. One gathers
that Mrs. Thornhagh Hewet was very delicate, and became
as time went on an absolute invalid. There are some
charming early letters from Barbara, while she was still

Miss Bab. She gives a natural girlish account of having been the May Queen at Rufford. She begs her aunt not to mock her and call her a Milkmaid Queen. " But after all," she adds, " what is there to be ashamed of, simple pleasures suffice for simple folk." It must have been a lovely scene in the Wilderness at Rufford, and if Lord Scarbrough happened to be present small wonder that he should be attracted by the May-day Queen.

Of the youthful days of Sir George, the kind and devoted brother, we have too few glimpses, but letters which will be introduced from time to time will prove what an exceptional man he was.

Gertrude Savile's Diary of 1745 does not spare any of her relatives. Even Miss Bab is misjudged by her aunt on one occasion. As to Mr. and Mrs. Hewet, her dislike for them increases with time. Sir George is only blamed for weakness in being taken in by Mr. Hewet.

Gertrude Savile's Diary.

"*July*, 1745.

Of dear good Sir George Savile.

" Not long ago I saw a letter from dear Sir George's Steward in Ireland wch says that extraordinary young man has given him orders in this time of scarcity (wch has been and still is very great in ye Kingdom) not only to forbear his Tenants there, but to excuse ye poorer from paying some half a year's Rent and some a year's Rent according to their necessity, and not only so, but allows £5 a week among the poor wch his Steward says keeps between 60 and 70 from perishing. O! God bless the worthy youth, God will bless him I doubt not, and I hope has raised him up to make him an Instrument of his Glory and of Good to man-kind, and to be a bright example. O gracious Creator keep him from the temptations and Snares wch his youth and Condition expose him to, in this wicked and dangerous World, keep him in his integrity and goodness of heart, in the Faith and Fear of Thee, In ye Belief and dependence upon Thy gracious Providence, and grant him thy Favour wch is better than Life and all y^e

injoyments of it, and Thy mercifull and powerfull protection
in all times of temptation, either from Prosperity or any
trouble or Affliction."

"*London, September 21st,* 1745.

"None sure so young, so extraordinarily distinguished
himself as dear Sir George, who wth ye first entered into y^e
Association for Yorkshire and Nottinghamshire both, and
went backward and forward from one County to another,
Raised and Desipplind men in both like (as I was told by
a wittness of it) an old and experienced officer, and, which
was most extraordinary, at ye generally (and most numerous
that ever was known) Association of Yorkshire he first proposed y^t what men were raised should go wherever his
Majesty should require."

"*October* 1745.

"Several Regiments of Troops raised in Yorkshire, 3 in
the West Riding. Lord Malton commanded all, in one of
them dear Sir George desired and had ye Commission of a
Captain, and raised his Company of 50 men (in Yorkshire) in
3 or 4 days, which was looked upon as uncommonly quick.
(He raised men, I don't know how many, in Nottinghamshire also but had no Commission there.) He was very soon
made a Lieutenant Col."

During the rebellion there was a panic among many
people, and it was thought advisable to send Miss Bab from
Shireoaks to her aunt in London. There appears to have
been considerable jealousy touching the guardianship of the
child, though it could hardly have been anticipated when
Sir George was still in the very heyday of his youth that
she would eventually become his co-heiress. The next two
letters were written by Mr. Mitchell to Mistress Gertrude
Savile :

"Eakring, 19th Oct: 1745.

"GOOD MADAM,

"I am very proud of the honour you have done me,
I assure you I neither wanted leisure nor inclination to read

Mrs. Savile's letter through and instead of growing weary, as you in your great modesty apprehended, my pleasure rose upon me, and increased to the end.

"I am exceedingly obliged to you for the tender of your kind offices and for all your engaging actions as well as expressions in favour of me and mine.

"I think you judged very right in sending your receipt to Sir George, tho' it would have been the same thing in effect whether it came in the first place to him, or to Mr. Elmsall or myself.

"I have been in some hurry, but it is pretty well over, we were one while alarmed with the rapid progress of the rebels, and fear'd they would have taken their route by our doors whilst we were utterly unprovided to dispute their passage. This put many of our ladies upon the thought of securing their persons and effects from insult and rapine by a timely retreat. Mrs. Thornhagh was not however of the number, for she could not persuade herself to fly from Shire-oaks, tho' in the neighbourhood of Worksop Manor; our apprehensions are now much subsided and I fancy our ladies begin to think themselves safe enough in their own houses. I most thankfully acknowledge your goodness in being so ready to receive my charming ward, but as matters now stand I believe there will be no need of removing her, and this might excuse me from offering you any advice upon her account, but as I have very little that I think needful to say to Mrs. Savile, I shan't trespas much upon your patience in hearing all. I should only beg you would afford her as much of your company and allow her as little of your servants, as may be and that you would carefully avoid to speak before her with the least terror or frightfull apprehensions of the rebellion. I believe you might hire a handsome coach or chariot with a coachman in livery by the month to be ready at call, ladies are better judges than men of young Miss'es expences, cloaths and the like. In these articles your own discretion would give you the best advice tho' in civility you might ask Mrs. Thornhagh's advice too.

"I can give you no certain account of D.N. only that his house has been searched, I believe in a very civil manner, and nothing found. 'Tis said he took the search unkindly, methink he should have invited the gentlemen to do their duty and not have laid them under the ungenerous and un-neighbourly necessity of demanding that they could not help insisting upon. There were many reports and other circumstances to render him suspected. Some of the reports upon examination were found false, and this I imagine has made the search less severe and scrutinous than it would other wise have been.

"I had the pleasure to observe no fright amongst my family but in one of my maids. My wife and girls are in good health, much obliged as well as myself to Mrs. Savile, and join with me in hearty acknowledgements.

"We have got Sir George's arms cleaned, repaired and made fit for use, he has eight men and horses with proper arms and accountrement at Rufford ready to move at the first call; he raised in Yorkshire thirty of his fifty men in less than two days and hoped to be complete in a few days more. I hear of no gentleman on his side that has shown more zeal upon the present occasion than Sir George and his brother Thornhagh have done.

"Mr. Elmsall and I have neither of us been wanting in the most affectionate advice to Sir G. in regard to his person. He has honoured me with a most obliging letter, and I think we may trust his discretion.

"He was under some difficulties with respect to the D. of K." (the Duke of Kingston?). "It was necessary in the present conjuncture that they should frequently meet and consult together with the neighbouring gentlemen, Sir G. had thoughts of making a sort of apology to his Grace, but I told him I thought such a step would be too formal; and that he had better take no notice of any former shiness; but treat His Grace the D. of K. as a gentleman concerned in the same glorious cause with himself: and when the present troubles should be over, he might return to his former distance and strangeness. This would be to meet the trouble by treating persons and things as they are; whether he has followed my advice or not I have not had the opportunity of learning.

"In a very numerous concourse of our noblemen and gentlemen I could not help thinking our dear Bar^t made the best personal appearance, but it may be I am a little prejudiced in his favour. However I have the satisfaction to be positive I was not much wide of the truth. He came this week to Shireoaks and is to return the next to Yorkshire to look after his new charge.

"I hear Miss Savile's maid has gone to London, but I here nothing of Miss herself, and am entirely ignorant how she is to be disposed of.

"I am with the truest respect, Madam,

"Your most obliged and faithful Servant,

"GILB^T MICHELL."

This letter is endorsed by Mistress Savile with the remark: "Does not know of Miss Savile's being come."

"Eakring, 3rd Jany: 1745-6.

"MADAM,

"I am exceeding sorry for the uncertainty and uneasiness you have undergone, I wish it had been in my power to prevent it.

"Mrs. Thornhagh honoured me with a letter of the 28th past, in which are these words. . . . I have had a letter from Mrs. Elmsall, whose opinion it seems to be as well as yours that I had best bring her (Miss Bab) down with us, especcially as no proper person is thought of for her to be with in Town: which I therefore will with pleasure do. . . .

"As this requires no answer I have given none to it; you see by it what you are to depend on, and it answers a good deal of your letter.

"I am so sure of Mrs. Savile's sincerity as well as my own that I am not afraid of any ill consequences from our misunderstanding each other, being fully persuaded that no mistake can happen between us which we shall not both of us be willing, and one of us at least able to clear up to the other's satisfaction; indeed I wonder there are not more mistakes between us two and between us and others than there are, so much are we both kept in the dark; when Miss came down to Shireoaks I was not consulted. She is to go up again for a small time upon account of the troubles; in this I am consulted and agree to it. Our apprehensions from the troubles lessen; upon this I advise against going; however she is sent and sometime after she is in town. I am told she is there, after this I am asked whether she is to come down again : though the only reason ever mentioned or insinuated for her going up is at an end. This is a specimen of my usual treatment; you will pardon me therefore for not giving you more light from time to time; I had it not to give, otherwise you should not have wanted it.

"I wrote to Sir G. and desired him to show the letter to Mrs. Elmsall, I asked them both about Miss Savile's board and instructions for you. Sir G. said immediately we could give you no less than Mrs. Thornhagh had, and he would consult Mrs. E. about instructions. The unsettled times have put my letter out of their thoughts, I believe, for I have heard no more of the matter. As for the board I think you ought to have at the rate of £80; the washing will be more than countervailed by the value of provisions and house room and the alterations you must necessarily make in your table.

"Miss Bab has given me a great deal of thought and concern, when I think of her sister, I see a very young lady just entered upon a new course of life in which a variety of cares and pleasures must call her off from a close attention to the child; none but relations can be both willing and fit to receive the young dear. And even these are very hard to be found, for of others the better sort value not the advantage of having her and dislike the trouble : the lower sort must not be wasted with her, a boarding school is the worst of all; I wish we could find a place for her, where her mind might be improved with knowledge, honour and generous sentiments with the whole train of virtues ; these are the things that should first and last be instilled into her with tenderness and address by precept and by example ; these will be of the most extensive and lasting advantage to her, they will form the true happiness and beauty of her whole being; music and dancing seem to me not to deserve much time or expence, they are little better than amusements at best and upon matrimony they are generally superseded by and neglected for the more valuable cares of a family.

"For some reasons above mentioned I fear Miss S. has not had all the care and attention paid her at Shireoaks which we could wish; I wish you would ask her how she used to spend her time there, whether she was much with her brother and sister, or in her chamber with her maid, or in the kitchen and amongst the lower servants; you will know the best times and manners of asking such questions. I am so much a stranger to the family that I don't know how to make these inquiries myself. I know not how to account for Mrs. T.'s late behaviour with regard to her sister, but upon the supposition that she wants to be rid of her and leave her in your hands. Poor dear Miss Bab, what must we do for her? I don't mean by this to throw her upon you, your health and happiness are dear to me and I know how inconsistent they are with her long and settled stay with you.

"Whether I have been treated with all regard that is due to my trust I wont determine, but I will venture to say I have not found that open and candid usage which my soul delights in and which I have experienced with inexpressible pleasure from one not so much obliged to it as those I complain of. I am told your nephew and my honoured ward has gained the love and admiration of all that know him in Yorkshire. My P.M. particularly treats him with the tenderness of a father. He has with great application made himself master of the military discipline and has taught it his men with such diligence and success that they are said to be the best company in the regiment.

"I would not delay a post in giving you what satisfaction I could. I have been forced to be short, but I hope I have not omitted anything necessary. The Plainness and sincerity I have used will make amends for the want of ceremony from our humble services, and best wishes attend Mrs. Savile and Miss.

"It is very cold, I can hardly write.

"Your most obliged and obedient Servant

"G. MICHELL."

To return to Gertrude Savile's Diary:

"*London*, 1745-6.

"Miss Savile left me. Considering I neither desired her coming, only made her wellcome w^{hn} sent to me, to my great inconvenience, desired directions about her again and again from Mrs. Thornhaigh particularly (and all else concerned wth her, even Mr. Thornhaigh) that I followed w^t I could obtain as near as I could, and as to w^{ht} I could not, I did my best, sacrificed most of my time and other sattisfactions to her, treated her wth great care and tenderness, regarded her in everything more y^n myself, Considering all this (however I might fail in prudence) I think I have both ye times of her being wth me, had a very ill return, the first time I lay'd it upon Mrs. Ogle to excuse as much as I could Mrs. Thornhaigh but this time I must think her ye principal even y^n, as well as now. I almost believe her being sent to me, or at least staying so long, was designed a snare; my new nephew her Husband (who is as far from a bright as a Polite Man) has been very rude, imprudently so I think. There must, there plainly is a design in Him and his Wife; his numerous Relations, cosens twenty times removed, to have not only the Child but her fine Brother in their management, how many have already aimed at this. The example she saw with her own fickle and too mean, bold and ungratefull temper made her behave much worse both to me and in all other respects, since her new Brother and Sister's coming and more and more so every day, so y^n I grew very much tired of my Charge, and am very glad to be delivered from it. I doubl my undertaking it will have ye same sort of consequences as my going to Rufford tho' forced by my Brother. She has been with me 16 weeks and 2 days this time, viz. from ye 20th Oct^{br} to this day, and 8 weeks and 2 days Two years ago, viz. from 14th Feb. to ye 13th April, in all 24 weeks and 4 days."

"*November* 8, 1747.

"Sir George came to town, and with him Mr. and Mrs. Thornhaigh, Sir George's elder sister, their Two children,

Miss Savile and Two sisters (viz. Tisy and Sally) of Mr. Thornhaigh, all to be at Sir George's House."

"*December* 10.

"Miss Savile began ye Small Pox. Sir George being ye best young Man in ye World did a most generous thing which none but himself would, viz. passed a Fine and Recovery to impower me to lett the House at Newcastle, wch it proved I could not do without."

"*London, April* 23, 1751.

"Sir George lent his House (wch could not be refused to ye persons who desired it) for ye use of ye young Prince of Wales, 'tis hard, almost cruel, to be forced from so fine, so convenient a House, on which his Father, and self has laid out so much money. He has his choice of any House in Town to be hired for him, and paid for and kept in repair (by ye King, I believe,) in lue of his own. He made choice of ye D. of Bolton's in Hanover Square, a most disadvantageous exchange; as indeed any House in London would be. He must never hope to have his own again I doubt. The King sent him thanks by ye D. of Newcastle. His and Leicester House are to have a communication made, as was w^hn the King was Prince."

On December 3rd Sir George wrote to his Aunt Gertrude a letter concerning the great novel of the period, "Clarissa Harlowe." It is most interesting in itself, and gives views on the subject of indiscriminate reading which ought to have weight at this time, when each year brings an encumbrance of literature which would certainly be the better for much winnowing.

The little touch of practical matter at the end is most characteristic :

"DEAR MADAM,

"If I have been an idle fellow at writing letters of late I may say I have been a diligent one at reading letters, having I believe had the perusal of no less than 700 or 800 between 8 or 10 persons on affairs of the last importance, and the subject so moving that was almost impossible to read some of them with dry eyes. If I am not mistaken you have read this correspondence and now I believe I need not tell you that it is the history of Miss C. Harlowe that I mean, and I shou'd be glad of your opinion of a book about w^h there are so many different and opposite sentiments. I wou'd ask you therefore if you think it is wrote with a good or bad design and whatever design it is wrote with whether it is likely to have more good or bad affects for affects it will have, if any book in the world ever have. I s^d be glad to know too whether you think the characters natural as well those of which you are a judge as those of which you cannot have a particular idea, as for example that of Lovelace with regard to which I only ask if you think it is possible in human nature; and this you may answer without having pass'd half a dozen years with a set of Mowbrays etc. etc. With regard to the consequences of the book the great question is whether he does or does not teach more iniquity in one part of the book than he can counterbalance by his moral reflections and catastrophe in another. Those who are against say (to bring one instance) that a girl had better never have the means of carrying on a forbidden correspondence put into her head than first be taught how to hide letters, pen etc. and then shewn the ill consequence of it. Those for it answer that we are all cunning enough to contrive what we like to do, especially if it be wrong and forbidden and that therefore it is better to be taught evil and at the same time warned against it than to be left to find it out, for we are all pleased with what we have the finding of. I am not at the end of it yet by above a volume. I cannot say but I'm pleased I have read it, but must allow that it w^d very well bear reducing to perhaps 3 or 4 volumes. You see I have taken care to rob you of the cause in your last and to give you a subject to write upon. I am sure it has found me one, for I have nothing to tell that signifies a farthing whether one knows or no. Lord this or Lord t'other very ill. The Duke of Ancaster marryd, all which releases me and displeases me just as much as that Thomas

Samson s^d be ill and Will Thomas marryd, which I s^d not write to you about. And now that you may not think me as long as Mr. Lovelace to John Belford Esq. I will conclude by assuring that I am your most aff^te nephew

"G. SAVILE.

"Shireoaks, Dec. 3rd 1750.

"Alas Business. I have your receipts for w^h am not sure that you did not expect a recpt. in your turn, but if I had not got them you w^d have heard from me before this. Woe be to the Hissers when I come.

"To Mrs. Gertrude Savile."

CHAPTER XIV

Marriage of Richard, Fourth Earl of Scarbrough, to Barbara Savile.—
Gertrude Savile's Diary

IN Barbara Savile's earlier letters to her Aunt Savile, she gives a very touching account of her first meeting with Lord Scarbrough, and subsequent letters allude with maidenly modesty to his first attentions, so that we are not surprised to find the following letter to his aunt from Sir George at Rufford, which foreshadows the union between members of the Savile and Lumley families :

"DEAR MADAM,

"I believe by next Wednesday's post I shall have the pleasure of acquainting you with the conclusion of our great affair. The Sandbeck family come here to-day; Friday next we shall all move into Lincolnshire. You must excuse the haste of this intelligence from

"Your aff^{te} nephew

"G. SAVILE.

"Rufford Sat. Dec. 23rd 1752."

Then comes the promised letter :

"DEAR MADAM,

"I have at last the pleasure of sending you the intelligence I promised you. Lord Scarbrough has not given us the slip any more and Mr. Ogle tied the knot yesterday in the Chappel.

"The morning was ushered in with solemn faces and low voices, and the afternoon concluded with Champagne and Burgundy.

"I write before anybody is up and so have no compliments but Newton's to send you.

"I think this is enough matter in conscience 'for one letter, so subscribe myself at once,

"Your most affec^te Nephew,

"G. SAVILE.

"Rufford, Dec: 27th 1752."

Mistress Gertrude Savile duly records the event in her Diary:

"Dec: 26, 1752.

"Miss Savile marry'd to ye Earl of Scarbrough, nothing that can seem to promise happiness wanting in ye match— his character extraordinary in all respects; long acquaintance, believe more than common—(especially among ye nobility) liking and love on his side, with a proper shair on hers—agreeable to all his Familie, as well as to hers—his first proposal was just before his Father dyed in last March —so afterword by him a day or two before Sir George went to France, wch shortened that good Brother's stay there. Since that time His progress to Matrymony has been as quick as prosperity and ye Lawyers would allow, except about a fortnight's delay from my Lord's illness. They were marry'd in Sr George's Chapple at Rufford, by Mr. Newton Ogle, the Dowager Lady and her Daughter being there. The Monday following they went (Sr George, Mrs. Thornhagh also) to a seat of my Lord's in Lincolnshire called Glentworth, where they kept open house for near three weeks, in extreem grandeur, had two French cooks from London, and Two Confectioners, in short heard that all made a great Eclat in ye county, were charmed with ye Bride and her Behaviour, and that my Lord's mother (as well as Himself) expresses great pleasure in her Daughter-in-law."

Glentworth seems already at this time to have become the favourite residence to the neglect of Lumley Castle. The magnificent hospitality, just referred to, and further described in the following letter, may account for the financial difficulties which must have saddened the later years of Lord Scarbrough's life, and certainly added to the sorrows of Barbara's widowhood. But nothing of this was foreshadowed when Mrs. P. Massingbred wrote the following brilliant description of the pageant to her daughter-in-law :

" I don't find the newspapers have yet given you an account of Lord Scarbrough's wedding; therefore I will. They were met near this Town by the Mayor and Aldermen— and L⁴ S. and Sir George alighted out of the first coach and mounted their horses, which as well as themselves were richly adorned with gold and silver, and attended by Mr. Chaplin himself, and mob. Then they proceeded slowly through the town, yᵉ Bride in an open Landau, and my Lord's mother; in Sir George's carriage was my Lord's sisters, Mr.—after Earl of—Ludlow, who is speedily to marry Lady Fanny, and Mr. and Mrs. Thornhagh (afterwards Hewett) and divers other post chaises with ladies' women, etc. They did not stop anywhere, but went on to Glentworth, but came again to the Low Hill assembly and was met there by Lord Veres, Lord Geo. Maners, Sir F. Dashwood, and many other Familys and most of the Lincoln ladys that had convenience of coaches. They keep open house at Glentworth in the most magnificent manner I ever heard ; Miss Whichcot who is at her Uncle's wrote her mother an acc⁵ of the 1st and 2nd days' entertainment as follows. 2 courses of dessert at dinner, 30 dishes at each, but not one she knew what it was, and she never dined worse in her life ; in the dessert she hoped to regale in some raspberry and cream, but to her great disappointment it was full of Ice (no gᵗ variety in this season) but to make amends they recommended some sweetmeats done in brandy. The dinner was by candle light and served in exceeding fine chaced plate, the dishes oval ; they danced till supper, the second course of which was gilt plate, a present from the last Prince of Wales, with his arms in the middle of each, candlesticks, salts, waiters, and changed with the courses. Everything as elegant as French cooks and confectioners from London can make it. The attendants numerous dress'd in laced cloathes and white silk stockings. Mrs. Amcotts and some of ye young ones and Mrs. Dymock went yesterday. I suppose they thought it proper because they used to visit the Dowg^r or else might have been excused, considering how much they oppose the present Lord's interest."

At the time of the marriage the family jewels were reset and added to. The accompanying list is a copy of the bill of one Peter Dutans. Not one of these jewels is in the possession of the present Earl. The list was found in 1898:

	£	s.	d.
A necklace of brilliants which cost	346	5	0
A nesclavage (what is that?) girdle with tossells, knot and ends	265	7	6
The horn of plenty which hangs to the necklace	167	7	6
As the esclavage was too short an addition had to be made which cost	37	7	0
The cross	187	7	6
A fine aigrette representing an eagle	96	0	0
One aigrette of different flowers tied with a knot	136	0	0
An aigrette pompon	98	0	0
Four circles of brilliants for the hair	41	0	0
A girdle buckle	108	0	0
A pair of 3 drop earrings in which my lady employed her two large drops and in which she furnished 6 side drops	130	0	0
Total price of the earrings in addition to stones supplied	325	15	0
A sett of five fine starrs	330	15	0
A brilliant hoop ring and a gold one	14	0	0
Total[1]	2024	4	6
Should be	2283	4	6
A small ring with flowers tyed with a knot of brilliants	5	5	0
His lordship's seal	13	17	0
For some brilliants to form several ornaments, watch and chain, etc.	74	5	0
Total	2117	11	6

This bill was settled in full November 8th, 1753.

[1] Total as reckoned in jeweller's bill.

A letter from the young Countess of Scarbrough to Mistress Gertrude Savile shall now speak for itself:

" Glentworth,
" January 27th, 1753-4.

" Does it appear possible in the nature of things, to have an excuse or good reason to give, for being in debt, many thanks for a very kind letter almost a month? it is not an absolute impossibility; if not quite so, and such a thing *can* happen, I am the person who can do it; nothing but a very great abundance of company or a confinement by illness, can, I am sensible, be an excuse for so long a neglect; and that I may appear rather yet more pardonable, I am going to plead both, for being so strangely long before I write to my dear Aunt Savile, whose very obliging letter demanded surely my earliest acknowledgements :—I will (not to tire you Madam) be as concise as possible ; in one word (as to the first) I can with truth assure you, that since our arrival here till within these 10 days I have literally scarce had a leisure hour, so great our hurry of company, with regard to the other part of the ten days I mention I have, disagreeably enough, spent in my room, being confined to it, by an inflammation in my eyes, (occasion'd by a cold I caught I know not how) and which, tho' not by any means a dangerous disorder, was an effectual prevention of my writing ; it has now almost perfectly left me, but I am much desired not to strain them with too much looking (on any thing) at a time ; and indeed Dear Madam, this is the first day I've ventured to write a word. I must presently take my leave but not till I have returned you my best thanks and with mine my Lord's, for your very kind congratulations and good wishes; pray then do us the favour to accept them and believe me to be

" Dear Madam,
" Your most dutiful niece
" and obliged humble servant
" B. SCARBROUGH.

" Shall I make excuses for this scribbling or no, past all

doubt it needs them, but whether that is not very formal is the question."

There is here no allusion to her little son, George Augusta, who was born in the preceding September.

Gertrude Savile's account of her long illness gives so much insight into various characters that she shall tell her own tale :

"*London, November* 18, 1756.

Tirrible Illness.

"My great Illness which thro' long breading grew so extreme violent that I could no longer go out of my Room after the 13th." She appears to have suffered terribly for about ten weeks from 13th November, "from which day I think I may date the extremity of my illness, at least keeping my room and almost my Bed to Jan^ry 21st 'twas near Two months more before I was able to go down Stairs." She complains of the behaviour of her relations thus :

Reflections about my relations.

"Relations 'tis too often experienced are not always the best Friends, often enemies, but never was that so remarkable, so general as it has been to me, and that not from the common cause, Interest clashing. My History in that Particular, were it worth reading or my time in writing would be ye most extraordinary I really believe of any Person's in the World. From my cradle (except in Two instances) tho' an object of contempt, and treated as a poor abject slave, without comon sense or Passions, or even feelling yet the greatest object of jealousie and Fear to most of them. Tell me (for I have much longed to know) Yee Philosophers, yee Studiers of nature or of Mankind, how is this compatible? that a dispised Idiot, a creature not thought capable of plotting, sure or so much as rational, should at the same time be the grand Butt for the most Machivilian Policy to shoot at? and this from my good Mother (for very good she was in most respects) down to my niece Hewitt—My Niece? Her behaviour in my great Illness gave occasion to my present reflections ; wch was almost as wonderful as my own History, considering her grand, only (I think) Characteristic is

Prudence, should add stediness, an uncomon one in a woman—say the men—rare indeed in all, yet not I think commendable if improperly apply'd. But she knows w^t she does, she has made herself too, too secure in ye good opinion of one (who I'm affraid she wants to make a fool of, I ought to thank her tho' for not in the least endeavoring to make one of me) whose regard and love is abundantly to Her and Hers, worth gaining, and keeping, with all her Art wish it may not be too easily gain'd and kept, and that she may make the least proper, gratefull return for it. I much doubt it, have good reason. She came to Town in the beginning of my illness, sent in form to notify it, my answer an apology for not waiting upon her from being extremely ill. After wch instead of coming herself (that was more y^n her Prudence thought necessary) she sent once a week, and sometimes (wch was still worse to me in 5 days) a common How-de-ye as if nothing was ye matter and that at unseasonable times, notwithstanding I always sent word I was extremely ill, beg'd her saucy Fellow not to knock so hard, wch he always did, so as often to wake me in a fright out of a slumber (wch then was a rare happiness). Nay tho' I sent my own Servant (lest hers might not deliver my messages) she still continued to plague me; till I both sent word to the Fellow not to come any more to my House and to Herself that I desired she would send no more to disturb me. Some time after that (for she let me be a short time unmolested) w^n due form required her return of a visit from one of my neighbours, about 6 weeks after ye beginning of my illness, w^n I was just able to sit up without a Blanket round me, she vouchsafed to call in person, not expecting or desiring to see me I dare say. I would see her out of curiosity at her unaccountable (as I thought) behaviour, and to put an end to her dredfull messages. With astonishing stediness (I could almost say a harsher Word) she wiped her mouth and with her constant formal demureness said she thought I did not choose to see Company, that any Body might not like that at all times, and as to my answers to all her messages, and wch I sent by my own Man (tho' some I'm

Mrs. Hewitt's behaviour in my illness.

sure she received) she thought proper utterly to deny except that part of my last wch desired she would send no more to me. That might serve a purpose in representing me as She wished. All this I think was stretching Prudence (wch my Brother called—tho' Himself was remarkably deficient in it—the chief virtue, and what he chiefly inculcated to her) to a crime and a very Shamefull one too. And as a still greater agrivation of her untruth in pretending not to know that I was really ill, I had at that time a letter from Ly. Scarbrough whose knowledge of my dreadfull illness was as Herself said from good Mrs. Hewitt. But Sir George was not to know it, nor had I the least regard (that's the grand point aim'd at) or inquiry after me from him of many months. Then indeed a very long letter pretty kind, expressed some consern, but mostly filled and (chiefly if not only) intended to excuse his dearly beloved sister from any neglect in acquainting him, blaming his own slightness and disregard, that no doubt he must and was sure he had been told of my illness, but that indeed he imagin'd 'twas only a cold and thought no more of it. O! good young man. 'Tis very uncommon but possible that Goodness itself, the strictest honesty and sincerity of heart, Truth and Honour joyn'd to the finest, brightest understanding—'Tis possible I say (however strange) that all these from prejudice and Friendship (carry'd to a degree of Inthusiasm) may produce effects wch one would suppose could only proceed from the very reverse of those fine qualities. O! Mrs Hewitt! how secure has Prudence (not the most laudable tho') made you? What lengths may you not go?"

Here the Diary enumerates some of the exceptions to the general treatment of Gertrude Savile's relations, the first being:

"My poor Cosen Newton," etc., etc. "My other exception, and that considering her youth and all

The two exceptions to the general treatment of my relatives.

other circumstances as extraordinary (but not so interesting) is Lady Scarbrough. Her whole behaviour indeed has been always courtious, obliging and (tho a countess) respectfull; her nature is Courtesy and Humility. She picques

herself upon showing that to all. `Now rightly judg^t charm-
ing qualities, espehily in the Great; tho only
assumed, if not to low and base purposes; but
in her not so. Her Lett^r (wch I mention'd before) upon Mrs. Hewitt's telling her of my
illness, was so excessive kind, may call it tender, that greater
could hardly be expressed by nearest and dearest Relations,
or w^t is more Friends, and this from a woman of quality to
a private gentlewoman! From a young niece to an old
Aunt! and Her not rich! from whom she can no more
expect then happily she wants anything! surprising tho'
scarce credible that all ye affectionate consern she expressed
was quite sincere, but if it was not, yet it showed a regard
that was greatly obliging. At least that she thought me
worthy of some regard which no other of my Relations did.
But disregardfully and truly indecently and inhumanly as
all my Relations treated me (except dear good Lady Scarbrough) I found Friends in almost strangers."

Lady Scar-
brough's great
goodness.

"*November*, 1756.

"I confess Sr George's neglect was some consern and occasioned (then and allways will)
wonder for he has still a good Heart, tender,
compassion^e! So I have heard his Father had, whilst young.
He grows more and more like him.

Sir George's
neglect.

"What rock so Firm that incessant dropping won't make
an impression on? What understanding so fine and bright
as to be incapable of any Sully? Wholly free from a Flaw
or one weak place, for ye cunning and artfull to work
upon?"

"*London, January*, 1757.

"Of all the various ways of dispensing Charity
I think none were so great or beneficial as w^t (I
believe) Sir George Savile set the example of (at
least his was ye first that I heard of) and what was after
follow'd by many, viz. obliging his tenants in Nottinghamsh^e
(at least) to sell their corn at a moderate price, and making
up the difference to them out of his own pocket, as no doubt
he and all the others did.

Sir George's
charity.

" (Risings in many places of the common People about the dearness of bread. Many mills pulled down.) "

" *London, April* 16, 1757.

" Lady Scarbrough brought to Bed of a Second Son. He was Baptized Richard after his father. Mr. Lumley (Ld Scarbrough's Uncle) and Sir George stood for him. She lay down in the country."

With the following curious critical opinion, which puts Cibber above Garrick, we will take leave of Mistress Gertrude Savile's Diary, to which we have been greatly indebted for much interesting matter. It certainly gives a fair picture not only of the habits of private life, but of the history of that disturbed period before the glamour of the Stuarts had quite faded from men's and women's minds, although the Hanoverian succession was already practically secured.

Doubtless Lady Scarbrough had often witnessed the performances of the actor-poet.

" *London, December* 11, 1757.

" Colley Cibber Esqr Poet-laureat Dyed in ye 86 year of his age. Tho he was very far I fear from being a good man, he wrote several of the most inofensive, modest Comedies (almost all of them even moral, sets Virtue in an amiable and Vice in an odious light) as well as the genteelest and most entertaining Ones that ever were acted. He was an excellent actor, particularly in the parts of a Fop, and a Villain, in those he has not yet been match'd, scarce ever will. He had left off acting some years, is the last of that truly compleat set of actors, in comparison of which ye present (even ye celebrated Mr. Garrick) are in my oppinnion but Strolers in a Barn—except Mrs. Pritchard who exceeds all I ever saw, indeed in all parts, Tragedy, Comedy and (before She grew too fat) in Men's. If I must except Mrs. Cibber too, 'tis only in very tender parts; she can do nothing but whine. There are some very good for Comick, odd, drole Parts, Woodwards and Shooter extraordinary and as y^e Stage or Stages go, Barry in Tragedy is very good. Poor Cibber ! "

CHAPTER XV

Masquerade at Harewood.—Letters to Aunt Savile.—Letters from James
Lumley to the Duke of Newcastle.

HATEVER differences of opinion may have
arisen from time to time, there seems throughout to have been a close attachment between
Sir George Savile and his two sisters, Mrs.
Hewet and Barbara, Countess of Scarbrough;
for the latter, indeed, he seems to have combined paternal
with brotherly tenderness and affection. From the numerous
letters that passed between brother Hewet, Barbara Scarbrough, Sir George Savile, and later the numerous sons of
Lord and Lady Scarbrough, we get pleasant glimpses of
happy family life at Shireoaks, Rufford, and Sandbeck.
Glentworth and Lumley Castle figure more rarely in these
records, but brother Hewet receives a fine salmon which
Lord Scarbrough brings from Lumley Castle, caught in the
neighbouring River Wear, which it is hoped will not be
unfamiliar through the description given in an earlier portion
of this Chronicle.

Another contributor of many letters to the family was
F. F. Foljambe (commonly called the three F's), who married
first a daughter of Mr. Hewet's, and secondly Mary Arabella, Lord and Lady Scarbrough's eldest daughter. Among
others he sends the following, which gives a very amusing
account of what was evidently a very startling scandal of
the time. Ladies seemed capable of being as lawless in the
end of the eighteenth as they too often prove now in the
twentieth century. Such a tale as he tells of a certain Lady
Worsley and two young ladies of family surpasses the worst

and company (more indeed the latter wch I actually think we are never w^thout) and thereby omitted writing, indeed I find I grow a worse correspondent than ever, and really I believe mine (at least I deserve it) will forsake me I'm so abominably near forsaking them, by my neglect. I don't know how it is whether I've less and less leisure or fancy I have, or whether I grow more stupid (I do almost fear I do that) at writing, or what I can't very well tell, but I really find now-a-days, if I write two letters, I don't mean to one person but in all, in three months I think I do mighty things. Don't you cry shame on me Dear Aunt Savile— however so long as I write to any body it shall be to you who are really very good to take up with my scribbles. Since my last, your little friend Georgy gave us a very great alarm, being taken very and suddenly ill and with such symptoms, as left us nothing to suppose but the small pox wch as (if it pleases God he lives and is well) we assign to inoculate him the next spring, we by no means wish it to prove, but after continuing so two days, it almost as suddenly left him and since he recovered his strength and spirits (w^h indeed were very much affected for some time after) he has been vastly well and wild to a degree, and his Sis and Bro."·(Richard, his mother's darling) "follow his example, the first you can easily suppose, the last as much I mean as a little soul of 5 months old can do. It will be on Georgy's account as I said that we shall not see London and so shall not think of coming long before the proper season for inoculation which I think is in March. Your last query as I think about our house, and you might indeed well look about and about again, for no such place exists, nor (from the jumble among the builders and people and My L^ds present uncertainty) do I know when it will, so that we must for the present make what shift we can.

"With my L^ds compts which he desires me to present,
 "I remain
  "Dear Madam
   "Your dutiful and affect^ate niece
    "and obliged servant
     "B. SCARBROUGH.

BARBARA, WIFE OF FOURTH EARL, WITH HER
SON, GEORGE AUGUSTA, FIFTH EARL
SIR JOSHUA REYNOLDS

the whole was over and the Commendam pass'd before I knew one word of it; or had receiv'd your Lordship's letter. Mr. Lumley was with me from your Lordship, & proposed to me to recommend Mr. Hammer to the Bishop of Durham for a Prebend in his Church: I told him I should most willingly do it if I had not procured, this last summer, the last Prebend in the Church, for the Head Master of Westminster School, Dr. Markham. Mr. Lumley then wish'd that I would recommend Mr. Hammer to the Bishop for a living, —I will certainly mention it to him and, if in decency I can, so soon after a great Favor from the Bishop, I will recommend it. If Mr. Hammer will find out any living in the gift of the Crown likely to become vacant, if it is not engaged I will endeavour to procure it for him.

"I am &c.

"HOLLES NEWCASTLE."

The holding a living or benefice *in commendam* is where a vacancy occurs holding such living commended by the Crown until a proper pastor is provided for it. This may be temporary for one, two, or three years; or perpetual, being a kind of dispensation to avoid the vacancy of the living. These *commendams* were granted to Bishops after they had ceased to be granted to lower dignitaries of the Church.

"MY LORD. The Place of Receiver of the Land Tax for the Division of Lindsey in the County of Lincoln being become vacant by the death of Mr. James Ward, I take the liberty of troubling your Grace with this & at the same time recommending Mr. William Hillyard to be his successor. Give me leave to assure your Grace that he is a Gentleman of the most unexceptionable character & in every respect qualified for the office & besides able to give the most undeniable security for his behaviour therein.

"In complying with this request your Grace will extreamly oblige me, more particularly so as it is in that part of the County where I reside & I shall allways look upon it as a mark of that regard your Grace has been so obliging often to express for me.

"Sandbeck May ye 10th 1760."

"Chester June yᵉ 10ᵗʰ 1760.

"My Lord. I take the liberty of giving your Grace this trouble if the Place of Mr. Bee to be in the Customs at Hull is not disposed of, I should take it as a favor if your Grace would confer it, on Mr. John Green of Lincolnshire, a person formerly in good circumstances but now in great distress. Your Graces compliance with this would be very agreable to me."

"My Lord. Being just inform'd that the Living of Thorfeild in Hertfordshire is going to be vacant by the resignation of Dr. Young now translated to the Bishoprick of Norwich, I take the liberty of troubling your Grace with this, & requesting it for the Revd. Mr. Hammer of King's College in Cambridge. I must remind your Grace that it is now above eight years scince you promised me to provide for him, & yet he has not obtain'd any thing. In a letter your Grace wrote me some time scince you wonder'd how I could doubt your intentions to provide for him, but surely My Lord when you reflect I have waited 8 years, is there not more than sufficient reason to doubt your Graces intention; but I hope your compliance with this request will convince me that I can depend upon you & as an additional weight to my application I must add that in a conversation I had with you two years ago you promised me the first good living that should drop.

"I can not I own sit down quietly & see every thing disposed of to the friends of others whose equall I think myself in ev'ry respect whilst mine are totally neglected.

"If the Person I recommended had any imputation upon his character, a refusal might with justice be given, but when he is in virtue & Learning equall to the better half of the Dignified Clergy I must even look upon his want of preferment as a great indignity offered me from that Government I have so diligently & unrewarded served on all occasions when call'd upon.

"If my present application, your Graces promise & the arguments I have urged prove fruitless I must confess all hopes of preferment from your Grace for Mr. Hammer will

all ranks of his People. If at any time this summer I should be within reach of Clermont, I shall certainly take an opportunity of paying my compliments there.

"Lincoln, June yᵉ 3ᵈ 1765."

Lord Scarbrough was made Treasurer of the Household on June 17th, 1765. He was also Deputy Earl Marshal of England, and his various duties seem to have taken him a good deal to London. When at his country homes, Glentworth, too seldom Lumley, and most often Sandbeck, we read of company and entertainments on a large scale. There is a description of a grand party at the latter place for the Doncaster Races, at which her Majesty was present. One can hardly picture good Queen Charlotte lending *éclat* to a race meeting. Speaking of Queen Charlotte, there is a letter from a Mr. Baynes to Mr. Hewit, written during October, 1784, giving the following information:

" Madame Hastings gained admission to the Queen [Charlotte] through Madame Schulemberg to present H.M. with diamonds and pearls to an immense value 14 *lb.* in weight."

What Court intrigue hung about those pearls and diamonds? Had she been as beautiful as her unfortunate contemporary, Marie Antoinette, there might have been a pendant to the Diamond Necklace romance.

Richard Lumley, the second son of Lord Scarbrough, gives an account to Uncle Hewit of the grand ball at Sandbeck, held on December 24th, 1780, and tells how they all sang glees and acted charades.

Rufford was as much home to the young Lumleys as any of the Scarbrough residences. Balls were of frequent occurrence, and there was plenty of hunting and shooting for the men.

CHAPTER XVI

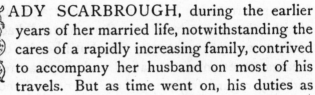ADY SCARBROUGH, during the earlier
years of her married life, notwithstanding the
cares of a rapidly increasing family, contrived
to accompany her husband on most of his
travels. But as time went on, his duties as
Deputy Earl Marshal of England and other important
posts about the King's person, necessitated Lord Scarbrough's presence in London. The claims of Parliament
also detained Sir George in the metropolis, and Lady Scarbrough spent her time at one of her homes, paying visits to
London from time to time. Sir George Savile underwent
much anxiety concerning Lord Scarbrough's affairs. The
family jewels were sold, and the plate was only saved by
being bought in by Lady Scarbrough's truly generous
brother. Seven sons and three daughters to be provided
for must have increased the gentle Barbara's anxieties.

Of these sons, George Augusta, Lord Lumley, whose
birth in 1753 has been mentioned, was plain, retiring, and
often ailing; probably the attack of smallpox in 1757
affected permanently both his health and spirits. At the
same time he was not wanting in ideas of his own, as will
be seen by the following letter to his kind uncle, Sir George
Savile. The letter refers to a riot at Eton in which he had
taken too prominent a part, and will be interesting to all
Etonians:

"Monday
"November 28th 1768.

" HONOURED UNCLE,

"The very kind, mild and affectionate treatment I
met with from you, at a time when I the least had reason

to expect it from my conduct, calls for my most dutiful acknowledgements; and I sincerely beg your pardon for having deferred paying them so long. The reception I met with from you at that time, and your kindness to me during the whole, I cannot be too much obliged to you for.—The situation I was then in, was as you may suppose a most disagreeable and unhappy one. I had inconsiderately withdrawn myself from the authority under which I was placed, and as inconsiderately bound myself to a solemn obligation not to return to it. I was under the disagreeable situation of either leaving school at a time, when I had just begun really to enjoy it; not only this, but likewise of giving the greatest uneasiness, vexation and displeasure to all who had any regard for me; or on the other hand, (as I then thought) returning to school with the notion of perjury on my mind. This you entirely relieved me from by persuading me fully of the inconsistency of the oath itself, and of the opinion in which I then was of the absurdity of it. For, (as in duty bound) I am under the highest obligation to you, and shall I hope always be truly. You was so kind as to lay aside the authority of one who had a right to lay down his opinion more positively, and if on the other hand I spoke and argued with greater freeness than became me I hope I was persuaded entirely of my error, I beg your pardon and hope I am forgiven. I cannot forget one thing that I by mere chance heard of. I mean the letter which you sent to Dr. Foster, and the kind manner in which it was done, which with long etc. of kindnesses I have received from you I shall with gratitude reflect on.

"I suppose you have heard what became of me after you saw me last? My Papa has told you that he sent for me about 6 o'clock, and left me in Audley S^t when he went to Lincoln Fields. I arrived at this place next day about 3 o'clock after dinner, and having first seen my Tutor and Dr. Foster, my Father went back to town and we parted friends on my promise that it should be the last time such a thing should ever happen.

" My Tutor treated me with the greatest kindness as indeed he did through the whole affair, to every body his

behaviour throughout is such as has I believe, gained him
the good will and good wishes of boys, Masters, and
parents, and was the single master to whom, when in a re-
bellious body, we paid the usual respect. He behaved to
us then as he had always done, with the greatest affection
and kindness, really sorry for what had happened, but without the least appearance of passion or resentment. This he
did while there was no occasion for more violent measures.
The next morning when we came back to Eton in order to
speak with Dr. Foster he immediately seized Grenville (one
of his pupils) and kept him at his house till his windows
were broke, and his wife thereby thrown into fits by the sight
of about a hundred boys battering the doors and windows
of his house. His conduct through the whole, has I think
merited the highest commendation and respect, and I shall
think myself wanting in gratitude as a scholar as well as a
pupil, if I did not give you my opinion with that of (I may
say) the whole school. He both spoke and acted as if he
really felt for every one of us. But to return to what I was
speaking of; I went into school at 5 o'clock and was flogged,
not for the thing itself but for the company in which I went
home as Dr. Foster said; for he had not intended to have
whipped me had I not gone off with Galby who, I suppose
you know, is expelled. With how much hastiness soever
our Master behaved before the rebellion he has since treated
us all with much more lenity and clemency than I s^d have
expected, but I am afraid the school will be hurt by our late
secession. The authority of the imposters is entirely taken
away, but I s^d guess it will not be long before it is restored.
The boys are except 10 or 12 all returned. I know little
other news about Eton, but what w^d be too tedious in a
letter. I have wrote the chief particulars that I recollect.

"It is now about a week to our breaking up when I shall
hope to see you well, till which time I remain Hon^d Uncle

"Your ever dutifully obliged and affectionate Nephew,

"G. A. LUMLEY S.

"I have sent you my Tutor's letter which you sent me
some days ago, directed to you in Leicester Sq^re."

and in particular young officers constantly hurt themselves and many dye by overheating themselves with dansing (much in vogue there). Of this Mr. Harrison observed many instances, and two in particular, remarkable healthy fine young fellows who dyed. The one illness which I mentioned above Mr. Harrison himself to have had, was by his business obliging him to go from *Passage Fort* to *Spanish Town* in haste. No horse or chaise was to be got and he was forced to walk it. It was 7 miles, excessive hot, and he paid for it by a bad fever which however from his good habit of body and former temperance, he got over in about a week. His own experience and his observation of others seems to have convinc'd him that there is no manner of need of being ill from the climate, which indeed he describes as a pleasant one likewise.

"With regard to Diet, beside what is said above about salt meat &c. (which there is no need to say much about because there is no great temptation to eat it for those who can afford better) Mr. Harrison adds that much mischief is done by the fruits of the Country, but not so much on account of their naturally unwholsome quality as by eating them unripe, and this is a great trap for strangers. Almost all the fruits of the Country have when not perfectly ripe an acrid or rather an *austere* (or sloe-like) taste. He tells me that he has eat *freely* of fruit, particularly oranges, without ill consequences. Excess however I do not mean to recommend. But he was very carefull to have them full ripe.

" Mr. Harrison has been very sollicitous to recollect the most material articles, and desires to be remembered to you with his best compliments, and on telling him what I have said he begs I will mention again the article of over dansing as having proved fatal to so many.

" I need not repeat what I said about the dews. On the whole, and from what I have likewise heard of the climate itself being mended of late by the clearing the Country, I conclude that there is nothing so fatal to the health as may not be guarded against by a very *attentive Care.*

" If your destination be not there all this is but a little paper and ink wasted and I shall be very glad of it.

"As to the weak sour punch advis'd for the dry gripes I find by Mr. Harrison's Acct. there are disputes about it. Some it agrees with and some not, and it is an unsettled point to this day.

    "Once more God bless you my dear Dic,

                  "Your affect Uncle,

                        "G. SAVILE.

"Honble Richd Lumley."

Richard Lumley's return from Jamaica was pretty rapid for that time, for in September, 1780, Lady Scarbrough writes to brother Hewet, mixing the first and third persons very quaintly:

"Good Mr. Hewet has afforded Lady Scarbrough and all at Sandbeck the utmost satisfaction in giving it under his own hand and seal that the bathing at Matlock has greatly benefitted him. I must not pass over a subject of exceeding great joy here. That dear dear Dic Lumley is safe arrived in England from Barbadoes and expected here. Dear Tom has got a little ship and is sailed for Oporto and was well his last letter." Tom was the third son and was in the Navy.

Richard, Lord Scarbrough, wrote many letters to his men of business between 1780 and 1782. Barbara's letters to Mr. Bassett, the agent at Glentworth, during this period were full of anxiety concerning her dear lord's health, but Lord Scarbrough himself seemed full of life to the last. His letters are bright and business-like; they do not hint at embarrassments which would have weighed down most spirits. In 1781 he had a serious accident which might well have cost him his life, but Lady Scarbrough thanks God that he is going on well. He was appointed Vice-Treasurer for Ireland, according to the "Gazette," on March 27th, 1782. His last letter was written on May 7th, 1782, and contains no suggestion of indisposition or of any special anxiety; but he died on May 12th.

Debts and difficulties of every kind increased greatly at this crisis. A letter given by the late Sir Charles Anderson, of Lee, to the Right Hon. Francis Foljambe, of Osberton, gives an account of an attempt made by the creditors of the dead earl to seize the body when it was being conveyed to the grave. The earl was buried at Saxby in Lincolnshire, and there was a scene as the *cortège* passed through Lincoln. The attempt was not successful, and as there is no allusion to the circumstance in any of the private letters one may believe and hope that the poor widow never heard of the circumstance.

The eldest son, George Augusta, who succeeded as fifth Earl, though, as we have seen, delicate in health, showed himself to be a man of ability. His letters are practical, manly, and very much to the point. He was anxious to do his duty by his family, and seemed full of tender concern for his mother. Troubles enough fell to her share during the years that succeeded her husband's death. The following letter to her brother was written a few months after her bereavement:

"MY DEAREST BRO.

"We have received your kind, satisfactory and sufficiently explicit letter which with my Son's enables me I think to be rather more decisive in my plan, a thousand thanks for it and with love and duty from May in particular. We are all well, Jack replaces the little boys at Eton about the same time I quitt this place, that will now be next Thursday. I propose to proceed and pass a few days or week at St^{ar} [?] and then, since as I've told my son, you both persist in making me (by not sooner deciding for me) too much my own mistress, I have now resolved on the halt you in your goodness hint at; by passing a week or four nights at Rufford which will answer the double purpose of my being within reach of early intelligence of the event I am anxious about, and also give my son's people at Sandbeck a little more notice of my coming, whatever orders you think necessary at Rufford, vous est le maître. But you must be assured I wish to give as little trouble and make as little fuss and be as little announced as possible. Your servants on the least hint and without even a hint at all are always too ready to serve and oblige me. They know your mind. I think I will write a line to Mrs. Sykes or Mrs.

Wilson, apropos to whom her nephew (the most peaceable, inoffensive and obliging creature) gains ground I hope sensibly, and dear Richard has a good opinion of him. I'm glad William A. does not want it this year, still more glad that Hull is likely to agree with you.

"Might not official accounts, if not letters, have been expected by this time from India?

"I pray God bless you too.

"Your ever faithfully affectionate sis:

"B. S.

' Saturday, 7th Sep. 1782.

"My son will tell you of a strange jumble which I fear I must have been the cause of, but I hope rectified."

The May referred to in this letter is the eldest daughter, Mary Arabella, who, as has been already said, became the second wife of Mr. Foljambe. The event about which Lady Scarbrough was anxious was the first wife's confinement. "Jack" was the fourth son, John Savile Lumley, born in 1761; and the little boys whom he was replacing at school were the fifth, sixth and youngest sons, Frederick, born in 1761, Savile Henry, born in 1768, and William, born in 1769. The last paragraph of the letter refers to the sailor, Thomas; while the son in the postscript was Richard.

The next letter, from Lady Mary Lumley, was written to her uncle about the same time:

"Saturday, Aug. 17th, 1782.

"MY DEAR UNCLE,

"The enclosed letter I received on Wednesday last from Mrs. Foljambe, and on account of three lines in the last page of it my dear mother wishes you to see it, as she is in some perplexity (as well as myself) in what light to understand what Mrs. F. says respecting our return into her neighbourhood: whether she speaks as *really wishing* to see us *before* her confinement, or whether her tenderness would not permit her to express a contrary wish, and she may have meant this as a gentle hint that she would like nearly over with Sir George Savile, the physician says he cannot last many days more." It is, however, curious that no mention occurs in the numerous letters written about this time of the actual fact of his death.

No man in the records of England's heroes more truly deserved the title of patriot. He refused the highest post that could be offered him, being convinced that he could serve his country best in a private capacity. In every relation of life he seemed above other men. The fierce light that beats on such lives, kings of men, never laid bare any flaw in his. The year before his death he wrote as follows to his nephew and heir, Richard Lumley, on the subject of his candidature for parliamentary honours as member for Lincoln in the room of his elder brother on his accession to the earldom. Lady Scarbrough incloses it to her son. Inside the wrapper in which, as she quaintly says, she has "lapp'd it up," she writes: "The within may be legible or *not*, *That* you'll judge best. But it *Deserves* to be written in Letters of Gold. Your ever affec. Mother B. S."

"Rufford
"January 12th 1783.

"DEAR DIC,

"Tho' I am not yet in the way of writing letters very much and am besides of course pretty much in arrear in the article of Correspondence even on businesses which should not be delay'd; yet I think it is too material entirely to neglect giving you a short line at least on the subject of your letter to Ld. S. which he has shewn me. Tho' my notions do not coincide perhaps exactly with yours on that Subject, yet I tell you fairly, I am very far from wondering at the light in which you see the business, or at the wishes you express. On the Contrary, I only wonder that you are so moderate about it, and are not run absolutely away with, and that you don't feel as absolute a necessity of being in P^t as of wearing Artois Buckles or of doing any thing else— *becoming your age and situation*—that is, in an other form of expression, *what others in your situation would do*. We are so much rul'd and Govern'd and *Ton'd and etiquetted*, even in our pleasures (of which one would think one had a

SIR GEORGE SAVILE, BART.

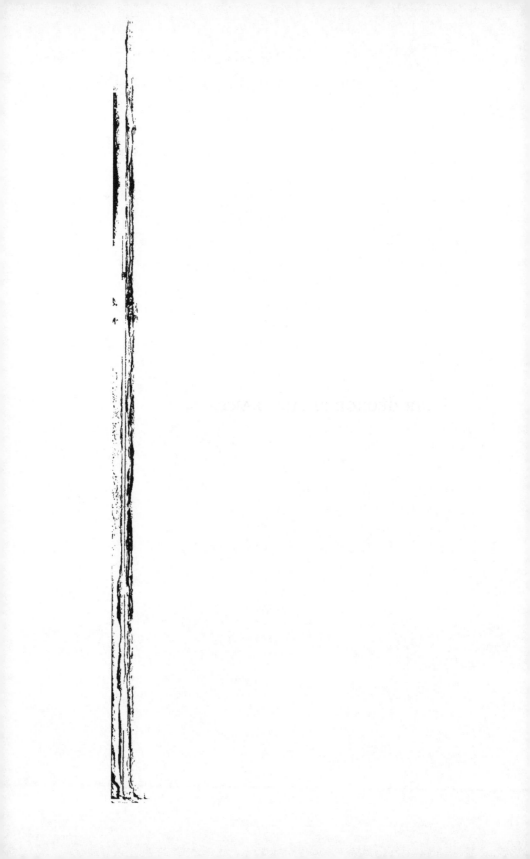

half,—selling dearer or worse goods ; so that probably they proved the dearest Votes of all.

"I say, do all these people bona fide owe much Gratitude? Were they *bought* or *employed* but for the *sake of their Votes*? On the other hand did they seek for any thing but to get, in one shape or other, the best price for their favour? A Bargain's a bargain. I am not quite sure that you have any more *right* than *reason* to expect any *gratitude*. I'll grant you, for once, therefore, it shall be a *female* Tyger who has devoured all your children but one, which therefore you depend on her *suckling* out of *Gratitude* to your *family*. Do not expect my dear Dick any Creature to act but according to its Interest and nature.

"I think it probable therefore that under such an explicit declaration as above mentioned you would not be first on the Poll. But then your adversary, who bribed, might be detected; you would petition. *Your* upright immaculate dealing would be manifest, and you would get your Seat. Whether your petition would cost you £1,000 or £10,000 I will not say, but I know your success would be very *doubtfull* to say the best of it. It is exceeding hard to bring Bribery home to the *Candidate* (then the sitting member) so as to *incapacitate* him : and it is heavy work to prove the *being bribed* seriatim and individually on a sufficient number of your opponents' Votes to cut him down to a minority. For instance, if my oppo^{nt} has 150 Votes, *all brib'd*; and I have 50, all honest. I must *prove above* 100 of his Voters bribed, or I do nothing if I prove only 99. He remains with 51—and if I prove only 100 he remains as good as I and it is a void election. I must cut off 101, or I don't get the Seat.—And yet all mankind shall know —not a soul shall entertain the least doubt of all his Votes being brib'd ; but he has been cunning enough (which is easy) to avoid *legal proof*. I should not in 20 sheets have half done with this part of the question. It is madness to look at the object with this expectation.

"I will only add that there will be no saying that you will be very cool and pull up and not run it thro' a Petit^{n}, if you are bent on y^{r} Poll. Not to mention your own

Eagerness now heated by the Contest, and *the scandalous behaviour of your Adversary* &c &c &c (and all the common rigmarolle Cant of the loosing party) how can you withstand all your friends clamouring round you and rolling upon you, if you have the spirit of a Man, not to desert their Cause. After they have manfully and honourably stood by you— in a public Cause—a virtuous Contest—to vindicate the Honour of Lⁿ it is *them* and their *honour* and the *Public* and the *public concern* that you are deserting; and all for the little mean consideration of a little Money. They only wish they had known you better before they adopted your Cause &c &c &c.

" You see you are no longer your own Master.

" Now the last supposition and the most favourable tho' I think far the most unlikely is that the Ton of Virtue prevails, the Freemen (mentis inopes) reject the dirty bribe and you are chosen—What good will it do you? In the way of Pleasure, have you a distinct idea or have form'd a competent judgement how much you may receive from it in the way of a public Place? Perhaps less than you imagine or do you look upon it in that light only? There would be less to say against the slovenly or maccaroni style of attending Parlᵗ if you had bought your seat in the usual honourable way ; having paid the Radicalls for their votes, what Right have they to expect you to attend except for your pleasure and to pass the time away till Almacks, after which it will be a *cursed Bore*. But as you are to come in quite on other principles, you will feel as if you had a *duty* to attend there, and not only on provincial businesses, such as your immediate Constituents may be concerned in (as turnpikes and other local matters) but as a member of Pᵗ for you are chosen not the member for Lⁿ, but chosen *by* Lⁿ *a Member of the National Senate.* This is a tough job sometimes, and I am persuaded you would not be quite easy in neglecting it. You must consult your own Mind and the turn of it, in this matter. I can only ask questions, no one can judge for another. Do you find your mind disposed to lay hold of great questions, and dig for Precedents in the Journals? This leads to the last question (or last but one) and indeed meets the powerful argument of pushing in your profession by Parliamentry Interest. I ask therefore, (after having dismiss'd the question of Pleasure) is it to be Profitable? How? Why if you will vote with the ministry you'll get a Reg^t or you may oppose 'em till they give you one. But you don't mean this: yet a man may by an honourable sticking to his party, get the Reg^t very honourably in the End, when they come in. The morality of this must be for your own thoughts. I confess it does not meet my Ideas. What man can say he is conscientiously using the best of his judgment on any great State Point when he is (right or wrong but very honourably) sticking to a Party in order to bring them into play that he may get this Reg^t as a reward for his fidelity to his Party and for having often come at an hour's warning (and in the hunting season) to vote on the right side (which he may know by looking at forces tho' he only gets to the House by 12 or 1 in the morning just in time to divide).

"But besides all this I do believe it is actually a loosing trade. Some indeed get money by horse-racing but calculate *all the money* spent in training horses and you will find it far exceeds *all the money* won in Plates. In like manner, few (infamous Contractors excepted) make their market of Parl^t I am persuaded.

"I have one article more material than all, it is that of *Qualification*. I do not believe that any but the Eldest Son of a Peer is exempted. A sham qualification seems to me no other than a direct fraud and evasion of the Law: a bad set-out for a Law maker.

"I intended at first to have stayed your stomach by a short letter and writ more fully afterwards, but when I had begun I thought it as well to go thro' while the ideas were fresh in my mind.

"Don't shew this letter to *any body*. I mean *strictly*.

"Dear Dic, Yours affectionately

"G. SAVILE."

The following two anecdotes help us to understand Sir George Savile's character. The first is contained in the interesting Autobiography of Eliza Dawson, afterwards Mrs. Fletcher, who was born at Oxton, near Nun-Appleton, the old home of the Milners. It is edited by her daughter, Lady Richardson, and contains many anecdotes of illustrious men :

" I think it was in the year 1779 that my father took us all to a review of the West York Militia, on Chapeltown Moor, near Leeds. The regiment was at that time commanded by Sir George Savile, whose speeches I had often heard my father read with peculiar emphasis and satisfaction, considering him the most patriotic and honest man in the House of Commons. He happened to be personally acquainted with Sir George, and meeting him accidentally that day he invited us all into his tent, and regaled us with wine, fruit, etc. He took me on his knee, and his good nature found amusement at my childish delight in all the pomp and circumstance of the review. For many a day after I enacted the glories of that day in the little garden at Oxton, shouldering my musket, rushing on to the charge, marching in quick and slow time. But the greatest glory of all was having sat on the knee of the great Sir George Savile. At that time Sir George's hair was thin and grizzled, and stood off from his face, and it much amused my father to find me frizzling, or, as I said, 'Sir George Saviling' my hair in the weeks after I had seen him. Sympathy with my father's high esteem for that good man's public virtue laid perhaps the foundation of my hero-worship."

The second anecdote, contained in a letter addressed to H.R.H. the Prince Regent (George IV.), does full justice to his legal acumen. The style is suggestive of a moral story in " Evenings at Home" and might well be entitled " The Biter bit":

" ANECDOTE OF THE LATE SIR GEORGE SAVILE, BART.

" Sir George had two Farms joining to each other, one of which he lett to a wealthy but very slovenly Farmer for £400 per annum, the other to a poor but very Industrious Man for £200 per annum, who kept his Grounds well cropt and in such good order that it soon became worth double the Sum.

combination occurred when there were still younger sons left to succeed to Rufford according to the testator's evident intention, for when the Hon. and Rev. John Lumley Savile succeeded to the earldom in 1832, he kept possession of Rufford.

CHAPTER XVII

Straitened circumstances.—George Augusta, fifth Earl.—Death of Barbara,
Countess of Scarbrough.

FTER the death of Sir George Savile, Lady Scarbrough's letters are pathetic in many ways. It is specially painful to realize, from her constant appeals for the remittance of her delayed jointure and the interest of her children's small fortunes, how straitened she often was for ready money. Lady Mary Lumley came of age in 1782, but was in no better plight than her mother. George, fifth Earl of Scarbrough, did not economize, and matters were complicated by his extravagance. His letters to Mr. Bassett seem sensible and practical enough, but his mother's letters too often mention shortcomings on his part, which helped to complicate her affairs. There were sales at Glentworth and Sandbeck, and the former seat ceased to be a residence for the family. For three years after Sir George Savile's death, Lady Scarbrough divided her time between Cransley Hall in Northamptonshire, a place she had hired, and London. In 1784 there was a great and what proved a fruitless search for some important paper connected with the Lumley colliery affairs. Lady Scarbrough writes in November of that year: "All I know relating to the papers in the Audley House at that sad period of sorrow you advert to" (her husband's death), "being that my dearest Bro^r, now gone too, assisted my poor son and Mr. Baxter at that time, looking over a great quantity of papers, many destroyed as being clearly useless. Where the undestroyed papers were moved to I am ignorant. It now just occurs to me that there is or has been lately a Box or Boxes in a low room (I think the Pantry) at Sandbeck in which I am pretty certain of Mr. Toone's telling me there were old papers which Mr. Brodrick on examination had found to be useless. To return to those above mentioned in Audley House, I think from some circumstance I heard, being then at Rufford, they were probably removed to Savile House previous to the sale in the spring of 1783 in Audley House. Since that, namely the last spring 1784, my son (Scarbrough) was advised that it was desirable he should clear Savile House of what belonged to him to some other place. The boxes, if there, would be sent by sea to Sandbeck. . . . All I can do besides I have done. I wrote immediately to Mr. G. Metcalfe, late Hall Porter at Savile House and also to Heph[r] Byram at the Nag's Head, Knightsbridge, that if either of them can give me intelligence of the Boxes they will let me know."

Lady Scarbrough goes on to say that she thinks Mr. Baxter should have had accurate information concerning them. On May 17th, 1786, the Hon. and Rev. John Lumley writes as follows on the same subject:

"Mr. Toone and I looked over all the Drawers and other places in the room I mentioned which were sealed up yesterday morning. Our search however was fruitless. I really am somewhat disappointed on this account as you and Mr. Tennyson will probably be. I really thought I recollected seeing some such papers as those you want upon a former search which was made by Mr. Foljambe, my brother Scarbrough, and myself in 1782. We found however to our surprize—A Will[1]—which whether of any consequence now at this time, I know not. I think I have understood from those concerned in my late Father's affairs that no *Will whatever* can in the least affect them. We also found some Acts of P[t] and papers relative to Willoughton, King's College, Acts for discharging some estates under the marriage settlements and settling others, as well as some papers relative to Lumley Castle and Cold Hesleton which I

---

[1] Probably a will of the second Earl of Scarbrough, still in existence at Sandbeck in his own handwriting.

took out for the chance of their being of any use to yourself."

These are of course the papers which have already been so frequently mentioned as giving so much information, and which are now arranged in boxes at Sandbeck.

George, Lord Scarbrough, seems to have taken life too easily, and to have acted too much on the principle of " Live and let live." His letters prove him to have had sufficient shrewdness and aptitude for business to have set matters straight if he would have regulated his expenses to his available means. Mr. Bassett in 1785 drew up a very clear statement of his means and of his liabilities, and prepared a plan which should have satisfied the creditors and yet have enabled Lord Scarbrough to live as befitted his station. But during all this time his poor mother was reduced to many straits. On one occasion she could not undertake a journey for want of means. However, in 1786 she gave up Cransley Hall and accepted her son Scarbrough's offer to make her home once more at Sandbeck. Between this place and London, with occasional visits to Bath, she spent the remaining years of her life.

George Augusta was an ardent sportsman, a constant attendant at race meetings, and assiduous in his attentions to widows, whose charms on more than one occasion nearly entangled him in the toils of matrimony. Bath seems to have been a favourite resort. He was a bad rider in spite of his devotion to sport, and accidents on several occasions endangered his life. He was certainly not a favourite with his family, though he was a more amiable and better-natured man than his brother John. His mother writes affectionately of and to him ; and it may not have been altogether his fault that she was so often and so sorely pressed for money. He inherited an encumbered estate. In 1790 Mrs. Foljambe died, and in 1792 Lady Mary Lumley married the widower, Francis Ferrard Foljambe, and this marriage seems to have given great comfort to Lady Scarbrough. She writes very happily on the subject to Mr. Bassett. In one of her numerous letters to her man of business towards the close of 1784, she mentions that her son Frederick is at Nun-

CHAPTER XVIII

Richard Lumley Savile's marriage.—Death of the fifth Earl and succession
of Richard.—Marriage of Frederick Lumley.

ICHARD, the second son of Richard, fourth
Earl of Scarbrough, and Barbara, had succeeded to the vast estates and picturesque
home of his uncle, Sir George Savile, in 1784,
and assumed the surname of Savile according
to the directions in the will, but three years elapsed before
he was established at beautiful Rufford. He was to receive
£1,200 per annum from the estates until all mortgages,
charges, etc., were reduced to within the capital sum of
£4,000. During the intervening years he had been assidu-
ously courting Henrietta Willoughby, daughter of Lord
and Lady Middleton, attending to his Parliamentary duties,
and giving what help he could to his widowed mother,
whose deserved favourite he had always been. For some
unknown reason his pretensions to Miss Willoughby's hand
were discouraged by both her parents. They seem to have
assumed that he was addicted to the fashionable vices with
which young men about town were credited. Never did
the course of true love run more roughly. The Rev. John
Eyre, his constant friend and confidant, bears testimony
to the remarkable excellence and uprightness of Richard
Savile's character. In one letter he asserts that he is indebted to him for taking a higher view of his own responsibilities. He declares that his life as a clergyman compares
very unfavourably with Richard's, and he consequently
bitterly resents the unjust estimate which Lord and Lady
Middleton had formed of him. Serena was the name under
which Miss Willoughby is mentioned in the letters which

are preserved at Sandbeck. Her conduct is deserving of the highest praise. While never swerving from her allegiance to her lover, she would not allow herself to correspond with him or meet him.

There is an amusing story told of Richard Savile—how he dressed up as a chimney sweep, blacked his face, mounted an ass, and in this guise obtained a sight of his Serena, if not a word with her. Was it on this occasion, one wonders, that he decked his steed with blue ribbons, and on being remonstrated with for wearing the wrong colours (the Lumleys were then ardent Whigs), he replied: " Blue asses were made to carry yellow laddies "?

However, his faithfulness finally overcame all objections, and Richard Lumley Savile was united to his Serena, the Hon. Henrietta Middleton, in June, 1787. The voluminous marriage settlement is in existence among the family papers. Thus we have the satisfaction of knowing that Barbara Scarbrough lived to see her most worthy son married to the object of his faithful attachment. John Eyre rejoiced most sincerely over this marriage. One surmises from his letters that he was a humble and distant adorer of Lady Mary Lumley. But he evidently recognized that his suit would not be entertained, and contented himself with doing his utmost to promote her brother Richard's interests. He condoled with the family on the anxiety that George, Lord Scarbrough's vagaries caused them. He seemed to fear at one moment that a fascinating widow really had entangled him beyond reprieve, and regrets that anxiety on this score is retarding the recovery of Lady Mary, then undergoing a cure at Bath, where the Earl had also taken up his quarters, but for the reigning widow's sake, not Lady Mary's.

The following song was written on the occasion of the marriage of the Hon. Henrietta Willoughby and the Hon. Richard Lumley Savile:

Why waves the fair Banner on Wollaton's Towers
  While the glad Strain of mirth sounds to Harmony dear?
'Tis that light-hearted joy steals on night's dreary hours,
  And the fairest, the noblest, the happiest are here;

And the dance and the song, every sorrow beguiling,—
    The frowns of old Time, or the threat'nings of care;
Here pleasure is tripping, and Beauty is smiling,
    'Tis the welcome of Honour, the feast of ye Fair.

What Harp wakes the strain from yon time-beaten Willow
    Where murmurs old Trent o'er the Bard's early grave?[1]
No dull sound of sadness now floats on ye billow,
    Tho' faintly yet sweetly it steals o'er the wave.
It bursts into gladness, 'tis joy's sprightly measure,
    Let the light step of Beauty the melody share;
That song which unfolds Hospitality's treasure,
    That welcome of Honour, the feast of ye Fair.

Hark the "Pibroch" of mirth in soul-cheering numbers
    Where Sherwood still sighs for ye sons of the bow;
Bold Robin's shrill bugle awakes from its slumbers,
    Oh! catch the glad strain e'er unheeded it flow.
All the records of mirth from wild minstrelsy streaming,
    In forgetfulness hush'd, shall no longer compare
With the sweet smile of gladness from eyes brightly beaming,
    With the welcome of Honour, the feast of ye Fair.

Oh! Blest are those hours their glad radiance darting
    O'er life's brighter day, midst the grapes purple bowl;
Let the lip of the fairest its sweetness imparting
    Speak one wish from the goblet which flows in each soul.
Long as Trent swiftly flows, his fair vallies beholding,
    Far, far from these Towers be each feeling of care;
Where beams that warm spirit whose bounty unfolding
    Spreads the welcome of Honour, the Feast of ye Fair.

During the years that followed his marriage Richard
Savile and his faithful Serena spent what were the happiest
years of their lives at Rufford. Several of her letters during
this period, written when "her dear, dear Love" was pur-
suing his Parliamentary duties or attending various race
meetings, are of too personal a nature for publication. They
are not dated, and it is most disappointing to find so little
family history in them.

It is much to be regretted that neither diaries nor visitors'
books were the order of those days, as many distinguished
people must have visited Rufford, and it is said that Mrs.
Siddons was once a guest there. George IV., when Prince
Regent, certainly was. But at times things were very quiet,
and Mrs. Savile writes on one occasion to her dear, dear

[1] Kirke White.

Mr. Savile (she never called him by his Christian name) that H. (the Hon. Mrs. Frederick Lumley) and her dear little boy are great comforts to her. "We two lone women," she writes, "help each other to keep up our spirits in the absence of our respective Lords and Masters."

In 1807 George Augusta, fifth Earl of Scarbrough, died. He escaped many riding accidents and the wiles of more than one fascinating but not desirable widow, and died at Bath of a feverish attack, which the violent remedies of those days subdued only too effectually. His brothers, the Hon. Richard Savile, the Hon. and Rev. John, and the Hon. Frederick Lumley, were summoned to Bath, and the man of business conveyed the mournful intelligence to the other members of the family. All due honour was paid to his remains. But his had not been a profitable career. He had considerably added to the burden already laid upon the Scarbrough estates; and Richard Savile made no secret of his reluctance to exchange his beautiful home at Rufford and his congenial Parliamentary duties for the state and dignity of an earldom, large scattered estates, and a considerably smaller income than the one he had enjoyed at Rufford. He is reported to have said that he gave up £10,000 a year and the most beautiful home in England when he became Earl of Scarbrough. However, he was not a man to shrink from his responsibilities, and he and his wife lost no time in complying with the terms of Sir George Savile's will. Had the gallant sailor, Thomas, lived, things might have been very different. As it was, John, commonly called "Black Jack" (did it refer to his cloth only, or also to his character?) became the owner of Rufford. As has been mentioned, he was educated at Eton, and thence went to Cambridge. He became Rector of Winteringham, Lincoln, and Thornhill in Yorkshire, and Prebendary of York. He made everything very difficult and greatly added to his brother's sorrow at leaving the home he so dearly loved. The magnitude of George Augusta's debts, and in justice to him it should be added the embarrassed state of affairs to which he succeeded, necessitated sales at Lumley Castle and Sandbeck. The sale at Rufford was of course between

Richard, now sixth Earl of Scarbrough, and John Lumley, who at once assumed the name of Savile, though he never lived at Rufford, but remained on at Edwinstowe. Tradition says that a gipsy prophesied that he would only enter Rufford to be carried in feet first, and would leave it to be carried out feet first; and this came to pass, though whether or not the event created the prophecy it is difficult to decide. There is no doubt that he was the least satisfactory and amiable member of that large family. His letters are always full of complaints, he is always wanting money, and insinuating, when he does not positively assert, that everyone takes advantage of him. His mother speaks of his wife, Miss Herring, as "his amiable consort." Poor soul! she had a hard life if all reports are true, or even half of them. At one time he is reported to have grudged her the ordinary necessaries of life. He was a miser and hoarded up money in all sorts of places. Bank-notes were found in the cellars after his death, defaced and valueless. He persuaded an old woman in Edwinstowe to let him bury a box in her garden. It was dug up after his death, and was found to be full of silver pieces, varying in value from five shillings to one shilling. No children having blessed the marriage of Richard, the new Earl, and his beloved wife, John and his children became heirs presumptive to the Scarbrough estates, and the Hon. Frederick Lumley to Rufford.

Richard and Frederick were the two brothers who were the most attached to each other. Frederick Lumley's only surviving granddaughter, the Lady Harriett L'Estrange, describes him as a tall, handsome man. He had married in 1786 Harriet Ann Boddington (the H. alluded to above), only daughter and heiress of one John Boddington, Secretary to the Board of Ordinance. The following is an abstract of the will of John Boddington of Richmond, Surrey, Esq., which is dated December 18th, 1784, and was proved on January 27th, 1785, by the executors named in the will:

" To my wife Sarah all my 4 per cent Bank Annuities, all my freehold and copyhold estates in Richmond and my dwelling house in Bedford Square.

"To my reputed daughter Harriot Ann Boddington £2000 in trust to my Executors till she attains the age of 18 or on her marriage, also my farm called Cookham Farm in Westerham and Eaton Budge, also a little farm called Bished in Westerham, my farms and Manor of Browns in Eaton Budge in Kent and Lingfield, Surrey, farms in Cranbrook and Tenterden etc. to her and her issue—remainder in default to my wife.

"The said daughter is now at Mrs. Beevor's in Dover Street.

"To Robert Drew my wife's nephew £1000. My wife Sarah, Cuthbert Fisher and Thomas Fitz-herbert Esq. executors. To whom residue is to go.

"The bodies of my two deceased children to be removed to the place of my interment.

"Witnesses, Michael Morris, Sen. and Jun.

"Henry Sayer of Lincoln's Inn."

From the following letter, written by the late Lady Georgina Milner to her husband's nephew, now Sir Clements Markham, C.B., it is evident that Mrs. Frederick Lumley was much appreciated by her sister-in-law, afterwards Lady Scarbrough. "My father Frederick Lumley was their only surviving child. My grandmother was dead before I was born. My grandfather married again [a daughter of Admiral Bradby, in June, 1819], and we never had any communication with the Boddingtons (probably because there were none) but little monies came from them. My godmother was Anne Fisher, probably a Boddington, and she left me a little money." Note here that Barbara Scarbrough refers in one of her letters to "my son Frederick's father-in-law Mr. Fisher." John Boddington married in 1772 Sarah Oare of Maidstone, daughter of the Rev. Mr. Oare. She was not Miss Boddington's mother, but she doubtless called her mother. Miss Oare, sister to Mrs. Boddington, married a Mr. Fisher, the husband of Anne Fisher. N.B.—Did Mrs. Boddington marry again, taking as her second husband another Mr. Fisher? Lady Georgina's letter continues: "My grandmother was I believe a charming person, and the most intimate friend of my old great-aunt, Henrietta, Lady Scarbrough (wife of the 6th Earl). It was her love for my grandmother that made Lady Scarbrough take us for her children."

Lady Scarbrough speaks with great affection of Mrs. Frederick Lumley. She visited the young couple at their first home at Cheam. In 1788 they came to live at Worksop, near Mansfield. Their eldest son, Frederick, had always been a great favourite; but now his importance in the eyes of both Lord and Lady Scarbrough was increased, if that were possible. It is very evident that all their hopes and aspirations were centred in him. They were both too amiable to express their feelings, but John's conduct during this trying time was evidently a sore trial to them.

And now occurred the last and most disastrous sale, which took place at Lumley Castle in December, 1807. Tapestries of probably priceless value, pictures of the utmost interest, furniture of probably every date, and smaller objects of interest beyond description were brought to the hammer. For twenty-one days this ruthless sale continued. The old housekeeper, a notable character, who lived to see Richard, Frederick Lumley's son, come to his kingdom, succeeded in saving a few fixtures and some family pictures, also a few pieces of furniture; but the magnitude of the sale can only be gathered from the lists and from the length of time it lasted. It must be borne in mind that there had been a sale after the death of the fourth Earl.

CHAPTER XIX

Sir William Lumley.—Captain J. R. Lumley.—Letters from Nelson and
Collingwood.—Marriage of Frederick Lumley and the Beresford con-
nexion.—Their children.—Letters from George IV. and William IV.—
Death of sixth and seventh Earls.—Litigation.—Beresford ghost story.

T has often been asked why there are no jewels
in the family, and why those sold in his father's
time were not replaced when Richard Savile
brought his countess to Sandbeck. Their
great-niece, Lady Harriett L'Estrange, gives
the following account:

" Plans were prepared and an estimate was submitted to
Lord and Lady Scarbrough. In those days jewels were
much more a mark of rank and position than in these
degenerate times. A countess was almost obliged to have
a tiara, stomacher, necklace and bracelets, while ladies of
lower degree were contented with the humbler stones and
quaint ornaments they called their 'trinkets.' When Lady
Scarbrough saw the price her lord would have to pay for
this insignia of her state, which amounted to £30,000, she
calmly said : 'We have no children; we lead as far. as
possible a quiet country life. I have been to Court without
jewels, and can, if it should be necessary, go again without
them. Your younger brothers have very inadequate fortunes. Let us spend the money on them.' Such a generous
wish was cordially responded to, and hence the absence of
jewels in the present generation, which led an Irish nephew
to describe the ninth Lord Scarbrough's wife as 'the barest
countess he had ever seen.' "

There is no mention of Savile Henry Lumley, the fifth
surviving son of Barbara, in any private letters of this
period. He married Mary Henrietta Tahourdin, daughter

of General Tahourdin, known to the younger members of the family as Aunt Lumley, but less reverently styled "Bags" by her elder nieces and her nephew Dick Lumley. She was a clever, witty woman. An old inhabitant of Tickhill now living near York says that Colonel Savile Henry Lumley was a very nice gentleman, but quiet. He was short of stature, but had a very pleasant face.

As regards information, it is far otherwise with the youngest and sixth surviving of the seven brothers, William Lumley, born August 28th, 1769, presumably at Lumley Castle, for the register of his birth is to be seen at Chester-le-Street. He entered the army in 1787, commanded the Light Dragoons in Ireland in 1798, became a Colonel before he was thirty, and was wounded at Antrim. He also commanded the same regiment in Egypt in 1801 ; served in South America, and commanded the advance forces at the capture of Monte Video in February, 1807. In 1808 he was serving in Sicily, and wrote the following letter, which is copied from the original in the British Museum :

"Pizzo di Gotto, Octr 28th 1808.'

"My dear Sir,

"I think you will not see any objection to the B.O. enclosed herewith. I leave it to you to translate, & explain it to your Corps. I am not fond of *Compliments*, & as I detest deception in any shape, I never pay false ones, but, under the circumstances of the case, I should not have felt satisfied with myself, had I not made some few remarks, upon your Corps being placed under my orders.

"I shall be obliged to you for a line, on your return from Head Quarters, or from Messina, in case your stay there shall be much prolonged, the period for which you will of course arrange with the Adj^t Genl.

"The bearer of this conveys the Weekly states etc. for Head Quarters.

"I remain, My dear Sir,
"Your faithfull

"Lt Col^l Lowe   "humble Servt
"Roy^l Corsican Rangers   "William Lumley
"&c. &c. &c.   "Brig^r Genl."

(Enclosed.)

"Pizzo di Gotto. Octr 28th 1808.

"B.O./ The Royal Corsican Rangers having been directed to occupy the Cantonments of Spadafora & Venetico, Brig^r Genl Lumley takes the earliest opportunity of expressing to that gallant Corps in general, & its not less gallant, as well as able Commander in particular, the real satisfaction he feels in having them placed under his Orders, Under every disadvantage of proximity to the Enemy's Coast, & various other unfortunate & untoward circumstances, The determined Defence made by Lt Coll. Lowe, & the Corps under his command, & the honorable convention enter'd into with the Enemy when obliged to cede the Island of Capri to a great superiority of Force, sufficiently prove the Value of the Corps, & how fully they are to be depended upon in any Situation & the very Terms of the Convention also prove how fully their Valor was appreciated & how much the Enemy had still to apprehend from them if driven to a final desperate resistance. Altho' the details of the recent transactions in that Island have not yet officially been made public, yet sufficient is already known to justify the Brig^r General in saying, that it was the misfortune not the fault of their judicious Commander to be obliged to evacuate the Post, where further resistance would have only occasioned an unavailing Loss.

"The Brig^r General has only to add that he entertains the sanguine Hopes of that Corps remaining under his orders, of his still having the assistance of their able Commander, untill an opportunity may offer, under less disadvantageous Circumstances, of proving to the Enemy that they are equally respectable, and equally to be dreaded in the Field, as they have been in the Post which they so gallantly endeavoured to maintain.

"A. STUART
"Ass^t Adj^t General."

Sir William Lumley became Major-General in 1811; and commanded the whole of the allied cavalry at Albuera under the gallant Marshal Beresford, for which he received the gold medal. An account of the battle will be found in the following letter, written by a Mr. Sutherland to the Earl of Scarbrough :

"Ulverston 16th June 1811."

" MY LORD

" A few days absence beyond the intended time of my return home, has occasioned some delay in sending back our dear General's letter which I now Inclose with my Thanks to you for allowing me so early a perusal of it.

" How gratifying must it have been to your Lordship to hear his conduct on the memorable 16th of May, so well appreciated by the Prince Regent & the Royal Brothers of York & Cumberland; & I do trust that their high opinion of Him will lead to an early Regiment. The Duke of York's reappointment is in his Favor, but independent of such a private motive, I am really glad that his Royal Highness is again placed at the Head of the Army, because I believe it will please all good & zealous officers.

" I strongly feel all the Englishman within me upon every success of our Arms ; but the Battle of Albuera excites a more than common Interest from the conspicuous share which Genl Lumley bore in it ; & this has set my head to work upon making a plan of it ; taking Marshal Beresford's public Letter for my guide, with a good Map of Spain for the ground. A bold attempt for a Ci-devant Volunteer ! And will your Lordship forgive my Presumption in offering you the inclosed copy of this attempt of mine to delineate the Military movements of that glorious Day ? It may afford you 10 minutes amusement, & I send it in the full persuation of your favorable construction.

" It forcibly strikes me that Genl Lumley has a proud & just claim to a considerable Share in the ultimate success of the Day, for it was his quick perception, & skilful Manœuvres with an inferior Force of Cavalry, which foiled that of the Enemy's attack, yet the very retardment of his movement would have had most serious consequences, by allowing the Left Columns of the French Infantry to effect their purpose of forcing the two Brigades of Genl Stewart's Division in their advance to Charge. As it was, both Divisions fortunately made their Charge at the same time, & therby completely vanquished the Enemy. In my Sketch, I have had the confidence to suppose some Manœuvres of our Dear General. I hope the news is authentic of his having overtaken the Enemy's Cavalry near Licrena & reduced their number, by killing, wounding, & taking upwards of 400 of them; & I hope too that the chief of these may prove to be the Murdering Lancers.

"I sincerely rejoice to hear that your Lordship, & Lady Scarbrough are well. I beg my very best Compliments to her Ladyship, & that you may both continue to enjoy good Health & all possible Happiness is the concluding Wish, of

"Your Lordship's

"Obliged & faithful servant

"THOS. SUTHERLAND

"Upon weighing my packet to your Lordship I find it too heavy for one Cover, & therefore my Battle comes separate."

It is to be regretted that "the Battle," which is preserved with the letter, cannot be reproduced, as it is very neat and clever.

The General wás made a K.C.B. in 1815, G.C.B. in 1831, became Colonel of the 1st Dragoons in 1840, was Governor and Commander-General at Bermuda and a Groom of the Bedchamber. He married (1st) on October 3rd, 1804, by special licence at Ulverston, Lancashire, Mary, second daughter of Thomas Sutherland, the writer of the above letter, who died in July, 1807. Poor soul! she must have seen very little of her gallant husband during those short years of married life. He married (2nd) in March, 1817, at Blyth, Nottinghamshire, Louisa Margaret, widow of Major Lynch Cotton, who survived him, and who died in Green Street on September 11th, 1859. Sir William died in December, 1850, aged eighty-one. I can remember Lady Lumley, and I have a faint recollection of seeing my great-great-uncle and of being rather naughty on the occasion.

There are one or two allusions to Sir William's gallantry among the family letters, and congratulations from Mr. Bassett on his well-merited promotion. There is a printed pamphlet referring to his work when Governor of Bermuda, and there are also despatches and documents amongst the papers at Sandbeck making honourable mention of him. It is much to be regretted that all his pictures, medals and everything that belonged to him were left unconditionally to his wife, who left them all in her turn to her sister, a Mrs. Sapte. A portrait or print of Sir William is being anxiously sought after by his old regiment, but in vain.

There is at Sandbeck a small bundle of very interesting letters written to the Hon. Frederick Lumley about his natural son, Captain J. R. Lumley, who was in the Navy and distinguished himself greatly during the operations of the fleet at the beginning of the last century. Two of them are from Captain Boyle, and the others from Lord Nelson and Lord Collingwood. They are given here entire, and furnish us with almost all the information we have as to this gallant officer:

> " H.M.S. Seahorse cruizing within
> the Hieres Islands 17th July 1804.

" SIR,

" I lose not a moment, well knowing that reports are sometimes circulated that cause much anxiety to the friends and relations of officers who have been in action to acquaint you with great pleasure that your Son tho' badly wounded in the left arm by a Musket Ball on the night of the 10th Inst in a most gallant Attack on the Enemys Coast is in a fair way of recovery.

" This attack was made by Boats from the Narcissus Seahorse and Maidstone; those of the Seahorse under the Command of my friend Lumley and tho' under a very heavy and galling fire of guns and Musquetry from the ships and shore the destruction of a French Convoy was effected by conflagration in the Port of Lavandour within the Hieres Islands in a most cool intrepid manner.

" I should do great injustice to my friend did I not mention him in the highest Terms which I already have to the

Commander in Chief who is much interested about him, indeed his amiable disposition has endear'd him to all on board and I assure you I never saw more universal anxiety shewn than is for his recovery which I trust you will shortly hear from himself and that you will believe me his sincere friend and

"Your most obedient

"Hum^{ble} Servt

"COURTENAY BOYLE."

"H.M.S. Seahorse off Toulon

"24th July 1804.

"SIR,

"Since my last of the 17th Inst it is with much grief I acquaint you that the Wound your Son received is of a much worse nature than was in the first instance supposed the Ball having pass'd thro' the upper Bone of the Left arm and also thro' the socket of the Blade Bone and fractur'd both so much as to make Amputation of the limb by taking the arm out of the Socket necessary; this operation was perform'd a few Hours since by the most Skilful Surgeons of the Fleet and my poor friend having made his mind up to the Loss bore it with the greatest firmness and fortitude, his age, good constitution and quiet of mind will I trust in God be the causes of his speedy recovery and I cannot doubt but his gallant conduct together with the severe loss he has sustained will lead to his immediate promotion; my anxiety regard and friendship for him must plead my excuse in taking the Liberty of pointing out that a moment should not be lost by his friends in making application to the admiralty to promote him to the Rank of Commander and indeed I trust he will not then be forgot but speedily after obtain the other step so much the wish of those acquainted with him and by none more than his sincere friend and

"Your most obedient Hum^{ble} Servt

"COURTENAY BOYLE.

"I must add the Surgeons have succeeded to the utmost of their wishes."

Lord Nelson's letter is as follows:

"Merton 31ˢᵗ August 1805.

"SIR

"I have received your Letter of the 24ᵗʰ Instant on the subject of your son's being employed in actual Service—and in answer I beg to assure you that I will feel great pleasure in mentioning Captain Lumley's name to Lord Barham, but I cannot presume to say that it will procure him imployment—the pension given to Captain Lumley for the loss of His arm, does not in my opinion at all interfere with his being imployed. My Eyesight being very indifferent I am obliged to answer this by my Secretary.

"I am Sir

"Your most obedient humble servant

"NELSON."

Lord Collingwood's letter is short, but very much to the point:

"The Ocean off Toulon

"Octʳ 4, 1808.

"SIR,

"I have the pleasure to enclose to you a Commission appointing you a Post Captain in the Vacancy made by the death of Capt. Campbell of the Trident—and as Rear-Admiral Sir Alexander Ball has selected Capt. Vincent of the Hind to be his Flag Captain you will at the same time receive an order to command the Hind by Exchange.

"I beg to express to you Sir the satisfaction I feel in promoting an officer of your distinguish'd reputation and zeal for the Kings Service; and congratulate you on it.

"I am Sir

"Your most obdᵗ Humble Servᵗ

"Captain J. R. Lumley   "COLLINGWOOD.

"H.M.S. Hind."

Lady Harriett L'Estrange remembers seeing Captain Lumley when she paid a never-to-be-forgotten visit to her grandfather in London, who was then married to his second wife, *née* Jane Bradley. Lady Harriett has a mourning brooch given to her mother in memory of Mrs. Lumley, and she remembers being taken to see her. She was ill and had probably been bled, for there were drops of blood on her face, which was otherwise ghastly white, making the contrast startling against her very black hair. Lady Harriett, in telling the story, said the impression made on her was so strong that no subsequent events have ever weakened it, and now in her old age the scene comes back as vividly as on the day it happened. Her grandfather and Uncle Richard Savile took her, young as she was, to the Opera. She was a very beautiful child, and the King (George IV.), who was very intimate with both, sent to invite the brothers to his box, and begged them to bring the lovely little girl with them. Lady Harriett remembers sitting on the King's knee and telling him he was much prettier than the other man, his brother, the Duke of York, and that his hair was nicer. One might say "Arcades ambo," but perhaps it would be high treason even to suggest that both wore wigs. Lady Harriett spent a sovereign that her grandfather gave her on a print of the King.

In 1810 Frederick Lumley lost his first wife. No letters are extant that mention the event. There is a miniature of her at Sandbeck, which does not suggest any beauty.

In 1812 his son, young Frederick Lumley, married Charlotte Mary Beresford, daughter of the Right Rev. George de la Poer Beresford, Lord Bishop of Kilmore. Her mother was Miss Bush, daughter of an eminent Irish statesman, and her grandmother was Miss Grattan, sister to the great Irish orator and patriot, Henry Grattan.

Many stories are told of Mrs. Beresford, who greatly dominated her family and whose influence will be seen at intervals in future pages. Sooner or later she generally got her own way. One of the quaintest tales was told of her at Bishopthorpe Palace, where Archbishop Harcourt, grandfather of the present Sir William, held almost regal state.

His Grace was very particular about the guests attending chapel. On the first morning Mrs. Beresford failed to put in an appearance. On the second morning the trusty henchman of the bishop came up to say that they were wait-

ing prayers for her and his lordship desired her to come.
" Tell him I am not dressed, Jeames," replied the lady.
" You are to come as you are, madam," was the imperturb-
able reply. " Tell him I'm ill, Jeames," screamed Mrs.
Beresford. " You must come, madam," was still the in-
exorable mandate. " Tell him I'm dead, Jeames "; and the
door was banged to and locked by the determined corpse.

Charlotte's brother, Marcus Gervoise Beresford, young as
he was, held a good fat living. Of him Tommy Moore
wrote the following hitherto unpublished lines :

I

The Rev. Ichabod Beresford,
   A strenuous fowler before the Lord,
One morning left his Parsonage House
   To hunt to and fro on the hill for grouse ;
When a Methodist person of mean condition,
   Of whose intent he had no suspicion,
Took his Reverence sharply to task
   About his gun and his powder flask,
Saying in sly sarcastic tone,
   " Which of the Apostles ever was known
After the feathered game to stray,
   Brushing the morning dew away? "

II

Replies the Reverend Ichabod,
   " What you say may be true, but not at all odd;
For those reverend gentlemen whom you mention
   Lived some time before the invention
Of Dartford powder and copper caps;
   And *that* may account for the thing, perhaps;
But I'd have you to know, my grim Precision,
   That those good men were famous at fishing,
And I'll venture to wager of wine a dozen
   Were Peter the Apostle or Andrew his cousin
Here in the flesh—beyond a doubt
   They would throw a fly now and then for a trout;
Or this breezy morning in spite of your gammon
   Would fish in the Boyne on the chance of a salmon."

The bishop's father was the Right Hon. John Beresford,
brother to the first Marquis of Waterford and Archbishop
of Tuam, created first Lord Decies. His wife was Nanette
Constancia, daughter of Michell de Ligondes, a cadet of

the noble family of Ligondes of Château Ligondes in Auvergne, and of Mademoiselle de Marcellauges, one of the *noblesse non titré*, of a very distinguished family of the Midi. Her grandfather was the Chevalier de Ligondes, who was a Knight of Malta. He gave up his Cross and was absolved from his vows in order to marry (when a prisoner in England with Count Tullard after the battle of Blenheim) the Dowager Countess of Huntingdon, whose third husband he became. The Countess of Huntingdon was the daughter and heiress of Leveson Fowler. She was the grandmother of the great Pitt. Her first husband was Thomas Needham, Viscount Kilmorey. It is not certain that she was the mother of the Comte Ligondes, but Constancia's great-grandson, Marcus Beresford, who died Primate of All Ireland, presumes that she was.

Mrs. Beresford was beautiful and clever. She was brought up in England with her future husband's sister, Lady Elizabeth Beresford, more familiar in connexion with the famous Beresford ghost story as Lady Betty Cobbe. (See Appendix to chapter.)

Constancia was devotedly attached to Archbishop Cobbe, Lady Betty's father-in-law. Lady Betty had brought her friend to Newbridge to save her from a threatened nunnery in France. When the Archbishop died she was inconsolable. Her confessor tried to console her, but she replied that her only consolation was that her old friend was in Heaven. "Ah! pour cela, mademoiselle, it is impossible to suppose that a Protestant Archbishop who had never shown the slightest sign of recanting his errors could obtain admission to Paradise." "Then," replied the girl, "if so good a man does not deserve to go to Heaven, certainly M. l'Abbé will not do so." And for her part she would not believe in a Church which denied salvation to her beloved Archbishop. So M. l'Abbé returned to France, and Mademoiselle de Ligondes became a Protestant and married her friend's brother, better known to history as Commissioner Beresford.

Thus Frederick Lumley's marriage added another link of historic interest to the family records. Charlotte Beresford was only sixteen when she became a bride, and was a lovely winsome Irish girl with "eyes of most unholy blue," as wild as a hawk, and as talented as she was daring. Her husband, who was barely twenty-five, had met her when his regiment was quartered in Dublin. The bridal pair received an almost parental welcome from Lord and Lady Scarbrough, who from this time centred all their hopes of the future on the young couple. Charlotte took the heart of the childless couple by storm, who regarded her maddest pranks as "only little Charlotte's ways." Though so young at the time of her marriage, she had already been wooed by Henry Southwell of Castle Hamilton, when she was a girl of fourteen in the hideous dress of that period: short sleeves, bare neck, long frilled trousers appearing well below the skirt, and sandalled shoes. The Frederick Lumleys made their home at Tickhill Castle, a royal demesne leased from the time of the destruction of the monasteries to the Lords of Sandbeck. There are many documents relating to this tenure in Lord Scarbrough's possession, deeds bearing the portraits and autographs of the several Queens Consort, as lands at Tickhill formed part of their marriage settlement. Tickhill was a most pleasant home. The moat, keep, and fine old gateway recalled the days of John of Gaunt, who, according to tradition, once resided there. The house is less ancient, but old enough to boast a traditionary ghost, which has an unsettling way of sweeping its hair over the face of any occupant of a certain bedroom. The walled gardens are charming. Mrs. Lumley added to her other talents a great capacity for floriculture, and as time went on she was able to compete with Sandbeck, often producing earlier peas, roses, and peaches than the larger gardens.

Richard George Lumley, the only son of Mr. and Mrs. Lumley, was born at Tickhill Castle on May 7th, 1813. His birth is recorded in the Red Bible at Sandbeck, which was the gift of his great-grandmother, Barbara, Lady Scarbrough, to his father. His godmothers were Henrietta, Countess of Scarbrough, and Mrs. Beresford, his maternal grandmother. His godfathers were Richard, sixth Earl

of Scarbrough, and his maternal grandfather, George de
la Poer Beresford, Bishop of Kilmore. A *contretemps*
occurred at the christening, which, it is said, cost the un-
conscious babe a fortune. His father sprained his foot so
badly that he could not be present at the ceremony. The
young mother quite forgot that a certain Gally Knight, a
devoted friend of her husband's, had been asked to stand
proxy for the absent bishop. He was present in the old
church at Tickhill, proudly prepared to undertake office
and to prove a truly Fairy Godfather by leaving him a sub-
stantial fortune. Mrs. Lumley looked round for a proxy in
the church when the christening party were standing round
the font, and unconsciously overlooking the suitable proxy
asked her young brother, Marcus, who had no suggestion
in those remote schoolboy days of future primatical dignity,
to undertake the office. So completely was Gally Knight
overlooked, that he was not even invited to the Castle to
drink the babe's health, or taste the christening cake. Mrs.
Lumley never realized what she had done, but Mr. Gally
Knight looked on the oversight as an intentional insult, and
young Richard lost a fortune.

Besides this son the Frederick Lumleys had three
daughters to complete the family group. Frances Charlotte
was born on July 11th, 1814. Her godfather was Sir
William Lumley, and her godmothers, Lady Frances Flood
and Lady Mary Arabella Foljambe, *née* Lumley. The
name Arabella was added in consequence. The second,
christened Henrietta Susan Beresford, but called Harriett,
was born on February 10th, 1816. Her godfathers were
the Hon. John Lumley Savile (Black Jack) and Lord
Decies, Archbishop of Tuam, brother of her grandfather,
the Right Hon. John Beresford. Her godmothers were
Henrietta, Countess of Scarbrough, her paternal great-
aunt by marriage, and the Marchioness of Waterford, the
same connexion on her mother's side. The third daughter
was Anne Georgina, born August 21st, 1818. Her godmothers were Mrs. Fisher, already mentioned, and Mrs.
Scott; her godfather, Mr. Marcus Beresford, the youthful
uncle who had stood proxy for her brother to the exclu-

sponsibility. Lord Scarbrough quaintly observes that his sister, Lady Sophia Lumley, and his brothers, Frederick, Savile Henry, and William, *not being healthy*, are not likely to require more than had already been supplied them out out of their brother's generosity to supplement their originally small fortunes. Savile Henry lived to be seventy-nine, and Sir William Lumley completed his eightieth year, both surviving Lady Scarbrough, whose good constitution, to which her husband alludes, failed her before theirs did.

Meanwhile the happy married lfe of Richard, sixth Earl of Scarbrough, was drawing to a close. The death of George IV. drew forth a touching letter addressed to William IV. by Lord Scarbrough; and it was cordially responded to by the Sailor King. These letters, which are preserved with that already given from George IV., are as follows:

"SIRE,

"Trusting to the unmerited kindness I have for 25 years experienced from your Majesty, as well as the well-known liberality which so peculiarly distinguishes your character, with every sentiment of respect and personal attachment, I venture to approach your Majesty in this mode, being at present prevented from performing this duty personally from severe Illness, lately much increased from anxiety of mind, for the last two months, and final loss of the Best of Sovereigns, and to me the kindest and most constant of friends. It is this month fifty years since his late Majesty had honour'd me with his countenance, and, if I am not too presumptuous may I venture to say, his private constant friendship. Will not then this plead my excuse? for thus approaching your Majesty to offer Lady Scarbrough's and my condolence on the loss which the nation in general has sustained, but which is irrevocable to those who were honoured with his late Majesty's private friendship.

"I am too unwell to take at present in Public the usual oaths of allegiance of supremacy, but when I venture to recall to your Majesty's mind, that my Ancestor, the first Earl of Scarbrough, in some measure brought about the Protestant Succession and finally set the Brunswick Family on the Throne of these Realms, your Majesty will not doubt that the sentiments in future to be ratified by oaths are deeply engraved on my Heart, added to a sincere personal attachment for kindness received from you, I have the Honour to be Your Majesty's most Humble and devoted Servant

" SCARBROUGH."

"Bushy House June 30th 1830.

" MY DEAR LORD,

" Your Lordship's letter has of course reached me and I rejoice if any part of its contents can fit me here. Your Lordship talks of indisposition. My best sincerest and kindest regards attend the amiable Countess. I lament with your Lordship the death of my poor dear brother, our late most excellent sovereign and friend. I can never forget that the first Earl of Scarbrough was one of the four peers who energetically assisted in establishing the Protestant Succession. Go my dear Lord into the country and return next spring in perfect health that I may enjoy the society of your worthy self and the elegant Countess

" Ever believe me My dear Lord

" Yours most truly

"WILLIAM REX."

Richard did not long survive his beloved sovereign, and in 1832 Lady Scarbrough was a widow indeed.

Richard, Lord Scarbrough, was an accomplished violinist, according to the record of an old servant of John Lumley Savile's, afterwards servant to Mrs. Frederick Lumley, whose letter to Lord Hawkesbury on this and other matters connected with the family follows. The Lord Scarbrough mentioned at the beginning is " Black Jack."

"24 St. Andrew Square, Edinburgh

"15th December, 1898.

" MY LORD

" I received your letter and I hope you will pardon me for not answering it before now; Lord Scarbrough was killed instantaneously. Before he went to London in the heir presumptive to the earldom. This position might have gone against him in the final judgement with regard to Rufford, so an amicable arrangement was concluded.

APPENDIX TO CHAPTER XIX

THE BERESFORD GHOST (BY LADY BETTY COBBE)

NICHOLA SOPHIA HAMILTON, afterwards Lady Beresford, was born on Friday, the 23rd of February, 1666. She was the younger surviving daughter of Hugh Hamilton, Baron of Lunge in Sweden, who was raised to the dignity of Lord Hamilton, Baron of Glenawly in the County of Fermanagh and Kingdom of Ireland, in the year of our Lord 1660. His father, Dr. Archibald Hamilton, of ancient Scotch family, was made Archbishop of Cashel in the year 1630. He was despoiled of his goods by the rebels in 1641, and with difficulty escaped with his life to Stockholm, where he died at the advanced age of eighty in 1659, and whence his son Hugh returned at the Restoration in the following year to take possession of the family estates in the county of Tyrone. Besides Lady Beresford, Lord Glenawly had a son and another daughter, Arabella Susannah, who was older than Lady Beresford by two years, and was married on the 1st of July, 1683, to Sir John Magill, of Gill Hall in the county of Down. Upon his death in 1699 she married Marcus, third Viscount Dungannon, and died in 1708, leaving no family. Lord Glenawly died in 1679, and was succeeded by his only son, William, who survived him but one year, and his large estates devolved equally upon his two daughters.

From some circumstances, of which no explanation is given, Nichola Sophia Hamilton was placed in childhood under the care of a person who professed the principles of Deism, and who had also charge of John, Viscount Decies, eldest son of Richard, first Earl of Tyrone, of Curraghmore in the county of Waterford. Lord Decies was about one

year older than Miss Hamilton. Their guardian dying when
they were respectively about twelve and thirteen, they fell
into different hands. The persons upon whom the care of
them now devolved used every possible exertion to eradi-
cate the erroneous principles they had imbibed, and to pre-
vail upon them to embrace revealed religion; but all in
vain. The arguments used, though insufficient to convince
them, yet staggered their former faith. Although they were
now separated from each other, their friendship remained
unaltered, and they continued to regard each other with a
sincere fraternal affection. After some years had elapsed
and they were both grown up, they made a solemn promise
to each other, that whichever should die first would (if permitted) appear to the other to declare what religion was
most acceptable to the Supreme Being, whether the religion
of Revelation or that of Human Philosophy, which they
had most unhappily adopted. In a short time after this
promise was made, Nichola Sophia Hamilton was married
in the year 1687 to Sir Tristram Beresford of Coleraine, a
wealthy baronet of an ancient English family, who was the
possessor of large estates in the county of Derry. No
change in condition could alter the friendship between Lady
Beresford and Lord Tyrone. The two families lived on
intimate terms, and were frequent visitors in each other's
houses. Sir Tristram and Lady Beresford had only one bar
to their happiness; they had three daughters, but no son to
inherit their extensive possessions.

In the beginning of October, 1693, they went on a visit
to Gill Hall, the residence of her brother-in-law, Sir John
Magill. They had been there but a short time when Sir
Tristram observed, on his lady coming down to breakfast,
that her countenance was unusually pale and bore evident
marks of terror. He was much surprised, and anxiously
inquired after her health. She assured him that she was perfectly well. He repeated his inquiries and said, "You look
so unlike yourself that there must be something the matter
with you." She replied that she was as well as usual.
"But," said he, "I see a black riband about your wrist; have
you sprained it?" "I have not sprained it, Sir Tristram,"

she replied, looking extremely solemn and agitated; "and I must conjure you most earnestly never to inquire the cause of my wearing this riband. If it were a matter that concerned you to know, I should not for a moment conceal it. But believe me it is not, and I pray you and all my friends never to take any notice of it hereafter, or to ask me any question on the subject."

Sir Tristram, seeing that she was greatly agitated and hardly able to speak, grew alarmed, and in order to tranquillise her at once promised never to trouble her with any furthur inquiry, adding that, should it be ever proper that he should know it, he was well assured that she would inform him.

The conversation here ended, but Sir Tristram saw that she was far from tranquil, and asked her if there was anything further upon her mind. "I am very anxious," she replied, "for my letters"; and she begged him to inquire if the post had arrived. She was told that it had not. In a few minutes she again rang the bell for the servant and repeated her inquiry, "Is not the post come in yet?" She was again told it had not. "Do you expect any letters," said Sir Tristram, "that you are so anxious about the arrival of the post?"

"I do," said she; "I expect to hear of the death of Lord Tyrone—he died last Saturday at four o'clock."

"My dear," replied Sir Tristram, "I never in my life thought you of all people superstitious; but you must have had some idle dream, which has thus disturbed and alarmed you."

At this instant the servant opened the door and delivered to them a letter sealed with black wax. "It is," she said, "as I expected"; and delivered the letter to Sir Tristram. "He is dead." Sir Tristram opened the letter; it was from Lord Tyrone's steward, and contained the melancholy intelligence that he had died on the preceding Saturday, at the very hour Lady Beresford had specified. Sir Tristam entreated her to compose her spirits, and to endeavour to tranquillise herself, so far as it was in her power. She assured him that she felt happier than she had done for some time,

and added, " I can communicate to you intelligence that I
know will give you pleasure. I am shortly to present you
with another child, and I can assure you that child will be
a son." Sir Tristram received the information with the joy
it might be expected to convey, and expressed strongly the
felicity he experienced at the prospect of an event so long
and so ardently desired. After some months Lady Beresford was delivered of a son. Previously she had been the
mother of daughters only. The eldest of these, Susannah
Catherine, was married to Hyacinth Nugent, Lord Riverstone; she died s. p. in 1763; Arabella died unmarried in
1732; and Jane was married in 1711 to George Lowther of
Kilrae, and had two sons, the younger of whom, Marcus,
married the sister and heir of Sir Edward Crofton of Moate,
Co. Roscommon. He was created a baronet, and his grandson's widow was created Baroness Crofton.

In seven years after the birth of his son Sir Tristram
died, on the 16th of June, 1701, at the early age of thirty-
four, at Coleraine, and was buried in a vault he had ordered
to be prepared beneath his pew in the parish church.

After his death his widow was inconsolable; she shut
herself up, avoided all society, and seldom left the house.
She visited no family but that of a gentleman who resided
in the same-village, who was a near connexion. She passed
a few hours at his house every day; the rest of her time
was devoted to solitude, and she appeared determined to
renounce for ever all other society. The gentleman's family
consisted of himself, his wife and a goodly group of young
children. The lady of the house had a brother, a colonel in
the army. He was a distinguished soldier, but very dissi-
pated and extravagant. Whether by design or accident he
paid a visit to his sister, and soon made up his mind to
mend his fortunes by marrying the wealthy and still handsome widow. We may gather from Lady Beresford's statement that he made his advances with great caution, as he
had probably learned from his sister her determination and
her state of mind. He had engaged her affections before he
made any demonstration of his intentions, and a favourable
opportunity at length occurring, he made a sudden declara-

tion of his affection for her, and obtained her consent without giving her time for reflection or consideration.

Her imprudence in forming such a connexion was manifest to all, and the event justified public opinion. She was treated by her husband with contempt and cruelty, while at the same time his conduct evinced him to be the most abandoned libertine, utterly destitute of every principle of virtue and humanity.

To this second husband Lady Beresford brought a daughter and a son, after which such was the profligacy of his conduct that she insisted on a separation. They parted for several years. But at length, overcome by the penitence he expressed for his former behaviour, his promises of amendment, and his persuasions, she consented to reside with him once more. In January, 1711, she became the mother of another daughter, and late in January, 1713, she had her second son. The day month she had lain in being the anniversary of her birthday, she sent for her daughter, Lady Riverstone, and to a few friends, to request them to spend the day with her. Among the first arrivals were Dr. King, Archbishop of Dublin, and the clergyman who baptized her. The Archbishop was an old friend, and had been for many years a near neighbour when he was Bishop of Derry. In course of conversation she observed, " I am forty-eight to-day." " No," said the clergyman, "you are only forty-seven. A dispute with your mother some years ago led me to look at the register of your birth. You were born on the 23rd of February, 1666, and you are just forty-seven years old to-day." Upon hearing this Lady Beresford grew ghastly pale. " You have signed my death-warrant," said she, "for this day is my last. I must therefore request you to leave me, for I have something of importance to settle before I die." When the clergyman retired, she sent to forbid the arrival of her company, and at the same time she requested the Archbishop of Dublin, her son Marcus, now nineteen years of age, and her daughter Lady Riverstone, to accompany her to her private apartment. Immediately on their arrival she desired everyone else to leave the room, and then said: " My last hour is nigh at hand, and I have something I wish to communicate to you before I depart. You, my Lord Archbishop, are not a stranger to the friendship that existed between Lord Tyrone and me: we were educated under the same roof in deistical principles, and when the friends into whose hands we afterwards fell endeavoured to persuade us to embrace revealed religion, their arguments, though insufficient to convince us, were strong enough to stagger our former faith, and to leave us halting between two opinions. In this state of doubt and perplexity we made a solemn promise to each other, that whichever died first should (if permitted) appear to declare to the other which was the true religion. One night when Sir Tristram and I were in bed I awoke, and discovered Lord Tyrone sitting by my bedside. I screamed out, and endeavoured to awake Sir Tristram. 'For Heaven's sake, Lord Tyrone,' I cried, 'for what purpose, or by what means came you here at this time of night?' 'Have you then forgotten our mutual promise?' said he. 'I died on Saturday at four o'clock, and have permission to appear to you to assure you that revealed religion is the only one by which you can be saved. I am further permitted to inform you that you are now with child of a son who will be married to my niece, and Sir Tristram will not survive his birth many years. You will then marry again a man whose ill-treatment will make you miserable. By him you will have two daughters and two sons, and in child-bed of your youngest son you will die on completing your forty-seventh year.' 'Just Heavens,' exclaimed I, 'and cannot I prevent this?' 'Undoubtedly you can,' said he; 'for you are a free agent, and may prevent it by resisting every temptation to a second marriage; but your passions are strong, and you know not their power; hitherto you have had no trial. I am not permitted to say more; but if, after this, you persist in your infidelity, you will be miserable indeed.' 'May I ask,' said I, 'if you are happy?' 'Had it been otherwise,' said he, 'I should not have been permitted to appear to you thus.' 'I may then imply,' said I, 'that you are happy?' He smiled. 'And how,' continued I, 'when the morning come, shall I be convinced that your appearance

more to reside with him, but not till I thought I had attained my forty-seventh year. This day I have heard from indisputable authority that I have hitherto lain under a mistake with regard to my age, and that I have only this day completed my forty-seventh year. I have not therefore the slightest doubt of the near approach of my death. Armed with the sacred hopes of Christianity I can meet the King of Terrors without dismay, and, without a tear, bid adieu to the regions of mortality for ever.

"When I am dead, I wish my daughter, Lady Riverstone, to unbind my wrist, and let my son with yourself behold it."

Lady Beresford here ceased for some time, but, resuming the conversation, she entreated her son so to behave as to merit the high honour intended for him from an union with the daughter of Lord Tyrone.

She then expressed a desire to lie down, to endeavour to compose herself to sleep. Lady Riverstone and Sir Marcus called her attendants, and quitted the room, having first desired them to watch their mistress attentively, and, should they observe the smallest change, to call them.

An hour passed and all was silent in her room; they listened at the door and all was still.

In half an hour more a bell rang violently. They flew to her apartment, but before they reached the door they heard the servant exclaim, "Ah! she is dead, my mistress is dead!" Lady Riverstone then desired the servants to quit the room. She approached the bed with Lady Beresford's son, and they knelt down by the bedside. Lady Riverstone lifted up her hand, and she found the wrist exactly in the state described by Lady Beresford, every sinew shrunk and every nerve withered.

Lady Beresford's son, as had been predicted, married Lord Tyrone's daughter. The pocket-book and the riband are in the possession of Lady Betty Cobbe, by whom the above is stated, and who, together with the Tyrone family, will be ready to attest its truth.

CHAPTER XX

Richard, 9th Earl of Scarbrough.—Ride in Wheatley Park.—Lady Georgina
Lumley.

THOUGH a martyr to gout, and often laid up for weeks together, Frederick Lumley was much beloved, and was a welcome guest in the numerous hospitable houses of York and Nottinghamshire. The following lines, describing him, were doubtless by some local poet. They were found in an old pocket-book belonging to his devoted daughter, Georgina, and are now among the few family relics at Sandbeck. They are printed on a half-sheet of paper, and were wrapped round three locks of hair, one fair Saxon curl already dashed with gray, entwined with a bright brown tress and a short crisp curl of pale gold:

On the Death of Frederick Lumley Savile, Esq., Tickhill Castle,
Yorkshire.

A gracious being beloved by all,
The spirit fled, for God did call;
By grace divine he had new birth,
And pure returned to parent earth.

No pride, no malice in his breast,
The wretched was his daily guest;
And social bliss did with him blend,
The widow's joy, the poor man's friend.

Patience came down with pearly shower,
For death had touched the parent flower,
To soothe the sorrow of the mind—
All feel the loss of one so kind.

A noble master—husband mild—
His manners gentle, undefiled:

He sometimes felt affliction's rod,
But close pursued his way to God.

And left behind a pattern bright
To all who linger here below,
A name to soothe affliction's blight,
And smooth the path of pain and woe.

This touching expression of feeling was felt by all who came in contact with Frederick Lumley. He was beloved by all.

His only son, Richard, had been educated as befitted his state at Eton, where he acquired the limited amount of learning demanded in those days, and greatly distinguished himself in company with kindred spirits in the accomplish-plishment of every imaginable prank. Captain Gronow in his " Recollections and Anecdotes" tells how "the old pupils of Dr. Keate in Paris, soon after Waterloo, gave him a dinner at Beauvillers. . . . After drinking his health, as the bottle passed gaily round, we took the opportunity of giving him a little innocent 'chaff,' reminding him of his heavy hand and arbitrary manner of proceeding. . . . We spoke of Sumner's flirtation with the fair Martha at Spiers's; of Mike Fitzgerald tripping up Plumptree, the master, on his way to six o'clock school; of Cornwall's fight with the bargee; of Lumley's poaching in Windsor Park " (Second Series, p. 44).

Dick Lumley also enjoyed the distinction of being one of the daring crew who stole the historic block from Eton, now a trophy at Curraghmore. When Earl of Scarbrough with sons at Eton, he was very reticent on the subject; but in November, 1884, at their last meeting, his eldest daughter's husband, the Hon. W. Orde Powlett, now fourth Lord Bolton, persuaded him to give him the list of the heroes: Henry, third Marquis of Waterford, Lord William Beresford, Richard George Lumley, Lord Alford, F. Kemp, Louis Ricardo and J. H. Jesse. I think it was the last named of whom Lord Scarbrough remarked, with a twinkle in his eye, that " he wasn't a good enough fellow to have shared the honours."

In September, 1827, Sir Francis Doyle and Dick Lumley

were guests together at Wheatley Park, the seat of Sir
William Cooke, and the baronet bard tells the following
amusing anecdote:

"During the summer holidays of 1827, I met with an
accident which might well have been a fatal one. . . . I was
riding through Wheatley Park with an Eton friend, Dick
Lumley, the present (no, now alas the late) Lord Scarborough. We rode from Sir William Cooke's house to see
the St. Leger run for—the St. Leger, I mean, won by Mr.
Petre's Matilda—a race which I afterwards described in
verse, not without success. Two Eton boys on such an
errand naturally began to race with each other as soon as
they could. I had been mounted upon a hot, hard-mouthed
pony, who could not be stopped, when once in his gallop,
under a hundred yards at least. Having taken the lead,
instead of keeping my eyes before me, I continually looked
back to watch Dick Lumley's progress, wide on the right.
(He, of course, was doing his best to overtake me.) Then,
happening to turn round, I saw with dismay a great oak
across my path, with its boughs stretching away on both
sides of my advance. What was to be done? This question
dashed through my mind. 'Shall I throw myself off?'
'No!' darted up the answer, 'I will take my feet out of the
stirrups, and give way to the blow the instant it comes upon
me.'" Then Sir Francis goes on with a psychological description of his feelings. He continues: "My tumble, in the
end, amounted to nothing. I rose from the ground little the
worse, though Dick Lumley rode up, crying out in rather
a reproachful tone, 'Why, I thought you were killed!' as if
I had no business to get off so cheaply. He honestly rejoiced, I have no doubt, like the good-natured fellow he
was, at my unexpected escape, but I fancied I could detect
passing through his mind a momentary flicker of something
like disappointment that he had not to gallop back to the
house and electrify its inmates with the melancholy tidings
that I was lying a corpse under that ill-omened oak-tree.
However, on finding me by no means a corpse, he made
the best of it, helped me to catch my pony, and we then
rode on, to take our places in the Doncaster stand, I with a

lump on my upper lip as big as a pigeon's egg, but otherwise none the worse. I have always felt glad to have been
able to go on my own way after what had happened, because
'The Doncaster St. Leger,' perhaps my most successful
poem, would otherwise not have been written" (" Reminis-
cences and Opinions of Sir Francis Doyle," pp. 65-67).

Another anecdote of Lord Scarbrough's pluck in riding
is told by "that great Professor of rough riding, the veteran
Dick Christian, of Chapel Street, Melton," in " The Post
and Paddock ":

" Now there's Lord Scarbrow, Mr. Lumley that was.
Dash me! what a go I once saw with him! We was out
with the Belvoir hounds, Sir James Musgrave and me at
the tail of the hounds going for Langar, before we got to
the Smite. We were in the middle field that goes down to
the Smite. I says, 'Sir James, here's the Smite; will you
have it?' 'We must have it,' says he. Mr. Lumley he
comes up between us, and at it he goes. He jumped the
water, but he couldn't get through the bullfinch on the other
side: back'ards he comes. I couldn't see him or the horse.
Sir James shouts, ' He'll be drowned, Dick,' when up he
comes again. I catched his horse, and out he waded, as wet
and as black as my hat. Well, he gets on to his horse as
plucky as ever, just as he was; off he gets, runs back again;
I didn't know for my life what he was at. Blame me, if he
didn't dive in, head foremost, to find his right stirrup; he
fishes it out of four feet of water, buckles it on, and over
he goes again. He got through the bullfinch that time, and
they killed the fox at Colston Bassett. Well, some of the
gentlemen gave him their flask, and they persuaded him to
gallop back to Belvoir, and change. That 'ull be nigh twenty
years since: I met him some four years after, when Mr.
Foljambe's hounds met at Grove, and I says, ' Do you recollect the Smite, sir?' ' That I do. I should like such a duck-
ing again.' So I told all the gentlemen about it; how
amused they were! I never saw such a thing in my born
days."

Dick Lumley was undoubtedly one of the most popular
men of his day. Handsome, manly, loving fun and mischief,

RICHARD GEORGE, NINTH EARL OF SCARBROUGH

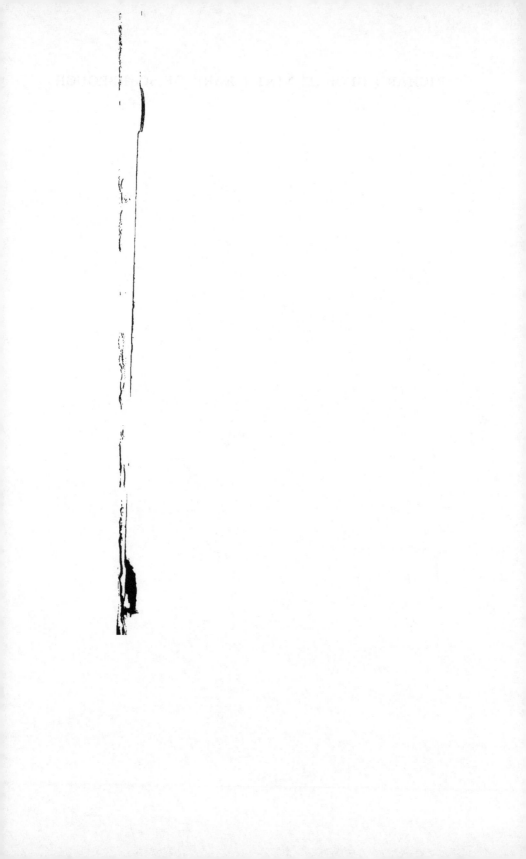

with more than a touch of Irish wit on a good foundation
of sturdy Saxon worth, he was welcomed in every house
and at home in every circumstance of life.

Of his three sisters, the two elder were already married
when their father died. Harriett, or, as she was christened,
after Richard Scarbrough's sweet wife, Henrietta, married
Edmund L'Estrange on November 5th, 1835. Harriett
Lumley was a very lovely girl, and Edmund L'Estrange
had only *Irish* expectations from an old lady who, as a
matter of fact, predeceased him but by a few weeks, living
to a fabulous age.

Harriett's grandmother, Mrs. Beresford, *née* Bush, and
niece of the great orator Grattan, did not favour the alliance,
and there is an amusing story told of the means she once
took to cut short a too long visit from the aspiring bridegroom.

On his return to the Palace at Kilmore after a long tramp
" Cock" shooting, he was greeted with " Ah! Neddy me
dear, I didn't expect ye back and I've just washed yer
room," an Irish equivalent for putting it by till next time.
Whether Neddy took the hint history does not reveal, but
he won his bride in any case. The marriage was celebrated
in London, and an old woman in the " Mizendew" (Maison
de Dieu) at Tickhill, still living, describes the rejoicings on
the occasion: " Little lamps twinkled behind every leaf of
the old ivy-clothed Castle. There was a bonfire at the top
of the keep and all the village was feasted."

Frances Lumley, the eldest daughter, married in 1836
Charles Hill, Colonel of the 7th Hussars, the regiment in
which young Richard Lumley was a subaltern at the time.

After her father's death, Georgina Lumley seems to have
divided her time between her beloved great-aunt, Lady
Scarbrough, and her sister, Mrs. Hill, who lived at Tickhill,
though not at that time in the old Castle, to which she and
her husband returned when her brother became Lord Scarbrough. She paid long visits to Nun-Appleton. Harriett
Milner writes in 1828 that Frederick Lumley is staying at
Nun-Appleton, at the same time as George Foljambe,
Squire of Osberton, whom she married. As will be remem-

were things of the past, and beautiful Castle Hamilton soon left the hands that had never really held the reins of ownership. Mr. Southwell had loved little Charlotte Beresford when she was only fourteen in short frocks, low necks, frilled trousers and sandalled shoes. It was said that he had even at this early date asked for her hand, and that her mother had even then favoured the alliance.

Richard Lumley and his sisters owed much to the racy Irish graft on their ancient Saxon stock. It is to be regretted that space will not admit of more anecdotes of this period. Richard Lumley was squire to his cousin Henry, third Marquis of Waterford, in the famous Eglington Tournament of 1838, the glories of which were so sadly marred by the pitiless rain that fell nearly the whole time.

It was during a delightful visit that I paid to the widow of the Knight of the Tournament in 1881 that she introduced me to Mrs. Heslop, mentioned many times in "Two Noble Lives," who had been custodian of the Castle in the days of Lord Waterford's bachelorhood. He only came there for shooting, and on such rare occasions as the return from crossing the border to take part in the great Tournament. I had better give the account of the arrival of the party in Mrs. Heslop's own words. She was a very old lady then, past eighty, but she lived to be ninety-three. Her memory was clear and her eyes like a hawk's. She was dressed in a high mob cap, and with quakerlike but most picturesque simplicity. "My beautiful lady," as I always called Lady Waterford, introduced me to the old dame as her Saxon cousin, Edith Milner, Dick Lumley's niece.

The old lady's eyes sparkled. "I mind him well, my lady; a limb he was, worthy to be his lordship's squire. Eh! but he was handsome, straight and tall, with an eye as blue as heaven, but with a glint of something else in it for all that. He was right bonny, was Dick Lumley. There wasn't a lass he couldn't have had for the asking, I was told, and I could believe it. But didn't they young lords wake up the old place. They must have the high table, and feudal times and all the rest of it, and such a noise of arms clashing, and wassail cups, and tilting and hawking and old-fashioned talk, as would have fetched all the dead out of their graves, if they could have had their way. It did seem quiet when they were gone, my lady, and I am glad to see one belonging to Dick Lumley, though she is only a lass." I reassured her by telling her that there was a blue-eyed, fair-haired son, and another with dark hair and eyes, besides daughters who divided the fair and the dark equally. She kept on saying, "I should like to see Dick Lumley again," and seemed to live much more in the past than in the present.

During that visit to Ford Castle, Lady Waterford took me to Flodden Field, where a Lord Lumley had fought. It is a long walk, but the time was pleasantly beguiled by our hostess, who told us many ancient traditions connected with the surrounding country. She reminded us how James of Scotland lingered at the Castle we had left behind, to the ruin of his own fame and the complete discomfiture of his gallant army. She showed us the positions the armies were supposed to have occupied, and almost fought the battle o'er again, so vivid was her description.

CHAPTER XXI

Marriage of Richard, Lord Scarbrough.—His Illness and Death.—Aldred, Tenth Earl.—Lumley Castle and the Dowager Countess of Scarbrough.

THE threads must now be drawn together with as much speed as possible, and this story finished up to date. Georgina Lumley went early in 1844 on one of her frequent visits to Nun-Appleton, and her diary records that it was in the old school-room there that the decisive word was spoken by William Mordaunt Milner, who afterwards became fifth baronet. She had been present at the Coronation of our gracious Queen Victoria, and had seen her open her first Parliament. She was married from Lady Scarbrough's house in Portman Square in 1844, and her brother gave her away. Lady Scarbrough lived to see her great-great-niece, the present chronicler of the records, and to wonder at the novel-sounding name that was given to her, in spite of its Saxon origin. " Georgina has got a daughter, and what do you think she is going to call her? Edith!" she said to her nephew's wife, then Mrs. Henry Willoughby, now Julia, Lady Middleton. She did not live to love and welcome Dick Lumley's bride, but died in 1846, leaving all she could, as her husband had done, to her beloved nephew, now heir presumptive to the Earldom of Scarbrough and Lumley Castle.

Richard Lumley married in October, 1846, Frederica, younger daughter of Andrew Drummond and of Lady Elizabeth, daughter of the fifth Duke of Rutland, and sister to the present Duke, better known as Lord John Manners, till the latter half of the last century, when he succeeded his brother. This marriage connected two more interesting and ancient families with the Lumleys.

But these records have already far exceeded the original intention of the writer, nor would it be possible in the life-time of many to do more than glance at the present home life and general events of interest. Perhaps some one may write the history of the nineteenth-century Lumleys as the present chronicler has dared to introduce those of the earlier centuries. Such a one will have diaries and papers close home to help him or her.

Richard Lumley succeeded to the estates of his cousin John on October 25th, 1856, as ninth Earl of Scarbrough. He inherited Lumley Castle, Sandbeck in Yorkshire, and Glentworth in Lincolnshire; but, as has been said, Rufford Abbey passed to other hands. The present owner, John Lumley, son of the Rev. Frederick Lumley, succeeded to his uncle, Sir John Lumley, created first Baron Savile, K.C.B., on his retirement from the diplomatic service, having been Ambassador at Rome and other places.

Lord Scarbrough had not been long in possession before a strange, mysterious malady, supposed to have originated in a serious fall from his horse, overtook him. He gradually lost the use of his limbs, and also during the latter part of his life became totally blind. It must have been a singularly bitter trial to a man who had been a noted athlete, skilled in all sports and devoted to outdoor life. He was struck down in the very prime of his vigorous manhood, but no one ever heard a murmur. He was always a cheerful, genial host to the friends he had made in his earlier, healthier years.

He was not able to take any active part in public affairs, and he only once used his prerogative as a peer, when he voted against the Irish Church Disestablishment Bill, which the Lords threw out, only to be compelled later to assent to it grudgingly. Lord Scarbrough felt very strongly on the subject, and made a great exertion to give expression to his feelings. He was supposed to belong to the old Whig party, but he did not wait for the Home Rule Bill to prove his loyalty to Church and State, but led the van of those honest men who after his death joined the loyal party. His Irish wit came out on the occasion, for when a brother peer remonstrated with him for appearing on the wrong side of the House, he answered: " You would not have me take the bread out of my poor old uncle's mouth, would you?" The head of the Irish Church was Marcus Gervoise Beresford, his mother's brother.

It was a singular and very sad coincidence that Sir William Mordaunt Milner, the husband of Georgina Lumley, who had represented York City as Member of Parliament from 1848 to 1857, should have been paralyzed about the same time as his brother-in-law, Lord Scarbrough. They had married within eighteen months of each other, and succeeded in the same year to fair inheritances. Both set a wonderful example of patience and resignation. Sir William Milner only survived the stroke of ill-health for ten years, and died in 1867 at the early age of forty-six. Lord Scarbrough passed the Psalmist's span, and died on December 5th, 1884, at the age of seventy-two.

The elder children of Lord and Lady Scarbrough were born at Tickhill Castle, where the first years of their married life, when still Mr. and Mrs. Lumley, had been spent. Their eldest son, Liulph, called after the "noble generous man" who lived at Lumley in the eleventh century, died in his twentieth year, just after the marriage of his eldest sister, Algitha, on August 13th, 1868, to William Orde Powlett, now Lord Bolton. They were spending their honeymoon at Lumley Castle, where at that time only a few rooms were partially furnished, when they were summoned back to take leave of their brother, Lord Lumley, a worthy son of his father. He had borne a long and trying illness with exemplary sweetness and patience. In a trembling hand, his father entered in the old red family Bible: " Died at Sandbeck, August 23rd, 1868, Liulph Richard Granby, Viscount Lumley."

The title descended to Aldred, the second son, who was born in November, 1857. He was gazetted to a sub-lieutenancy in the 7th Hussars, the regiment in which, as we have seen, his father had served, in 1876, and served in Natal during the disastrous Boer War of 1880-1, which

has now so amply been revenged. He left the army in 1883, and succeeded his father as tenth Earl of Scarbrough in 1884. He married in March, 1899, Cecilia, daughter of Cecil Dunn Gardner, and widow of Robert Ashton. In the following year he took part in the South African campaign as second in command of the 3rd Regiment of Imperial Yeomanry.

On March 31st, 1901, a daughter was born, christened Serena Mary Barbara, the first daughter born to a reigning earl for more than one hundred and fifty years.

Meantime the fair daughters of the house, his sisters, had all left the parent nest in quick succession. The second, Ida, married on September 7th, 1869, Viscount Newport, eldest son of the Earl of Bradford, to whom he has since succeeded. Lilian married on August 3rd, 1871, Lawrence Dundas, now the Marquis of Zetland. Sweet little Sibell ("We call her Si belle because she is so beautiful," her loving elder sister, Ida, said, when the little maid was only four years old) married, first, Lord Grosvenor, son of the first Duke of Westminster, to whom her son has now succeeded, on November 3rd, 1874. Lord Grosvenor died on January 22nd, 1884, at Saighton Grange; and she married secondly, on February 7th, 1887, George Wyndham, whose career promises to be a brilliant one. The third and youngest son, Osbert, married on May 3rd, 1892, Constance Wilson Patton, whose mother married, secondly, the Marquis of Hertford. By the death of her only brother she became the heiress of her grandfather, Lord Winmarleigh. The title became extinct on his death. There are two sons of the marriage, Richard and Roger, and one surviving daughter, Lilian.

We cannot do better than end, as we began, with beautiful Lumley Castle. As has been said, at the beginning of the last century it was neglected, and only a few rooms were furnished. Now all that is changed, as it has become the residence during the winter and spring months of Frederica, Countess of Scarbrough, who bravely faces the rigours of a northern winter for the sake of the home of her husband's ancestors. She knows a great deal about old furniture, and has gradually gathered together many old carved wooden settles and tables, such as might originally have been used by the Lumleys of three hundred years ago. The part of the Castle which she has made so homelike and habitable consists, besides the Barons' Hall, of a suite of rooms connected by galleries, comprising the dining-room, music-room and drawing-room. Her private apartments are in another part of the Castle. To reach them you cross what was once the portcullis chamber. Bright flowers succeed each other in the flower-beds around the old Castle walls; wild flowers bloom in the lovely Dene, where Lumleys of old culled herbs and simples for the cure of maladies and the healing of wounds. The poor and suffering for many miles round love the present Lady of Lumley as their forefathers cherished her predecessors. She is always gladly welcomed among her own people, and by the miners of Great Lumley. The foundation stone of the church, built some forty years ago, was laid by her eldest son, Liulph. She well deserves the lines dedicated to her in the " Lily of Lumley":

> Out of Time's dust, whelmed there when faith was young,
> I snatch these records of an ancient race :
> How for the truth, despising all things base,
> A delicately nurtured lady clung
> To life's deep word, nor feared the iron face
> Of violent death with bitter pangs that wrung
> Her wounded spirit, faithless friends among.
> All this she did through God's exceeding grace.
> Lady ! not only that her honoured name
> To thee entrusteth its futurity,
> But that, like her, armed with a faith divine,
> Thy graciousness could steal itself to be
> True if death threatened, if such need were thine
> I dedicate this legend unto thee.

APPENDIX

ACCOUNT OF THE LUMLEY ESTATES

LORENCE OF WORCESTER in his account, given in Chapter I., says that Liulph "had many possessions far and wide throughout England by hereditary right." However this may have been, his immediate descendants seem only to have held lands in the County Palatine of Durham. This Liulph's son, Uchtred, is said to have held the manors of Little Lumley and Heselden. The original family house was at Great Lumley, a mile south of the site of the present castle. The remains of the old manor house were traceable till recent times, and the cottage on its site is still pointed out. Liulph and his family removed, as we have seen, to Durham when the Normans were ravaging the country, and he was murdered there. The date of the foundation of Lumley Castle is unknown, but it is said to have been begun by Sir Robert Lumley in the reign of Edward I. (see p. 9), and enlarged by his son, Sir Marmaduke. The earliest existing portion is the west side of the quadrangle, the east front of which originally formed the exterior front. Sir Marmaduke's son, the great Sir Ralph, obtained leave from King Richard II. and Bishop Skirlaw of Durham to make his manor house into a castle, the bishop's licence being granted in 1389 and the king's in 1392, and it then assumed its present form. It is a quadrangle with an area in the centre, having at each angle massy square towers, embattled and machicolated; the whole being built of freestone, of a bright and beautiful tint. The east front, which retains all its original magnificence, extends 175 feet, and almost overhangs a deep wooded ravine, through which the Lumley Beck meanders till it joins the Wear. Three stages of masonry rise above each other with mullioned windows, heavily grated with iron; and a bold and stately entrance tower with its machicolated gallery and flanked by turrets forms its centre. Over the gate are six shields and crests carved in the stone which show its date. There seems to have been originally a domestic chapel in the castle, as a licence for celebrating service there was granted by Cardinal Langley to

Sir Thomas Lumley in 1432 (see p. 20). The castle remained unaltered till the time of John, Lord Lumley, who took such an interest
in his ancestors. He greatly altered the appearance of the castle,
though the extent of his changes cannot be traced now owing to
more recent "improvements." The whole of the windows of Tudor
character looking into the outer court and on the west, north and
east quadrangles date from his time. Also the fireplace in the great
hall and many of the internal decorations.

We shall best give an account of the castle at this time by quoting
from the Red Velvet Book, already referred to, which is an account
of the castle and of the family generally, drawn up by order of John,
Lord Lumley, at the close of the sixteenth century. It begins thus:

"AT LUMLEY CASTLE.

" At the first entrance into the Castle there standeth on the out-
side of the gate six auncient scutchions with their crests, viz: of
K. Edward the 3th quartering the armes of France sans nomber."
(A heraldic term, the same as *semée*, powdered.) "On the one side
the Armes of the Lord Pearcy. On the other side the armes of the
Lord Nevill: under them the armes of the Lord Lumley; On the
one side the armes of Baron Hilton, on the other side the armes of
Graye of Northumberland. All auncientlie cutt in hard stone.

" Within the gate, a faire scutchion of whyte marble with my Lord
Lumleys Armes. On each side a table picture, cutt in whyte marble,
the one representing the memorie of Sir Robert Lumley, the other
of Sir Marmaduke Lumley in the raignes of K Edward 2 and King
Edward the 3 who were the begynners, and laid the foundacon of
this Castle. The inner porch is adorned with 18 great scutchions of
whyte marble, having the Armes ingraven of my Lords Auncestors
inhabiting there, since the Conquest. On each side of the Porch is
written in Touche," (a sort of alabaster,) " and guilt *In Longaevi tem-
poris monimentis curiosus oculus est iniquus judex.*" (In the monuments of long time a curious eye is an evil judge.)

" In the midst of the Court standeth a Condeth," (the old form of
conduit,) " of 17 foote high with two bolls of whyte marble, standing
upon foure great pillers of whyte marble contayning my Lords
Armes, and my Ladie Elsabeths, his second wife.

" In the uppermost front of the Hall, there standeth a great
statuarie on horsback, as bigg as the life, wᵗʰin an arch of stone, in
Hall. memorie of King Edward the 3 in whose tyme the most of
this Castle was built, wiᵗʰn this arche also standeth sixe small
pictures, in whyte marble in memorie of his six sonns, viz:
Edward Prince of Wales, Willm̄: of Hatfeild who died yong, Lyonell
Duke of Clarence, John of Gaunt Duke of Lancaster, Edmond of
Langley Duke of Yorke, Thomas of Woodstock, Duke of Glocester.

" Upon the same front there are also Foure livelie statues all wrought in white marble in memorie of K Henry the 8, King Edward 6, Quene Marie and Q Elizabeth, in whose raignes his Lo^p lived.

" In the nether end of the hall against the skreene a Rich Lavatorie of touch and whyte marble contayning in height 20 foote.

" A long table of walnuttree.

" Thirtene Emperors heades of mouldworke garnishing the hall about.

" Sixe most rare heades of beasts, whereof one most rare to be seene, viz: a heade of some fallowe deare, as maie be supposed not unlike to a platiceros his heade. The scantling is from the outside of one palme to the other 7 foote and 4 ynches. The bredth of the palme is 2 foote and 10 ynches, the height of the horne from the setting on of the heade is 3 foot and 10 ynches; The length of the heade onelie is a foote 10 ynches and a half. The compasse of the eye is 7 ynches, betwixt the eyes 10 ynches, the Compasse of the beame in the smallest place is 9 inches, the length of one tyne of the horne is one foote 5 ynches; the compasse of the bigger tooth is 5 ynches, the compasse of the fore teeth 4 ynches.

Beasts.

" An heade of an Eliphant.

" The heade of a Strepsiceros." (An antelope with spiral keeled horns.)

" A Staggs head carrying nyne in the topp.

" A Heade of a Bezar." (A Bezoar-goat is a kind of gazelle.)

" A Heade of a beast called Geȋns." (A chamois.)

" The clawe of a griphyn, verie wonderfull, it carryeth in length 3 foote 10 ynches, the compasse of the rounde is 8 ynches and a half.

Birde very wonderfull.

" A faire table wherein is written in letters of golde verses, touching the vanitie of the worlde begynnynge as followeth."

Then follows a Latin poem, which is still to be seen on the walls of the banqueting hall, where however it is differently divided. It is there headed by the words " Theatrum Mundus, Spectator Deus." (The World a Theatre, God the Spectator.) The following is a translation of the poem:

" The world is passing away, a fact known indeed, a fact ever to be noted.
Known to thee, may it be known to the world, the world is passing away.
The world is passing away, not the world, that is, this fabric of the world,
I say, but the glory of the world, the world is passing away.
The world is passing away, quickly the name is passing, with the name the
    world.
But more quickly than the name of the world, the world is passing away.
The world is passing away, there are three things, was, is, will be, these three
    forces
Move the world, these three proclaim, the world is passing away.
The world is passing away, flying as time, as a river, as gold.
It is sufficient to say as the world, the world is passing away.

The world is passing away, nothing is certain, but the certainty of its passing.
In the world nothing is sure but this, that the world is passing away.
The world is passing away, there is nothing in nothing, but nevertheless its departure
Does not pass away; depart, error, thou being ruler, the world is passing away.
The world is passing away, nothing that thou seekest is sufficient when thou hast sought it.
The world has possessions, what it has it rejects, the world is passing away.
The world is passing away, am I strong? I shall not be, am I beautiful?
I shall not be; am I rich? I shall not be; the world is passing away.
The world is passing away, death follows life, the narrow the unfettered,
The long the short, the cowardly the gladsome, the world is passing away.
The world is passing away, the world which really fails in everything,
Which is ignorant that it fails in this one thing, the world is passing away.
The world is passing away, Christ does not pass away; worship not that which passes away,
Thou sayest, I do not pass away, without me this world passes away.
The world is passing away, as often as I reiterate it the world will cease
To pass away, I will cease to say, the world is passing away.

World; farewell to thee: flying me, then I will follow thee,
Thou wilt sometimes follow me, world farewell to thee.

To be, to have been, to be about to be, are three flowering things without a flower.
For at the same time everything will perish that was, is, or will be."

" Above the statuarie of tyme theise verses," of which again we give a translation :

" With winged shoulders, irrevocable time flies, the triumphing laurel conquers, the very sharp scythe cuts.

" Shall I build up, or pull down the statue of time? time the devourer of all things, has extinguished the names of our ancestors, their life and memory, it has devoured their marble, ivory, silver, golden monuments. When the succeeding years have followed into that time, and have threatened to cast into the darkness, in that long series of years, that progeny which it has brought forth, I should be powerless among the spoils of time, if a triumphal statue were consecrated. But time possesses all things, so that it would not be right to envy time its trophies and we ought to give thanks as to a common parent of truth, virtue, life, our nobility. By time are begotten the pedigrees of the Caesars, the sceptres of empire have increased, the atmosphere of honour pleases, is seized, is honoured, is destroyed.

" Time flows on, we gradually pass on and rush along; the sweet rewards of virtue alone remain."

Then follow three charters, in abbreviated Latin, very difficult to read. They are connected with the lands at Heyford, which came into the possession of the Lumleys by the marriage of Sir Roger de Lumley with Sibilla, eldest daughter of Hugh de Morewick (see page 9 and pedigree, page 13). The first paper is a concession from Robert Lumley, knight, to Roger his brother, of "all lands and all my tenements together with the mill at Harleston and the advowson of the church of Heyfford and with all my villeins and their chattels according to law which I had in the vills of Harleston, Heyford and Brynton Colyngtre and Brochole." It is dated March 20th, 1305.

The second in the book, but the first in order of time, is the final agreement on February 3rd, 1278, between Roger de Lumley and Sybil his wife, plaintiff, and John de Roseley and Beatrice his wife, she being the third daughter of Hugh de Morewik. It acknowledges that lands at East Chynington, West Chynington, Morewike, Ryneley and Hudspecht in the County of Northumberland, and Harleston, Heyford, Brynton Colingtre and Brochole in the County of Northampton belong to Roger and Sybil. This is the father of the Robert and Roger above.

The third, dated May, 1304, is an account of the Morewick family and of lands belonging to them at Dodford.

Then follows a rough pedigree of the Morewick connection, and of the younger branch of the Lumley family, descended from the Roger de Lumley mentioned above.

Next comes a copy of an inscription still to be seen on the walls of Lumley Castle, tracing the descent of the family from Liulph, of which the following is a translation, the original being in Latin:

" Liulph a noble and generous minister of the Anglo-Saxon race, a very renowned man, who far and wide throughout Anglia had many possessions by the law of heredity ; when, in the time of King William the first, Conqueror of the English, the Normans everywhere were fierce and cruel, and because he greatly loved Cuthbert, Bishop of Durham, recorded among the saints, removed with all his possessions to Durham and there indeed became dear and acceptable to Bishop Walcher so that nothing seems to have been done without his counsel: whence he aroused the hatred of many until he was killed by a certain Gilbert and other wicked ministers of the said Bishop. In revenge for whose death the Northumbrians cruelly slew Walcher the innocent Bishop at Gateshead A.D. 1080. By Aldgitha his wife, the daughter of Aldred Count of Northumberland Liulph begat a son Uctred, the father of William de Lumley the first of his name, from the place of whose domain the surnames of his descendants are chosen. Hugo Bishop of Durham wished this William, the son of Uctred, to enjoy that freedom from taxes which certain of the Barons in his Bishopric enjoyed, and he obtained a charter of King Henry II. William, not unmindful

of so many benefits left his vill of Dictonia in Alverstonshire to this
Bishop and his successors; (the wife of this William was Julia of
Hesilden). From the first William sprang the second, from the
second the third, who by the daughter of William Dawdre Knight
begat a son Roger, the husband of Sybil co-heiress of the renowned
Baron Hugh de Morewick. Of them was born Robert who by Lucia,
sister and heiress of Thomas, Baron de Thweng, begat Marmaduke,
the first deserter of the paternal arms, having retained the insignia
of the maternal branch. He begat, by Margaret Holand, his wife,
Ralph, a strenuous knight, whom King Richard II in the eighth
year of his reign raised to the dignity of Baron of the kingdom;
having married Eleanor, sister of the first Earl of Westmoreland, he
begat John, who by Felicia de Redham, his wife, begat Thomas, by
whom Margaret, his wife, daughter of James Harrington, Knight,
brought forth George, the husband of Elizabeth, heiress of Roger
Thornton Esquire by whom he became the father of that Thomas,
who by a natural daughter of the great King Edward IV, begat
Richard. He, marrying Anne sister of William Baron Coigners
left as heir John, the husband of Joan daughter of Henry le
Scroope of Bolton the unparalleled Baron, the grandfather of John,
last Baron of Lumley; here deposited in a sepulchre in certain
hope of a future resurrection, by his grandson whom George the son
by Jane co-heiress of Richard Knightley Knight had left sole heir.
This last John was twice happily married, that is to Jane elder
daughter and co-heiress of Henry Earl of Arundel; and also to
Elizabeth daughter of John Baron Darcy, a woman not only of an
ancient pedigree and race, but which is greatly to be praised with
virtues of modesty, truth, and conjugal love. Of the former of these
marriages were born two sons, Charles and Thomas, and an only
daughter, Maria, hardly indeed seeing the light, but most tragically
in their infancy they were taken up to heaven."

The description of the arms which follows next is also translated
from the Latin:

"The genealogy of the Lumleys. They in the earliest times bore
six silver parrots on a red shield. And for the Crest over the collar
intertwined of silver and red, a silver pelican erect on a gold nest
wounding itself in the breast by pecks with its bill, and pouring the
blood over its young, is conspicuous above the helmet. But afterwards, having married the heiress of the Barons of Thweng, having
set aside the former (as was the custom in those early days) they
usurped their arms instead of their own, namely a red fess between
three green parrots on a white shield."

The arms are very beautifully emblazoned, and then follows a
pedigree, splendidly illuminated, in the form of a family tree, ex--

tending over ten pages. There is also a table tracing back the royal family to its original source, some of the letters being gilt:

DEUS.

"Adam; Seth: Enos: Cainan: Malaleel: Jared: Enoch: Mathusala: Lamech: Noah: Sem: Bedwus: Wala: Hatra: Itermod: Heremod: Seldwa: Beau: Tatwa: Getha: Fringolduff: Frethewlf: Freolater: Frethewald: Woden: Beldai: Broand: Freothegar: Frewin: Wig: Egla: Elesa: Certic: Creodda: Cuthricus: Ceaulinus: Cuthwinus: Cutha: Ceolwaldus: Kenredus: Ine: Ingels: Coppa: Offa: Alcmundus: Egbrithus: Athulfus: Alfredus: Edwardus senior: Edmondus: Edgarus: Ethelredus: Edmondus Ironsyde: Edwardus: Margareta Scotorum Regina: Matildes Regina Anglorum: Matildes Imperatrix Romanorum: Henricus Secundus, Rex: Johannes Rex: Henricus 3, Rex: Edmondus Bolingbrok secundus filius, Henrici. 3. Comes Lancastriae primus: Henricus comes Lancastriae secundus:"

Then we have shields of all the families into which the earlier Lumleys intermarried, again very beautifully emblazoned and arranged, and showing a careful study and good knowledge of heraldry.

The remainder of the book is taken up with:

" A Certyficate from Mr. John Lampton Stewarde of Howseholde to John Lord Lumley, of all his Lo: monumentes of Marbles, Pictures and tables in Paynture, with other his Lordshippes Howseholde stuffe, and Regester of Bookes. Anno 1590."

This consists first of nineteen pages of paintings of furniture, in which the marble is well depicted, but there is an utter and curious want of perspective. The rest is of great interest and must be given in full. "Statuary" here means a large picture. It will be noted that Lord Lumley possessed pictures of all the famous men of the time, as well as many more ancient. The famous Shakespeare portrait, which was sold at the beginning of the nineteenth century, had not yet come into his possession.

" A note of Pyctures caryinge the
fowrme of the whole Statuary.

These sorted together
for the memorye
of yor Lo: house.

The statuary of Adam and Eve
The Statuaryes of xvi^{en} Auncestors of yor Lo: lyneally descending from the Conquest unto yor self.
⟨ The Statuary of yor eldest sonne Charles.

The Statuary of bothe yo[r] Lo: wives.

The Statuary of old tyme.

The Statuary of Kinge Richard the seconde, delyvering the wryte of Parliament to Ralphe the first Barron of Lumley, called by him the eight yeare of his Reigne

The Statuary of King Henry the eight and his father Kinge Henry the seaventh joyned together, doone in white and blacke by Haunce Holbyn.

The Statuary of Kinge Henry the eight alone doone in oyle coloures

The Statuary of his sonne King Edward the sixt drawne by ~~The Statuary of the Lord Darley, after King of Scotts.~~

The Statuary of Quene Anné Bulleyne.

The Statuary of the Duches of Myllayne, afterwards Duches of Lorreyn daughter to Christierne King of Denmarke doone by Haunce Holbyn.

The Statuary of the Duches of Parma, Regent in Flaunders, Base doughter to the Empero[r] Charles the fiveth.

The Statuary of King Phillip King of Spayne.

The Statuary of Henry of Burbon King of Navarre and of Fraunce

The Statuary of Willm̄ Nassau Prince of Orange, murthered by Balthazar Geraertez, a Burgunyan gent.

The Statuary of the Princes his last wife, daughter to Colligny Admyrall of Fraunce and widow of Colligny.

The Statuary of the last old Earle of Arundel Fitzallen, Lo: Chamberleyne to k: H: 8. and K: Edw: 6. and Lo: Steward to Quene Mary and Q. Elizabeth.

The Statuary of Willm Harbert first Earle of Pembrooke, created by King Edward the sixt Lo: Steward to Quene Elizabeth.

The Statuary of Thomas first Lo: Darcy of Chiche created by King Edw: 6. Lo: Chamberleyne to the said K: Edw: drawn by Garlicke.

The Statuary of the Lo: Charles Howard of Effingham, Lord Admyrall of England.

The Statuary of Sir Christofer Hatton Knight, as he was being vice-chamberleyne to Q. Elizabeth, who afterward was Lo: Chancelo[r] of Englande.

The Statuary of the Lorde Darneley afterwards K: of Scott and his brother Charles Stewarde in one table.

The Statuary of Robert Dudley Earle of Leicester.

The Statuary of Edwarde Earle of Oxfourde.

The Statuary of yo[r] Lo[p] selfe in yo[r] Parlyament Robes.

The Statuary of Monseur brother to Valois laste Kinge of Fraunce in the robes of y[t] order.

The Statuarie of Counte de Horne   } in the Robes of theire
The Statuary of Counte de Mounteny }   order.
The Statuarie of Robte Earle of Sussex   Anno 1593.
The Statuarie of Thomas Lord Broughe in his Robes of the Garter.

PICTURES OF A SMALLER SCANTLINGE.

The Picture of King Richard the Second.
Of King Henry the fourthe.
Of King Henry the fiveth.
Of King Henry the sixt.
Of King Edward the fourthe.
Of King Richard the third.
Of King Henry the seaventh.
Of Quene Elizabeth his wife.
Of Prince Arthur their eldest sonne.
Of King Henry the eight.
Of King Edw: 6. being Prince.
Of Quene Marye, drawne by Garlicke.
Of Quene Elizabeth as she was comyng first to the Crowne.
And agayne, as she was the xxxth yeare of her Reigne.
Of Stephen Batre Kinge of Powland.
Of Sigismond Kinge of Poland sonne to John Kinge of Swethland.
Of Sigismonde Batre Prince of Transsilvania aº 1595.
· Of Phillip sonne to the Kynge of Spayne that now is.
Of the Duke of Richemond, base sonne to K: H: 8.
Of the Duke of Buckingham.
Of the first Duke of Northefolke Hawarde.
Of the seconde Duke of Northfolke.
Of Thomas the third Duke of Northfolke, doone by Garlicke.
Of Thomas Earle of Surrey.
Of Thomas his sonne the 4 Duke of Northfolke.
Of Phillip his sonne afterwards Earle of Arundell.
Of Charles Brandon the first Duke of Suffolke Lo: great Mr.
Of the Duke of Somerset Seymar Lo Protector to King Edw: 6.
Of his brother Lord Admirall Seymer.
Of the last Earle of Arundell Fitzallen, drawne twise by the famous paynter Steven.
Of his sonne the Lord Mautrevers.
Of the first Marques of Winchester Pawlet, Lo: Treasorer.
Of the Lo: Marques of Northampton Parre, Lo: great Chamberleyne.
Of Thomas Earle of Northumberland, executed at Yorke.
Of the first Earle of Southampton Writhesley, Lo: Chauncellor.
Of the Lo: Robert Dudley, Mr of the horse to Quene Elizabeth.

Of him after he was Earle of Leicester Lo: Steward, twisé drawne bye Seigar.

Of the Earle of Southampton Fitzwillm̄s Lo: Pryvie Seale.

Of the first Earle of Bedfourd Russell Lo: Pryvie Seale.

Of the second Earle of Essex Robert Devereux, M^r of the horse doone by Seigar.

Of the Lo: Clinton, afterwards created Earle of Lincolne, Lo: Admirall.

Of Ambrose Earle of Warwicke, generall at Newhaven.

Of the firste Earle of Shroesburie.

Of the olde Earle of Lyneux.

Of Gilbert Earle of Shrewesburye that now is.

Of the Lady Margaret Douglas his wyfe.

Of the Pope Juliùs secundus.

Of Cardynall Woolsey Lo: Chauncello^r

Of Anthony Grandville Cardinall and Bishopp of Arras.

Of the Cardynall Poole.

Of the B. of Winchester, Steven Gardyner Lo: Chauncello^r

Of the B. of Rochester Fissher.

Of the old Lo: Henry Morley, A° 1523 done in water colo^r by Albert Duer.

Of the Vycount Mountague Browne.

Of yor Lo: doone by Steven.

Of the first Lorde Sheiffeild, slayne at Norwiche.

Of Arthure Lo: Gray of Wilton, Lo deputie of Ireland, doone by Seigar.

Of the first Lo: Willougbye Peregrine Bartue.

Of Thomas the first Lo: Crumwell, Lo: pryvie seale, and vice-regent to K: H: 8.

Of the first Lo: Wentworth, Lo: Chamberleyne to K: Edw: 6.

Of the first Lo: Riche, Lo: Chauncello^r of England.

Of Thomas the third Lo: Darcy of Chiche, doone by Hulbert.

Of the last Lord Braye.

Of the first Lo: Burghley Cicill, Lo: Threasorer.

Of Sr Anthony Browne M^r of the horse to K: H: 8. and K: Edward ye 6.

Of Sr Nichls Carewe M^r of the horse to K: H: 8.

Of old Sir Thomas Lovell Threasorer of howseholde to K: H: 7.

Of Sir Henry Guilfourd Coumptroller to K: H: 8. drawne by Haunce Holbyn.

Of Sir Thomas Moore, Lo: Chauncello^r, drawne by Haunce Holbyn.

Of old sir Thomas Wyatt.

Of the yonger sir Thomas Wiat executed.

Of Sr Thomas Hennege, Vice chamberleyne.

Of Erasmus of Roterdame, all this eight drawne by Haunce Holbyn.

Of Sir Willm̃ Winter, doone by Seigar.

Of sir Frauncis Walsingham Secretary.

Of sir Willm̃ Peter Secretarye.

Of his sonne sir John Peter.

Of sir Willm̃ Drury slaine in fraunce drawne by Seigar.

Of sir Nichl̃s Bacon Knight Lo: Keper of the great Seale to Q: Elizabeth.

Of Sir James Wilfourd Capten of Haddington.

Of sir Phillip Sidney, Lo: governoʳ in Zealand.

Of sir Frauncis Drake the great Navigatoʳ (doone by Seigar) who sayled round about the worlde.

Of Sir John Lutterel, who died of the sweat in K. Edw: 6: tyme.

Of Sir John Haukins Treasurer of the Admiraltie drawne by Hubbert.

Of Mʳ Thomas Candishe who sayled round about the worlde.

Mʳ Churchyards picture.

An old man fancying a yong woman.

Of Mʳ Edward Dyer of the Corte, drawne by Hubbert.

Of Mʳ Edw: Shelley slayne at Mustleborough feilde, drawen by Haunce Eworthe.

Of Mʳ Thomas Wyndeham drowned in the Sea returneinge from Ginney.

Of Sir Edward Kelley rare for his knowledge in Alcumistrye.

Of the Earle of Salisburie, Cecill.

Of Julius Caesar.

Of Henry the third Empoʳ husbande to Mawd the Empresse.

Of Maximilian the Empoʳ grandfather to Charles the Vth.

Of Charles the Vth Empour.

Of Steven Batere King of Poland 1583.

Of the Duke of Savoy Regent in Flaunders doone by Jaques Pindar.

Of the Duke of Parma, Regent in Flaunders.

Of the Duke of Alva, governoʳ in Flaunders, doone by Anthony Moorey.

Of the Duke of Askott 1583.

Of the Duke of Sert.

Of the County Egmond executed at Bruxels, drawne by Steven.

Of the Duke of Burbon, slayne at the sackinge of Rome.

Of Henry Valoys last of that name, king of Fraunce, murthered.

Of Henrye Duke of Guyse murthered by the said kinge.

Of Albertus Cardinall of Austria now governor of the Lowe Countryes.

Of Andrew Dore Prince of Melph.

Of Phillip de Roye a councelor to the K. of Spayne.

Of Balthazar Geraertez gent, a Burgunyan, who murthered the Prince of Orange.

Of President Vigilius, a great Councello[r] to Charles the Vth, drawne by Jaques Pindar.

Of Haward a Dutch Juello[r], drawne for a Maisters prize by his brother Haunce Eworth.

Of Sebastian Gabote the great Navigator.

Of Ignatius de Loyola first founder of the societie of Jesus.

Of Franciscus Xaverius firste of the Jesuites whiche brought the Christian faythe unto y[e] Indians.

Sir Thomas Stukeley slayne wth the thre Christians kings

Of Bocchas.

Of Petrarke

Of Dante

Of Oriosto

Of sir Gefferey Chawcer knight.

Of Buckenel the Scott.

Of Raphael de Urbino, the great paynter.

Of Willm̄ Somer, K: H: 8: notable foole.

Of Theophrastus Paracelsus.

Margaret daughter to Duke of Anioy and wife to K. Henry 6th.

Of Elizabeth wife to King Edw: 4.

Of Margaret Countesse of Richemond and Darby and mother to K: H: 7.

Of Quene Katheryn, mother to Quene Marye.

Of Quene Jane, mother to K: Edw: 6:

Of Quene Katherin Parre, last wife to K. H: 8.

Of Isabel wife to Charles the Vth Empo[r], mother to K: Phillip.

Of Mary Quene of Scottes, executed in Englande.

Of Elizabeth Q: wife to the Frenche Kinge, Charles the 9:

Of Isabel daughter to Phillip the second K: of Spayne.

Of the Duchesse of Savoye.

~ Of a Frenche Duchesse.

Of the olde Countes of Salisburie behedded.

Of the olde Marquesse of Dorcett syster to Sir Edw: Wootton.

Of the Counties of Shroesburie 2 ẁyffe to the first Earle of Shroesburie, eldest daughter to Richard Earle of Warwicke, Beachampe.

Of the Ladie Margaret Lenox.

Of the Duchesse of Somersett, Stanhop.

Of Mary Duches of Northfolke, daughter to the last old Earle of Arundell Fitzallen doone by Haunce Eworth.

Of the Lady Marques of Northampton borne in Swedlande.

Of the Countes of Huntington, daughter to the Duke of Northumbrelande.

Of the Countesse of Lincolne, daughter to the Earle of Kildare.

Of the Countesse of Warwicke, daughter to the Earle of Bedfourd.

Of the Countesse of Essex wife to the 2 Earle of Essex & widow to sir Phillip Sidney.

Of Marye daughter to Sr William Candishe wyfe to Gilbert earle of Shrewesburye y^t now is.

Of the Lady Jane Graye executed.

Of the Lady Katheryn Graye, maried to the Earle of Hertfourd.

Of the Countesse of Arundell second wife to the late old Earle of Arundell Fitzallen, daughter to Sir John Arundell of Lanherne in Cornewall.

Of the Countesse of Arundell, wife to Phillip Earle of Arundell, daughter to the Lo: Dacres of the northe.

Of yor Lo: first wife daughter to the old Earle of Arundell Fitz-allen drawne by Steveñ.

Of my La: yor second wife daughter to the Lo: John Darcy of Chiche, drawne by Hubbart.

Of the La: Darcy of Chiche wife to Thomas the third Lo: Darcy.

Of the La: Guilfourd wife to Sir Henry Guilfourd Coumptroller drawne by Haunce Holbyn.

Of an Italian gentlewoman drawen by her selfe and presented to the olde Earle of Arundell in Italy.

Of a Dutche Ladye.

Of an Italian gentlewoman in great reputacon wth her husband for her beawty.

Of Shores wyfe concubyne to K: Edw: 4.

Of a bride of Constantinople.

Of Mary Magdalen, drawen by Frauncs Flores.

Of Lucretia drawne by Cornelius Vancleave of Anwarpe.

Of Pompeia.

Of Cleopatra in water colours.

Of thre Italian Ladyes.

(*Added later.*) Off Mary Medices daughter to Francise Duke of Thoscane and to Joan of Austria, and wife to Henrie of Borbon Kinge of France.

OTHER PICTURES AND TABLES.

A speciall picture of Christ cast in mould by Raphael de Urbino brought into England from Rome by Cardynall Poole.

Thre notable peics of hangings, One of Christ his passage with his Crosse to his Passion, The other of his passion, And the third of his Judgement doone by Henry Houmfray, Thes were thos especiall peices, y^t honge in S^{ct} Magnus churche at the bridge foote in London. } geve away.

. A large picture of o^r blessed Lady with Christ her sonne in her Armes.

A large table of the Passion of Christ crucified, doone by Mr Schore of Utright.

A table of the fower Evangelists, supporting Christ.

A picture of S^{ct} Hierome.

The picture of our Ladie wth Christ in her armes togith^r with St Catherine and St Jhon Baptist on Canvasse.

The Passion of Christ cutt in black stone.

A great large table in folds of the Passion, very auncient and notable.

A table of Sainct Pawle preachinge.

A large table of Charité doone by Vincent of Macklen.

A large table of Noe, doone by Fraunce Flores of Anwarpe.

A large table of the Rape of Helena, drawne by Cleave Haunce of Anwarpe.

A table of a young man fancying the riche old woman.

A large table of the maner of banquetting in Flaunders.

A table of Anchises and Aeneas.

A table of Juno and Jupiter.

A table of Venus and Adonis.

A table of Dives and Lazarus.

A table of the building of Babell.

A table of Judith and Holofernes.

A table of the sale of Joseph by his brethren.

A table on the conyng prospectnie of death and a woman, doone by Hilliarde.

A table of the Ticlenes of Fortune.

A counterfeyt of an old booke.

A table of Cookerye.

Two large tables of China woorke.

A table of Hercules.

The 9: worthies in roundels enealed.

A great table of the birthe of Christ.

A great table of the fower Evangelistes.

A great table of the conversion of S^{ct} Pawle.

A great booke of Pictures doone by Haunce Holbyn of certeyne Lordes, Ladyes, gentlemen and gentlewomen in King Henry the 8: his tyme, their names subscribed by Sr John Cheke Secretary to King Edward the 6 wch booke was King Edward the 6.

~~The picture of Sr Edward Kelley, who was the~~ ~~of golde in~~ before

A great table of the temptacions of S^{ct} Antony.

A great table of a Dutche woman selling of fruyte.

A pycter of St Francis.

~~The old Morley Henry, doone by Albert Dure.~~

The Picture of Lodovicus Orioustus the Poete done by Lucios the payte[r].

The picture of Count de la Marche who wan Bryll in Holland for the Prynce of Orange.

Other Pictures in small of Christ, our Ladie and his Saints, wrought upon brass, and adorned wth marbles and marble Pillars.

Sum of the valew of the picture 623[£].

Imago Christi	S[ta] Ursula	S[ts] Bernardus
Christus crucifixus	S[ta] Dorothea	S[ts] Ambrosius
Christus spinis coro-	S[ta] Agnes	S[ts] Hieronimus
natus	S[ta] Clara	S[ts] Anselmus
Salvator 12 annor.	S[ta] Margarita	S[ts] Tho: Aquinas
Salvator portans	S[ta] Justina	Venerab. Beda
crucem humeris	S[ts] Joseph cum puero	S[ts] Sebastianus
Salvator portans	Jesu	S[ts] Hiacinthus
mundum.	S[ts] Petrus Apostolus	S[ts] Thadeus
Imago beatae virginis	S[ts] Paulus Apt$\overline{\text{us}}$	S[ts] Franciscus
portantes Jesum	S[ts] Philippus	S[ts] Rocchus
Beata virgo Maria	S[ts] Jacopus apt$\overline{\text{us}}$	S[ts] Anthonius abbas
Mater dei	S[ts] Symon apt$\overline{\text{us}}$	S[ts] Laurentius
S[ta] Maria Magdalena	S[t] Jhon Apt$\overline{\text{us}}$	S[ts] Anthonius de
S[ta] Maria Magdalena	S[t] Thomas apt$\overline{\text{us}}$	Padua
Titiana	S[ts] Matheus	S[ts] Didacus
S[ta] Caecilia.	S[t] Lucas	S[ts] Thomas Cantuari-
S[ta] Catherina	S[ts] Marcus	ensis
S[ta] Catherina Senen-	S[ts] Jhon Baptist	S[ts] Nicholaus
sis	S[ts] Bartholomeus	S[ts] Dominicus
S[ta] Martha	S[ts] Mathias	S[ts] Franciscus de
S[ta] Barbara	S[ts] Andreas	Paula
S[ta] Lucia	S[ts] Stephanus	S[ts] Benedictus
S[ta] Apollonia	S[ts] Jacobus ·	S[ts] Ludovicus rex
S[t] Agatha	S[ts] Augustinus	Galliae
S[t] Helena	S[ts] Gregorius doctor	S[ts] Peter Martyr"

"A SUM̄ARYE of certayne stuffe within your Lo: houses the xxii[th] of May Anno 1590 the Inventoryes of the partyculers remaynyng in bookes subscribed by John Lambton, gentleman, steward of household to yo[r] Lo: and under the handes of the severall wardropers there.

Sutes of hanginges of arras, sylke and tapistre . .	lvii
Turkye carpettes of sylke	xi
Carpettes of velvet for tables and wyndowes . .	xv
Other Turky Carpettes	iiii[xx]xv (95)
Testers 12, Sparvers 3, Pavylions 3, Canapies 6, &	
Feild beddes 4, wrought with gold, sylver and sylke	xl

Coveringes and Quyltes of sylke	xl
Chares of clothe of gold, velvet, and sylke . . .	lxxvi
Quisshins of clothe of gold, velvet, and sylke . .	cix
Stooles of clothe of gold, velvet, and sylke . .	iiii^{xx} (80)
Pallet beddes with their bolsters	lxxv
Pyllowes	iiii^{xx}
Lyvereye beddes	iiii^{xx}xv (95)
Woolbeddes	xxxii
Counter poyntes and Coverlettes . . .	lxix
Fustyans	liii
Rugges	ciii
Woollen Coverlettes and blankettes	lv
Travyses of sylke for wyndowes	xxi
Bedsteades gylt	iiii
Bed steades of walnuttre and markatre . . .	xxiii
Bedsteades of weynskot	xl
Chares of walnuttre and Markatre	xvii
Stooles of walnuttre and Markatre	lvii
Fourmes of walnuttre	xx
• Tables of walnuttre and Markatre	xxv
Tables of marble	xiiii
Cubboordes of walnuttre and Markatre . . .	viii
Chares of read Spanishe lether	ii
Stooles of nedlewoorke cruell	x
Stooles of read Spanishe lether	vii
Stooles of waynskot	cxviii
Cubboordes of Waynskot	xliiii
Tables of waynscot	l
Andirons of Brasse and parcell Copper, paires . .	xlii
Great standing wynd Instruments with stoppes .	viii
Vyrgynalles paires	v
Rygalles paires	ii
Jryshe harpes	ii
Lutes	viii
Howboyes	x
Bumbardes	iii
Crumpe hornes	iiii
Retorders	xv
Vyolens	xiii
Vyoles	xli
Sagbuttes	iiii
Cornettes	xii

The Stuffe estemd
5380.

The Armo^r valewed . . iiii^c iiii^{xx} xvii viiid (£480. 17. 8.)
The Plate & sylver vessell

The Library Registred in a boke wryten by Alcocke, my L: of
Chechester his L: servant, A° 1596 with all the rest of my boks
my selfe have dysparsed sundery ways."

It is much to be regretted that this Library Register is not to be
found among the numerous interesting manuscript books of this
time found at Sandbeck.

After the time of John, Lord Lumley, Lumley Castle remained
unaltered until the eighteenth century. Richard, the first Earl,
planned several alterations, but died before he could carry them
out, so they were executed by his son, Richard, the second Earl.
The stuccoed decoration of the Banqueting Hall is said to have
been the work of two Italians, who came to England for the purpose.

The following fragment of a letter has been found among the
papers at Sandbeck. It seems to have been written in the second
half of the eighteenth century. "We set forward for Newcastle.
I saw on our way Chester Church in which there is nothing curious
but the monuments of the Lumley family from the conquest—from
thence we went on to Lumleye Castle w^h is quite a perfect Building
not in the least injured by time Tis all of a most beautiful stone:
has four large fronts built round a Court, and a fine Tower at each
Corner: it stands high has a great deal of Wood about it, & commands a fine distant view on all sides: tis the most magnificent
House I ever saw, tho' many are more decorated: the Hall is a
vast size, and wel proportion'd but entirely plain White walls hung
with old Family Pictures: its plainness sets off the Dining Room
it leads to, w^h is the largest I ever saw, & finish'd in the most
beautiful wrought stuccos both Top and Sides, that ever was be-
held: the Furniture, as marble slabs, glasses chimney piece etc was
all equal: There common dining Room where the Possessor of this
Grand Mansion was lolling alone we did not see: besides this there
is a long string of magnificent rooms all furnish'd with Crimson
Damask—over wch was hung fine Family Pictures: overhead the
Rooms were equally magnificent: & from the Towers a most
glorious prospect: but nothing is more admirable than the Kitchen
Servants' Hall & all the offices on the ground flour—& what they
call hunting & shooting apartments on the same Flour any of us
private Folks, in our own Houses shou'd reccon very grand well-
finished apartments. I have been particularly particular, in the
account of this House, because Miss Jenny had such an inclination
to see it and to know what sort of a place it was so if you please
you may let her know the loss she has had."

A very different opinion of the Castle is given in a letter written
by Lady Carlow to her sister Lady Louisa Stuart on July 7th, 1781.
"Lord Scarbrough's 2 places in one of which is a fine Abbey in
ruins, the other Lumley Castle hardly worth seeing."

An account of the first of the disastrous sales mentioned on p. 265 is given in a letter written to Lady Louisa by the Duchess of Buccleugh, dated Dalkeith Palace, 3rd August, 1784. "We drove through Welbeck & Worksop Parks & theyn joined the old Road at Doncaster and plodded on except stopping at Lumley Castle to see if there was anything worth bidding for at the auction. I never saw anything so completely melancholy and neglected as the place. The House is a very good one and many tolerable pictures but none very good—A great many of the Scarbrough family which will sell for nothing I daresay. It is quite a melancholy thing to think of a great family place so entirely destroyed, indeed all his places will be the same for everything in general is to be sold. Luckily this Lord Scarbrough is a poor creature & I suppose does not feel it much."

For a long time the Castle was uninhabited, but the ninth Earl again used it at intervals, and at his death in 1884 it became the residence of the Dowager Countess, as was said before.

The original estates in Durham comprised, besides Lumley Castle, lands at Great Lumley, Cold Heselden, Houghton le Clay, Houghton le Spring, etc. The Great Lumley estate early became the property of the younger branch of the family. So did also, as we have seen, the Heyford estates. The various lands gained through the marriages with heiresses have been noticed in the course of the History. We have fourteen MS. books of the time of John, Lord Lumley, of lands in his possession, the first being dated 1581 and the last 1606. They are written in Latin, with, at the end, "A Breife declaration of one yere begonne the nynth of September . . . and ending the viith of September . . . Of stores, Acates, flower, fewell, Boordwages, Forrayne paym^{ts}, wyne spices etc."

Below is a summary of the account of the estates in the last of these books:

In Sussex. Lands at Stansted, Westborne with Prinsted, Singleton, Charlton, hundred of Box, with Stockbridge, Halinge, Leefarme, Lowdham, Kyndforde Rectory, Oldshoram, Overfolde, Hasfolde, Stoughton. Value £1,460 6s. 11d.

In Surrey. Lands at Cuddington *alias* Nonesuche, Westchayme, Estchayme, Ewells. Value £185 18s. 9½d.

In Kent. No places mentioned. Value £21 7s. 8d.

Towrehill. (Lord Lumley, as will be remembered, had a house there.) Value £109 6s. 8d.

Kylton in Yorks. Value £216 17s. 7d.

Harte in Hartlepool, Durham. Value £343 14s. 5d.

Lumley, Domain and Castle of. Value £295 12s. 8d.

Northumberland. Wytton, etc. Value £86 19*s.* 8*d.*
Total £2,720 14*s.* 4½*d.*

When Elizabeth, widow of John, Lord Lumley, died, all the property in Surrey came to his sister, Barbara, married to Humphrey
Lloyd, grandfather to Dr. Robert Lloyd of Cheam. Also, as we
have seen, the Towerhill property was left by Lady Lumley to her
nieces, so that probably Richard, father of the first earl, only
inherited the Lumley property. His wife inherited lands in
Gloucestershire, about which there are many papers at Sandbeck,
but we hear nothing further about them.

But the greatest addition to the lands held by the Lumleys was
that made by James, Viscount Castleton, to his cousin, Thomas
Lumley (see p. 179). These estates were best described by quoting
a paper, recently found at Sandbeck, called a "Rentall." It is
undated, but the writing shows it to have been drawn up about the
year 1680. In the original the names of all the tenants are given
and the value of the land held by each; but these names are here
omitted and the totals only given except when there is anything of
interest:

" A perfecte Rentall of the Righte Hon[ble] the Lorde Castletons
Estate in Yorkshire:/

	£	s.	d.	£	s.	d.
Roach Abbey (5 tenants) . . .				90	8	4
Stone (5 tenants)				33	8	8
Marris & Spittle (3 tenants) . .				32	13	04
Bawtry. Mr. Lister & Mr. Phillips .				5	15	4
Maultby (10 tenants) . . .				39	13	4
Sandbecke						
The Domaines	60	0	0			
(6 tenants)	28	0	4			
Thornborry hill . . .	6	0	0	94	0	4
Stainton (5 tenants) . . .				47	3	4
Bagley						
(4 tenants)	70	1	0			
Carrhouse	28	0	0			
Stainton Woodgrave . .	2	0	0	100	1	0
Braitwell						
The Tythes	60	0	0			
Stainton Cheife Rents . .	2	19	6			
Maultby Cheife Rents . .	2	10	0			
Sladhooton Cheife Rents .	7	5	1			
Austerfeild Coppiehold Rents .	5	7	10	78	2	5
Besides Coppiehold Fines there at the						
will of the Lord						

	£	s.	d.
The folds The severall Tenants there .	40	0	0
Sandbecke Parke The Compasse about 4 miles			
The outwoods Containinge severall hundreds of Acres			

	£	s.	d.
Sum totall per Ann: besides Woods & parke	561	6	1

A perfecte Rentall of the Righte hon^ble the Lord Castletons Estate in Lincolnshire:/

	£	s.	d.	£	s.	d.
Reresby (9 tenants)				274	0	0
Stainton (16 tenants)				315	1	8
Scotherne						
(10 tenants)	78	6	0			
Scotherne parsonage . . .	55	10	0			
Widd. Cole for Stowpark . .	90	0	0	223	16	0
Scotherne Coppiehold Rents yearly besides the Fines which are arbitrary .				10	0	8
				233	16	8
Tetney Grange						
(16 tenants)	52	11	2			
Item for lands lay at Thoris . ·	1	1	0			
Idem for Windles	0	4	0			
Tetney frehold						
(15 tenants)	137	11	8			
Osgreby tyth meadow . . .	1	6	8	192	14	6
Holton						
Mr. Thompson per tyth . .	32	0	0			
(3 tenants)	12	6	8	44	6	8
Willoughton & Blyborough						
The hall and ground therunto belonging	60	0	0			
(9 tenants)	139	18	8	199	18	8
Hackthorne (5 tenants) . . .				(hole).		
Fristrop						
Clerke farme	7	10	0			
(5 tenants)	29	4	0	36	14	0
Middle Rasine (4 tenants) . . .				26	0	0
Moreby & Wilkby. (2 tenants) . .				12	6	8
Fillingham						
(14 tenants)	58	7	4			
Maulthouse	2	0	0	60	7	4
Kursney (13 tenants)				168	19	0

Tofte and Newton	£	s.	d.	£	s.	d.
(33 tenants)	328	0	10			
Longholme	3	13	4			
Stannyholds	5	0	0			
	336	14	2			
Moreby free Rents	4	1	5	340	15	7
Skegnes (24 tenants)	758	19	5			
paid out of Skegnes as Appears by severall Tenn^{ts} which Mr Rutland Saund has onely for life per Ann.	300	0	0	1108	19	0
Saxby (3 tenants)	108	0	0			
paid besides by the Tenn^{ts} there to my Lords brothers . . .	442	0	0	550	0	0
paid besides by the severall Tennts of Willerton & Blyborough to my Lady Saunderson my Lords Aunt for her life	300	7	4			
Willoughton Monke Mannor Copiehold Rents	7	15	6			
Stow per Ann.	30	0	0	338	2	10

There is in Lincolnshire aboute 500 acres of wood not valewed & there is I thinke lefte out of the Rental of Skegnes the marsh which is now Improved cont. above 80 acres let to Mr Whittingham & Jo: Saunderson per ann. at £50.

The estate may be improved more than is given in, in the Rentall as followeth

Yorkshire/

	£	s.	d.
The demesne of Sandbecke in the particular is but £60 per Ann. but is worth above £100 per Ann.; to be added	40	0	0
Mr Hunt is but £35 per Ann. which is £50 per ann. to be added	20	0	0
		(sic)	
Carrhouse is but £28 per Ann. which should be £36. To be added	8	0	0
Braithwell Tythes £60 per Ann. which were alwaies untill letten to your Servant £70, to be added . . . , ...	10	0	0
Sandbecke Parke not valewed which is £120	120	0	0
The outwoods not valewed which are £100 per Ann. & if your Lp pleased might be much more the grasse besides the Wood . .	100	0	0

	£	s.	d.
The wood yearly to be Sold & so continue for ever	500	0	0
Coppiehold fines etc.	10	0	0
	808	0	0

Lincolnshire.

	£	s.	d.
Mr Rutland Saunderson pays but £80 which was formerly £130 to be added . . .	50	0	0
Stow parke £90 per Ann. which should be £100 to be added	10	0	0
Stainton Lordship much undervalued			
Scotherne Coppiehold Fines which are arbitrary not valewed			
Willoughton given in at £500 per Ann. which may be improved to £1000 per Ann. . .	500	0	0
Fillingham if your Lordships & Mrs Wray Estate were united: that lordship is improvable £500 per Ann.			
The like in Owmby & other places where your Estates are intermixed			
Tofte & Newton improvable when you please	150	0	0
Skegnes improvable 4/³ or 5/³ per acre according as other landlords lets which will come to above £200 per Ann.	200	0	0
	910	0	0

No yearely valew set upon Lincolnshire woods.

Mortgage
 £2000 to Hanson out of Skegnes.
 £500 to Pym out of Skegnes
 500 to Thomas Hindleby out of Friskney.
 300 to Halley out of a Ferme called yᵉ Folds in Maultby & Tickhill.
 200 to Fullingham out of Carhouse ferme in Tickhyll
 1000 to Hall out of Stow parke.

(Endorsed) For the Right Honble the Lord Viscount Castleton.
  Leave this at Mr Alexanders house over against the Crosse Kayes Taverne in Bedford Streete in Covent Garden. London."

In describing these places that which excites most interest is the first named. The ruins of the ancient abbey of Roche lie in a deep valley about three miles south-west of the town of Tickhill, the upper part running nearly east and west, the lower north and south. It is so concealed by high lands as not to be seen till one is just upon it, especially when coming to it from the direction of Sandbeck, all that side being a very high rock of stone, whence doubtless the abbey had its name. A natural phenomenon, probably heightened by art, contributed to induce the Cistercian monks from Newminster to make choice of this spot; for among the accidental forms which portions of the fractured limestone had assumed was discovered a resemblance to our Saviour on the Cross. This image was held in considerable reverence during the whole period of the existence of the monastery, and devotees were accustomed to come in pilgrimage to "our Saviour of the Roche."

On the arrival of the monks in 1147 they were welcomed by Richard le Builli, Lord of Maltby, and by Richard, son of Turgis, called also de Wickersley, who owned the valley, their lands being divided by a stream. They agreed that on whichever side of the water the monks should choose to build their abbey, they should be joint founders of it. According to Burton it was on July 30th, 1147, that Richard le Builli granted "to GOD and to S. Mary and the monks of Rupe" all his wood along the middle way from Eilrichethorpe to Lowthewaite, and so to the water which divides Maltby from Hooten, also two sarts which were Gamel's with a great field near and common pasture for one hundred sheep, six-score to the hundred, in the soccage of Maltby; while Richard, son of Turgis, granted to them all the lands from the borders of Eilrichethorpe to the brow of the hill beyond the rivulet which runs from Fogswell and to a heap of stones which lies in Elsi's sart, and beyond the road as far as the wool-pit and by the head of the field at Hartshow to the borders of Slade Hooten; all the land and wood within these boundaries and common of pasture through all his lands and five carats in his woods of Wickersley.

John, son of Richard le Builli, confirmed his father's grant, and Pope Urban III. by his Bull dated 1186 ratified all grants made to these monks and exempted them from tithes.

The following account of the Abbots of Roche is translated from a document, given in Dugdale's "Monasticon." The original was formerly in S. Mary's Tower, York, but unfortunately it has been destroyed:

"Memorandum. that in the year of grace 1147 was founded the house of Rupe on the 3rd of the Kalends of Augusts" (July 30), "whereof brother Durand was first abbot for 12 years" (1147-1159); (they have coined the word *abbatazavit*), "after him Dionisius for another 12 years (1159-1171), and after him Roger de Tickehilla for 8 years (1171-1179), and after him Hugh de Waddeworth for 5 years (1179-1184), at which time was bought Koreby Grange" (this must

and Convent of Roche of divers grants of lands and releases made to that house, viz., by Henry, son of Richard de Walcringham, of lands in Walcringham and Walcre with the pasture called Elger-oxgang, pertaining to the town of Walcringham; by Richard, son of Henry, son of Richard de Walcringham of lands in Walcringham; by Adam, son of William de Walcringham of a toft in the town of Walcre with the ferry pertaining to that toft, and land in Walcringham; by Henry, son of Robert Arnewy, of Walcringham, of lands at Fritheshend and of pasture in the common of Walcringham; by Henry, son of Robert, son of Arnewy de Walcringham, of lands in Upper Walton and Walcringham and a meadow in Monkeboye; by Henry, son of Robert Mamurri of Walcringham, of lands and pastures in Walcringham and of a piece of reclaimed land which they held of the gift of Roger the chaplain, and of the service and homage which Henry, son of Isabella, owed to him for a tenement in Walcringham; by Adam, son of William of Walcringham, of land in Drengesflete which they held of his fee of the gift of Roger de Osberton, and of the service of Geoffrey of Fulham, and for a plot of ground there called ' Morfurlong,' and lands in Schepewyk and Walcringham; by Geoffrey, son of Alan de Trenta, of land in Walcringham, with the homage of Walter de Misterton, the service due for land in Cormanhaghe, pasture appertaining to land in Walcringham and the service of Geoffrey de Fulholme, and of John, son of Roger, and also of lands in Walcringham and meadows at Helpol, Monkebothe and Walcringham."

On October 29th, in the same year, a licence was granted for the alienation in mortmain to the Abbot and Convent of Roche by Henry de Cokewald of a messuage, twenty acres of land and twenty acres of meadow in Roxeby; by Alan, son of Warin de Roxeby, of a messuage and a bovate of land in the same town; and by Hugh de la Wyk of a toft and two and a half acres of land in the same town, all of which are of the fee of the abbot, and are worth 23s. a year according to their true value, as appears by an inquisition made by John Abel, escheator this side Trent, and returned into the Chancery, in part satisfaction of a licence granted to them to acquire lands, tenements and rents to the value of £10 a year. On December 8th, 1315, protection with clause nolumus was granted for one year to the Abbot of Roche.

Among the Close Rolls of Edward II., there is a parchment, dated York, December 16th, 1318, in Latin, to this effect: " The King to his beloved Abbot and Convent of Messenden. He requests that they will admit into their house, William Bellard, ' charetter,' who long served the king and his father, whom the king is sending to them, and that they will deliver to him the necessaries of life in food and clothing according to the requirements of his estate, and that they will cause letters patent to be made under the common seal of their house, granting the same to him, writing back an account of their proceedings herein." " In the same way the underwritten are sent to the underwritten"; and among these: " Nicholas Taunt to the Abbot and Convent of Roche, afterward on the 10th day of March to the Prior and Convent of Chacumbe."

William was elected abbot on December 9th, 1324. During his time the Pope sent three mandates to Alan of Cosneburg, D.C.L., who was the Archbishop of York's proctor at the court of Rome, and in each case he sent a concurrent mandate to the Abbot of Roche, the Prior of Bradewell, and another. In the first of these, dated January 23rd, 1328, reservation is made to Alan de Cosneburg, Canon of Wells, of a dignity or office in the same, notwithstanding that he is rector of Hikilton in the diocese of York, and has a canonry and prebend of St. Mary's, Stafford, value twelve marks each, and has papal provision made to him of a canonry of Wells and the prebend of Yatton. Hikilton is to be resigned. This provision is renewed on May 1st, and here Hikilton is still mentioned as one of his benefices. There still seems to have been some difficulty in his path, as further, on February 25th, 1330, provision is made to him at the request of William, Archbishop of York, of a canonry of York, with reservation of a prebend, notwithstanding that he is rector of a moiety of Roderham, and has a canonry of Wells and the prebend of Yatton, of none of which is he able to obtain possession; and is rector of Hikilton, value 12 marks, and has canonries and prebends of Ripon, value 100s., and St. Mary's, Stafford, value 12 marks, there being an appeal to the Pope against him, touching the prebend of Ripon. Also on June 14th, 1329, when the Pope sent a mandate to John de Kilnhurst of the diocese of York, with reservation of a benefice in the gift of the Abbot and Convent of St. Mary's, York, he sent a concurrent mandate to the Abbot of Roche, Alan de Conesburghe, Canon of Wells, and another named.

These, for convenience' sake, have been grouped together, but there are two other notices of Roche in the Patent Rolls for 1329. The first is only a protection "with clause nolumus" for one year for the Abbot of Roche, dated October 24th; but the second is more important, as showing the lawlessness of the times. On November 20th, a commission of "oyer and terminer" was given to John Travers, Robert de Scarburgh, William Bassett, and Adam de Hoperton, on complaint by the Abbot of Roche that Edmund de Wastenays, knight, Thomas and Edmund, his sons, John de Herthill, chaplain, Hugh Roer, prester, Ralph de Thorpe, carpenter, John, son of Alice de Kyneton, John de Clsource, Robert de Wales, William Kirkeman, William, son of Emma de Herthill, Robert de Wastenays, and others entered his dwelling-house at Totewik, co. York, seized and took away sixteen oxen and one hundred and sixty sheep, value £30, besides other goods, broke his windmill, threw it down, and cut its timber into small pieces, and assaulted his servants, and expelled them from the said house.

The next abbot was Adam of Gykleswyk, who was elected in 1330; but there is some confusion, as in Dr. Hutton's "Extracts," besides this entry there is another later, to the effect that Adam, elected Abbot of Rupe, made obedience and was blessed March 20th, 1346-7. In 1333 a grant was made to various convents, and other religious bodies, that their grants towards the expenses of the marriage of Eleanor, the king's sister, should not prejudice them or their successors as a precedent; and among these one was made to the Abbot and Convent of Roche, who had given twenty shillings. On February 3rd, 1334-5, protection with clause nolumus was granted for one year to the Abbot of Roche. On November 22nd, 1345, John de Warenna, Earl of Surrey, granted to the Abbot and Convent of Roche the advowson of the church of Haytefield in Yorkshire; but in the following reign of Richard II., this seems to have been claimed by the Hospital of St. John of Jerusalem in Clerkenwell, as we find a ratification of the grant made on July 14th, 1379, provided that the abbot finds thirteen monks to celebrate divine service daily for the good estate of the king and his mother, Philippa, while living, and for their souls after death.

Meanwhile there had been two new abbots, Simon de Bankewell, who was elected on October 25th, 1349, and John de Aston, who made obedience and was blessed by the archbishop on November 23rd, 1358. On June 26th, 1380, a chantry of one chaplain was founded in the chapel of St. Mary, on the north side of Thorp Salvyn, co. York, granting to him for his support a messuage there and a yearly rent of fifteen marks, issuing from two messuages and ten shops in the parishes of St. Michael and St. Peter, Cornhill, and St. Olave, Mugwel Strete, London. The first chaplain, who must be resident, is to be Sir John de Shirokes, and on the voidance of the chantry by cession or death, the Prior and Convent of Wirsop, in the diocese of York, are within fifteen days to bestow it on a fit man; failing them, the Abbot and Convent of Welbek; failing them, the Abbot and Convent of Roche.

After this there is a long blank of over fifty years, during which we do not even know the name of the abbot. Burton gives the name, Robert, in 1396, which has been copied into the various histories, but he gives no reference, so that we cannot authenticate the statement. The documents in the Record Office for this period have not yet been catalogued, and Dr. Hutton even fails us here. He only tells us that on June 7th, 1438, a commission was issued to bless John Wakefield, Abbot of Rupe, and later we have from him, what is very rare, the mention of this abbot's death, as on August 7th, 1465; John Gray was elected Abbot of Rupe after the death of John de Wakefield.

In 1479, David, abbot of the new monastery of the Cistercian order, and visitor of the monastery of St. Mary de Rupe, in the diocese of York, certifies to the Lord Archbishop that John Gray, Abbot of Rupe, has resigned in July, and that William Tykell was elected the same day. After that, they succeeded each other rapidly, as Thomas Thorn became abbot on December 10th, 1486; William Burton on February 28th, 1487-8; John Morpeth on August 18th, 1491; and John Heslington on December 13th, 1503.

In Henry VIII.'s reign we can again obtain access to original documents, through Brewer's "Letters and Papers of Henry VIII." The first notice of Roche is that on October 1st, 1514, the abbot's name is mentioned among the recognisances of the repayment of loans.

The following letter was written to Wolsey in 1526: "Please it your grace to be advertisede that where as hertofore for certeyn resonable considerations your grace did respit and differre the confirmation of thabbot that in your Monasterie of Fontaunce within your diocese here. Commaunding unto us that after góode knowledge by dewe performance hadde aswell upon his devoute vertuouse and religous liffyng as of his activitie, wisdom, and policie, not only in the observaunce and kepyng of the Religion, but allso in the advauncement and profitt of his house in the temporalities; we shulde in time convenient certifie your grace of his abilitie unto the said Rowme. So it is that according to your said most honorable commaundment, we have with good diligence indevorde our selffs to knowe and to have dewe intelligence in the premisses and as we doo perceyve the said abbot, that is not only of good and vertuouse liffyng and well lernede, but allso he is right wyese, discreit, politike, and of goode experience, and gravitie and after our poore mynde he is the most able persone within the convent there to have the said Rowme, and we trust verayly yf it may so stande with your most graciouse pleasur: that he will hereafter so discreitly and wiesly governe the same that it shall not only be to the pleasur of god and contentation of your grace but allso to the great and singler profiet and advauncement of your saide monasterie in time to com. In consideration wherof in our most humble names we besuché your grace to be good and graciouse lorde unto hym, commaunding hym to be admitted and confirmed abbot theré, accordynge to the statutes and anceant customs as well of Religion as of your saide monasterie and allso to gyve and graunt unto hym your paternall benediction; and Jesus preserve your grace. From York the XXIIII daye of September

"Your most   servant, Bryan Higdon.
"Your moste humble and perpetuall bondman, William, thabbot of Ryvall.
"And your assured servitor, John, thabbot of Roche."

Tithe of herbage for pasture for 24 beasts, 18s.

Tithe of pannage for pigs, 1s.

Tithe of woods there, viz. 1 *fuell tree* from payment of the bailiff, 1s.

Great tithes in Hatfield, £8.

Thorne, £7.

Steynford, £5.

Tenth of fens, £1 10s. 0d.

Wool and lambs, £2.

Oblations, £2.

Small & private tithes, £12.

Mortuary fees, 6s. 8d.

Tithe of eel ponds at Braithmere, 11s. 0d.

> Average yearly total, £41 14s. 8d.
>
> Total value to the aforesaid monastery £261 19s. 8d.
> of which

REPRISALS

Returned rents

Rents returned annually to divers persons as the lord of Sprotburgh from the land in Marr and Barnby, 12s. 8d.

To the bailiff of the King's Wappentake at Stafurth from the said land, 1s.

To Roger Fretwell from land in Bramley, 7d.

To the King's chaplain at Connesburgh from land in Doncaster with a share in £11 from a quarter of the mill of Connesburgh, 2s. 6d.

To the chaplain of Steynforthe, 4s. 2½d.

Total to the bailiff of the lord of Stafurthe wappentake from land in Sladehoten, 6d.

To William Fitzwilliam knight from one tenement there, 3s. 6d.

To the Castle of Tickhill, 6d.

To the hospital of S. Leonard of York from land in Raynesfeld, 2s.

One quarter of wheat paid to the mill of Connesburgh from land in Brathewell, 6s. 8d.

To the bailiff of Tikhill per annum to the hospital of S. Leonard of York from land in Sandebek, 2s.

To the prior of Blida [Blyth] for a parcel of land in Sandebek, 1s.

To the bailiff of the King from Bers in the Honour of Tikhill, 10s. 10d.

To the king's bailiff from the wappentake of Straford, 6s. 8d.

From lands in Lumby and Austen with hereditary rights at Westines for land there, 1½d.

To the lord of Haddon for land in Quasshe in the county of Derby, £1 10s.

To the Cathedral of Lichefield from the aforesaid land, 6s.

To the prior of Blida for land in Tortworth, 1s.

Total per annum, £4 12s. 2d.

Alms.

Distributed annually in alms at the Lord's supper, £1.

Wax burning continually before the altar of the foundation of Rich. Furnivall, £1 9s.

Distributed in mass celebrated for the soul of Thomas de Bella Aqua per annum, 5s.

Total, £2 14s.

Fees.

Fees to divers persons as to William Fitz-William, knight steward of Armethorp, £2.

To Miles Wyn bailiff there, £1.

To John Grene bailiff and receiver of Barnbye, 10s.

To Thomas Grene steward of Thrustonland with rights, £1.

To Henry Gillott bailiff there, £1.

To Henry Whithede bailiff of Hilbright, £1.

To Thos. lord Burgh steward of Rokesby, £1 6s. 8d.

To Robert Thornabye bailiff there, £1.

Total per annum to Robt. Burton bailiff of Sturrop with rights, 10s.

Totals as aforesaid, £9 6s. 8d.

Pensions and for money paid for the Synod and for Curates.

Money annually paid from the Rectory of Haitfield as for the pension annually paid to the Vicar there, £15.

Pension annually paid to the Archbishop of York at the Synod, £7 10s. 4d.

And annually paid to the Chaplain of the King from Haitfield, 7s. 9d.

Total, £22 18s. 1d.

Amount of reprisals, £39 10s. 11d.

Clear value therefore to the Abbey, £222 8s. 5d."

Meantime the accusations made by Wycliffe against the monasteries had been repeated again and again. The first commission issued in 1489 by Pope Innocent VIII., at the instigation of Cardinal Morton, for a general investigation throughout England into the behaviour of the regular clergy, brought many evils to light, but had no good result. In 1511 a second investigation was attempted by Archbishop Warham, and a third by Wolsey twelve years later; but in each case, though exposure of crimes followed, no remedy was found. Finally, in the summer of 1535, Cromwell issued a Commission for a general Visitation of the religious houses, the universities, and other spiritual corporations. The persons appointed to conduct the inquiry were Doctors Legh, Leyton, and Ap. Rice. They began their work at Oxford on September 12th, and it spread from there all over England. On January 7th, 1535-6, Legh dates a letter to Cromwell from Roche Abbey. The result of his visit is found in the "Report of the Visitation of the Monasteries," kept at the Record Office. The original is in Latin, of which the following is a translation:

"Rupe alias Roche. Guilty of licentious practices, William Hela, John Wheland, Robert Reme, Henry Willson, John Doddesworth. John Robynson, suspected of treason against his Majesty, and imprisoned at York. *Superstition.* Here was made a pilgrimage to the image of the Crucifixion, found (as is believed) in the stone and held in reverence. *Founder.* The Earl of Cumberland. *Annual rent.* £170. *Debts.* £20."

The last Abbot of Roche was Henry Cundall, as we know by the documents at the time of the Dissolution, but there is no note of the date of his succession. On June 3rd, 1538, Sir John Nevyell, who seems to have been intimately concerned in the movement, wrote to "Dr. Lee," as he spells him, as follows:

"I have been in hand with the prior off Munksburton and he is almost att a poyntt for the resygnation off his hous unto the hands off the Kyngs hands and my good and gracyes lord and yours, trysting in my good and gracyes lord and yours to helppe hyme and his brethren to some resonabyll pensyon that they may pray for the kyngs soule." After protestations of devotion and declarations that he will receive no promotion nor fee more during his life, he continues: "The abbot off Royche is comyd upp, use hyme nowe as youe thynke best your sellfe, notwithstanding we have resavyd your lesse [lease], butt itt cane nott be sealyd to [till] he come down."

The document by which the abbey was surrendered is also in the Record Office. The original is in Latin, of which this is a summary:

"To all faithful Christians to whom these presents may come. Henry, abbot of the Monastery of S. Mary, the virgin, of Rupe, York, of the Cistercian order and Convent in that place. Know that we the aforesaid abbot and convent, of our unanimous consent for divers causes, have given, conceded, and by this charter concede etc. to our Lord Henry VIII, by the grace of God King of England and France, defender of the faith, Lord of Scotland, and Supreme Head of the Church of England, All our Monastery and

Abbey of Roche, with all its possessions in the counties of York, Lincoln, Durham, and Nottinghamshire, and elsewhere in England, Wales and the Marches thereof. Given on the 23 day of June, in the 30th year of Henry VIII. [1538]. Signed by me, Henry, the abbot, Thomas Twell, sub-prior, John Happe, Nicholas Collys, Thomas Wells, John Dodesworth, Thomas Cundall, Richard Fyshburne, Thomas Modylt, Thomas Acworth, Chr. Hyrst, William Care [Carter], William Helsey, John Robinson, Richard Mosley, Thomas Huythe."

The next document quoted is the scheme of pensions for Roche Abbey:

"The abbot for his pencion, £xxxiii. vi/s. viii/d.
The suppryour, £vi. xiii/s. iiii/d.
The bourser, £vi.
XI prestes monks every £v, £lv.
IIII noveces every lxvi/s. viii/d, £xiii. vi/s. viii/d.

Thabbot to have his books and the iiiith parte of the plate, the cattel, the houshold stufs, a challes, a vestment, and £xxx. in money at his departure with a convenient porcion of corne at discretion.

"Every monk to have at his departure his haulf yeres pencion by way of rewarde, and xx/s besides towards his appareil. Every monk to have his pencion and capacite free. Every servaunt by way of reward to have his haulf yeres wages.

"The kinges majestie to pay the debts of the house."

This last document is dated June, 1538, and the following probably belongs to the same time:

"This be the inventorye of all lands and guids pertening to the Monasterye of Roche by estimation.

Per lands and tenements pertening to the same monasterie in divers places, £222 or therabotts by estimation.

It. platte att the same monasterye, a crosse with a shanke parcell gilte.

It. VII chalics whereof 1 lent.

It. 1 croche parcell gilte.

It. a tabernacle wyche lyis in plege for £40.

Item 2 salts gilte with 1 cover.

Item 1 standing cupe with cover, parcel gilte.

Item a whitt boulle.

Item a alte cupe, parcell gilte.

Item masers 6 [saucers].

Item spoons 32.

Item catale pertening to the same.

Seats in ye Choir, wherein ye Monks set when they said service; which were like to ye seats in Minsters and burned them and melted ye Lead therewithall: alltho' there was wood plenty within a Flight Shot of them: for the Abbey stood among ye Woods and ye Rocks of Stone: in which Rocks was Pewter Vessels found that was conveyed away and there hid: so that it seemeth every Person bent himself to filtch and spoil what he could: yea even such Persons were content to spoil them, that seemed not two days before to allow their Religion, and do great Worship and Reverence at their Mattins, Masses and other Service, and all other their Doings: which is a strange thing to say; that they that could this day think it to be ye House of God, and ye next day ye House of ye Devil: or else they would not have been so ready to have spoiled it.

"But it is not a thing to be wondered at, by such Persons that well marketh ye Inconstancy of ye rude People; in whom a man may graft a new Religion every day. Did not ye same Jews worship Christ on Sunday, that had done to them much good many ways, and cryed on Fryday next following, Crucify Him?

"For ye better Proof of this my Saying, I demanded of my Father, thirty years after ye Suppression; which had bought part of ye Timber of the Church, and all ye Timber in ye Steeple, with ye Bell Frame, with other his Proveners" (purchases) "therein, (in ye which Steeple hung viii, yea ix Bells; whereof ye least but one, could not be bought at this Day for £xx which Bells I did see hang their myself, more than a year after ye Suppression), whether he thought well of ye Religious Persons and of ye Religion then used? and he told me yea: For said He, I did see no cause to ye Contrary: Well, said I, then how came it to pass you was so ready to destroy and spoil ye thing that you thought well of? What should I do, said He, might I not as well as others have some Profit of ye Spoil of ye Abbey? For I did see all would away; and therefore I did as others did.

"Thus you may see that as well they that thought well of ye Religion then used, as they which thought otherwise, could agree well enough, and too well, to spoil them. Such a devil is Covetousness and Mammon! and such is the Providence of God to punish Sinners in making themselves Instruments to punish themselves, and all their Posterity from generation to generation! For no doubt there hath been Millions of Millions that have repented ye thing since, but all too late. And thus much upon my own knowledge touching ye Fall of ye said Roche Abbey: which had stood about 300 years: For ye Church was dedicated by one Ada, then Bishop of Coventry in ye year of our Lord God 1244."

At the end of the MS. is the following note: "Began to transcribe this MS. on S. Nicholas his day ye Patron of our College, viz. Dec. 6, and finished it December ye 10, 1745. I have not observed ye old spelling of ye original, tho' I have ye language of that time which is false English throwout according to our present speech; and I have also divided it into Paragraphs.

"WILLIAM COLE."

Nothing is known of the monks after the Dissolution, except that Thomas Twell, named above as sub-prior, was a small bene-factor to the church of Sheffield. Willis says in his " History of the Mitred Parliamentary Abbies" that in 1553 "Henry Cundall received £33. 6. 8. at which time here remained in charge, in fees £1. 6. 8., and these following pensions, viz.:—to Thomas Twell £6. 13. 4., John Dodsworth £6., Richard Fysheburne, Thomas Harrysonne, Nicholas Tolles (Collys), Thomas Middletonne, Henry Wilsonne, William Carter, Thomas Wells, £5. each. John Robinson and Richard Morysley £3. 6. 8. each."

The first secular owner of the abbey cannot with absolute cer-tainty be discovered. Willis says that in the 38th of Henry VIII. (1546), the site of the abbey was granted to William Ramsden and Thomas Vavasour, but does not give any authority for the state-ment, and it is probably incorrect. The earliest deed relating to the abbey now to be found at Sandbeck is dated June 23rd, 1546, and is a licence of alienation from James Banke to Thos. Hewett, citizen and clothworker of London, of all lands at Roche Abbey, and states that it was first possessed after the dissolution by Henry, Earl of Cumberland. He, it will be remembered, is mentioned in the report of the visitation as the founder. This James Banke is probably the one who received the rents at Sandbeck, etc. (see p. 356). On Feb-ruary 12th, 1563-4, a licence of alienation was granted to Thos. Hewett to sell the house and lands of Roche Abbey to Richard Hunt of Manchester, and the indenture between them is dated April 4th, 1564, the sum paid being £600. The next owners were two brothers, William and Hugh Frankland, and Joyce, the wife of the former. The deed of sale is missing, but Richard Hunt's quit-claim is dated November 30th, 1566. On March 2nd, 1583, William Frankland having died, his widow, Joyce, sold her half of the pro-perty to Hugh, who had evidently been living there, for £260. On September 26th, 1599, Hugh Frankland made his will, leaving the abbey to his wife, Johan, for her life (his brothers, Ralph and John, being trustees), and after her death to his brother William and his son Ralph. The next deed to do with the house is very puzzling, as it is a licence of alienation for Ralph Frankland, one of the trustees, and his son William, to sell the land to Richard Frankland, son of John, the other trustee. Richard seems to have got into difficulties, as he mortgaged the lands for his wife's settlement. On July 31st,

1616, John Frankland, and Richard his son, sold the abbey to Ralph Hansby for £2,000, and on May 21st, 1617, this Ralph gave the land to his grandson, John Wandesforde. He kept it for ten years, and on October 25th, 1627, he sold it to Nicholas Saunderson for £1,800. In consequence of this sale, the following paper was drawn up, which was docketed: "The particular of Roche Abbey as it is letten and as it was letten before, 1627:

"The Rentall of Roche Abbey as it is now let

The parcells of ground.	The rate per acre.	The farmers and tenants and the rates how they were letten 8 years agoe.
	£ s. d.	
The ground within the walls the close called Sockens close and nether oxclose	11 10 0	£16 10s. 0d.
The milne with the over todeholes and nether todeholes the milne yard Marle pingle foure closes and Rochton's wife her pingle	29 0 0	To Lawrence Yates. £32 6s. 8d.
The highe leas hardsall flatt Clayton's close over oxclose and grange wood	23 0 0	£29, To William Misterton, and James Fretwell.
The house wheren one Widdow Scott now dwelleth wh: a pingle occupieth with the same	1 0 0	Widdow Scott.

(In margin) M^{dem}. she is of charity abated 12^d in her rent, which abate^t is only at the will of the landlord.

Parte of Walker's meadowe lyinge next to Sheepcote bridge	3 15 0	To Hughe Yates,

(In margin) This was only let for a yeare upon necessity and will yield more. £8.

Parte of Walkers meadowe lyinge betwixt that which Yates occupieth and the part of Jo. Hunt.	1 3 0	To James Fretwell

Over Lyme Kilne feilde nether Lyme kilne feild Hellwood Hellgreene Cotes Croft a pingle at Sheepecoate brigge lath yard well yard wood yard pt of Walkers meadowe pt of North wood

The parcells of ground.	The rate per acre.			The farmers and tenants and the rates how they were letten 8 years agoe.
	£	s.	d.	
for these hath bene offered by lease but paide but prte:	21	0	0	To John Hunte £23 13s. 4d.

(In margin) M^d Hunt haveing no lease thereof paide but from yeare to yeare for ever xx£

Three pts of Norwood	2	17	3	To James Fretwell
One pt of Norwood	2	9	2	To Robte Saunderson
One pt of Norwood	3	10	0	To Mr Hatfeild
Suma total £99 4s. 5d.				

(In margin) M^d the lease of these pts was made 16 yeare agoe and five yeares are yet in beinge upon expiracion whereof it may be much improved.

	£	s.	d.
There may be yearly raised of underwood and the growth still to continue, viz. 30 loads at 18^d the load	2	5	0

Woods as they are valewed

		£	s.	d.
The growinge timber and trees worth	in grange wood 80 trees at	26	13	4
	in Norwood at	23	6	8
	in grange wood 60 trees at	12	0	0
	w^thin the walls 3 oakes			
The house & barne & saltehouse	3 ewes at	4	0	0
	In the Helwood were worth	20	0	0
	The underwood for kiddinge & Celinge	30	0	0"

In a rough paper, dated 1633, the rental of the abbey was computed at £113 3s. 4d., while that of Sandbeck was about £100, besides about £30 for lands at Maltby and Bawtry.

Meanwhile the noble abbey was falling into ruins, undisturbed until towards the end of the eighteenth century. In 1774, Richard, fourth Earl of Scarbrough, called in the aid of "Capability Brown" to improve the grounds of Sandbeck Park, and in the agreement drawn up between them, which is given in full below (p. 366), occurs the following: "To finish all the valley of Roach Abbey in all its parts . . . with Poets feeling & with Painters Eye." In order to do this, the architect took down parts of the abbey and used the stones to make sham waterfalls. He also turned the course of the stream, and did other mischief which is thus described by a contemporary, William Gilpin, Prebendary of Salisbury:

"Roche Abbey stands in the centre of three vallies, each of which is about a mile in length; but otherwise their dimensions as well as

Horbiri, Robert de Wykersby, knights, Walter then seneschal of Tykehill, Peter de Waddeworth, William de Steinton, John de Monteby, Hugh de Scelhale, John de Wluethwait."

The right of possession seems, however, to have been disputed, as there is a document quoted in Dugdale's "Monasticon," unfortunately undated (but Richard, as we have seen, was abbot from 1238 to 1254), of which the following is a translation:

" To all who are about to see and hear these letters, and especially to the twelve knights elected to make the great assise between Robert de Veteriponte and the abbot of Rupe, Richard de Boyvill, eternal greeting in God. Wishing you to certify on the oath which you are about to make I testify in truth by the existence of God and by the baptism with which I have been baptized and by the knighthood with which I was dubbed that on St. Giles's Day in the year of the Lord MCCXLI my Lady Ydonea de Builli in pure and free will and in full power of her body with great deliberation of mind gave to the Church of Rupe all the manor of Sandbec with the ploughlands, and all other things in it and all pertaining to it in the presence of many of her friends and liegemen there present, Sir John de Croxton, Sir Thomas de Bury, Sir R. de Boyvill knights, Lord J. de Monby. On the morrow of S. Giles the charter of this donation was written and sealed with the great seal of the domain and the private seal on the morrow of the Nativity of the Blessed Mary next following."

Sandbeck continued to belong to the monastery until its dissolution, when it became the possession of Richard Turke with the other lands; but in 1552 it was sold to Robert Saunderson, who died in 1582, and who built a house at Fillingham. The date of the original house at Sandbeck is very doubtful. Hunter in his " History of Doncaster" claims the honour for Sir Nicholas Saunderson, son of the above Robert, whose name appears in so many deeds, and he certainly lived there, as a letter written to him on December 16th, 1582, is addressed to " Nycholes Saunderson the yonger at Sandbeck or elles wheare." But the following paper, recently found at Sandbeck, suggests that he only added to a house already there:

" Articles covenanted & agreed upon the xxith day of Februarie 1626 Between Sir Nicholas Saunderson of Fillingham in the County of Lincolne Knight & Baronet of the one partie & Richard Marshall of Ashby in the said County rough mason of the other partie as followeth

" Imprimis it is covennted & agreed on the behalfe of the said Richard Marshall that he shall undertake & begin a new house of the said Sir Nicholas Saunderson at Sandbeck in the County of

Yorke where it is lefte & bringe up the rough walls chimneys & gavell ends & all other worke thereof belonginge to the bonde of a rough mason untill the whole worke to be finished wth bringinge up of the walls.

"Itm̄ the said Richard Marshall doth covēnt to beed & ioynt all the outwalles thereof wth handsome scupled stones & to make the courses wth stones of a thicknes as neare as they may be.

" Itm he doth covēnt to bringe up the chimneys to the settinge on of the shafts & to make them so that they shall avoid smoake & cause no offence when fires are made therein.

"Itm he doth covēnt to arch over all the doores chimneys & windowes in the said buildinge so as there shalbe no use of anie Lintells in the same.

"Itm̄ he doth covēnt not to leave the said buildinge after it be begun but to keepe eight trowells continually on worke besides their servitors and to begin the worke the weeke next after Easter at the furthest & so to continue until the walls of the said worke be finished.

" In consideracon thereof the said Sr Nicholas Saunderson shall allow unto the said Marshall one roome about the said house for him & his people to lay their bedds in.

"Itm the said Sir Nicholas Saunderson shall paie unto the said Richard Marshall for everie roode of the saide worke beinge seaven yards in length & one yard in height the chimneys beinge measured but single measure & the doores and windowes beinge sufficiently arched as aforesaid the some of foure shillings a roode and the said Marshall is to have the doores & windowes allowed in measure.

" Itm the said Sr Nicholas Saunderson is to bringe all the stones lyme and sand w^thin fortie yards of some part of the said buildinge and to provide such stuffe as is fitt and needfull for the same.

" Itm the work shalbe measured at everie story height and the said Richard Marshall shall receive about £5 together ward (?) or so much as his worke comes to.   marke

"Sealed & delivered in the presence of Richard R Marshall
   Will Thomlynson
   Thomas Hyles.

M^m that I Richard Barkworth of Netleton in the Countye of Lincolne Rough mason doe Covñnt for my selfe my executors & assignees to undertake and well to performe and finishe the worke & covennt thereabout w^thin written in such maner and forme and for the same price that Richard Marshall hath undertaken the same and for performance of the same I binde my selfe mine executors & assignees firmly by these presents unto Sir Nicholas Saunderson of Fillingham in the said County of Lincolne knight and Barone.

In wittnes whereof I the said Richard Barkwith have hereunto set my hand and seale the twelfth day of March 1626

" Sealed & delivered
in the presence of   Ric. Barkworths marke
Will Tomlynson
John Dunstons

(Endorsed.)

" Ric. Marshalls Articles for buildinge the house at Sandbeck 1627 Ric. Barkw^th of Nettleton for the same. arrant knaves both for they performed nothing accordingly but gott my money & wold never mesure their work."

This paper shows that there was a house of some kind already there, as besides speaking of bringing up the rough walls, there was a place for Richard Marshall and his men to put their beds. We have no further record as to how Sir Nicholas finished his house when the two masons turned out " arrant knaves." The present house was probably built by Richard, the fourth earl. As has been mentioned, this nobleman had his grounds laid out by " Capability Brown," and the deed executed between them was as follows:

" September the 12th 1774.

" Then an Agreement made between the Earl of Scarbrough on the one part & Lancelot Brown on the other, for the underwritten Articles of work, to be Performed at *Sandbeck* in the county of York—(to wit).

" Article the 1st. To compleat the Sunk Fence which seperates the Park from the Farm, & to build a Wall in it, as also to make a proper Drain at the Bottom of the Sunk Fence to keep it Dry.

" Article the 2nd. To demolish all the old Ponds which are in the Lawn, and to Level & Drain all the Grounds where they are,

" Article the 3rd. To Drain and Level all the ground which is between the above mentioned Sunk Fence, & the old Canals mentioned in the second Article, To Plant whatever Trees may be thought necessary for ornament in that Space discribed in this Article, & to sow with Grass seeds & Dutch Clover the whole of the Ground wherever the Turff has been broke up or disturbed by Drains, Leveling, or by making the Sunk Fence.

" Article the 4th. To make good & keep up a Pond for the use of the Stables.

" Article the 5th. To finish all the Valley of Roach Abbey in all its parts, according to the Ideas fixed on with Lord Scarbrough (with Poets feeling & with Painters Eye) beginning at the Head of the Hammer Pond, & continuing up the Valley towards Loton" (" als Loughton," put in by Lord Scarbrough) " in the Morn, as far as Lord Scarbrough's Ground goes, & to continue the Water & Dress the Valley up by the Present Farm House, untill it comes to the Seperation fixed for the Boundary of the New Farm. N.B. The Paths in the Wood are included in this Discription & every thing but the Buildings.

"The said Lancelot Brown does Promise for himself, His Heirs Executors & Administrators to perform or cause to be Performed in the Best manner in His or Their Power between the Date hereof & December One Thousand Seven Hundred and Seventy Seven, the above written five Articles.

"For the due Performance of the above written five Articles The Earl of Scarbrough does promise for himself His Heirs Administrators & Executors to Pay or cause to be Paid at the underwritten Times of Payment Two Thousand Seven Hundred Pounds of Lawfull money of England—and three hundred Pounds in consideration of, & for the Plans & trouble Brown has had for his Lordship at Sandbeck, previous to this Agreement. Lord Scarbrough to find Rough Timber, four able Horses, Carts, & Harness for them, Wheelbarrows & Planks, as also Trees & Shrubbs.

"The Times of Payment

" In June 1775	.	800
Feb. 1776	.	400
June Dº	.	400
Feb. 1777	.	600
On finishing the work . . .	.	800
		£3000

(Signed) SCARBROUGH
LANCELOT BROWN."

(The second payment of £400 has been erased and £200 is put at the top.)

Several slight alterations have since been made, and some considerable ones in 1899.

Stainton is mentioned in Domesday in connection with Hellaby and with Dadesley, which is generally considered to be the old name for Tickhill. Land there belonged, as it did at Maltby and Bawtry, to Roger de Builli, and the account of it is as follows:

"In the Manor of Dadesley Stainton and Hellaby, Elsi and Seward had 8 carucates of land rateable to value and there may be 8 ploughs there. Now Roger has in demesne there 7 carucates and a certain knight or soldier of his had 2½ carucates. There are 54 villeins and 2 bordars having 24 carucates and 31 burgesses and 3 mills worth 40s. There is a priest and a church and 2 acres of meadow; wood pasture land 3 quarantens long and 1 broad. In the time of Edward it was worth £12, now worth £14. In the Manor of Stainton Seward had 2½ carucates of land rateable to gelt, there may be 1 plough. Now Roger has there 1 carucate and 2 villeins and 3 bordars who plough with 2 oxen. In the time of Edward it was worth 20s., now 16s."

The earliest subinfeudatory was a Hugh de Stainton, who lived in the middle of the twelfth century. It then passed into the hands of many families till it came to Sir Edward Stanhope, who sold it with other lands to Sir Nicholas Saunderson on April 2nd, 1627.

Bagley is a small district of Tickhill. Braithwell is mentioned in Domesday as part of the land of William of Warene:

"To him belongs the soke of Bradewell 11 carucates. In Brade-welle are 16 sokemen and 20 bordars with 16 ploughs. There is a church and a priest. Wood pasture 1 quaranten long and 1 broad."

Before speaking of the Lincolnshire property, a few words must be said about Glentworth, now one of the principal places belonging in that county to the Earl of Scarbrough, but not mentioned in the deed we are now describing, as it had not come into the possession of the Saundersons when the paper was drawn up. Glentworth is a village eleven miles north of Lincoln, and was formerly the seat of the Wray family, Sir Christopher Wray, knight, Lord Chief Justice of England, having built a splendid mansion there out of the profits of the Royal Mint, granted to him by Queen Elizabeth. He seems to have been a very remarkable man, and there is a high eulogy of him in Burke's "Extinct Baronetage." He died May 8th, 1592, and is buried in the chancel of the church at Glentworth. He was succeeded by his son William, who was created a baronet by James I. in 1612. The baronetcy became extinct on the death without issue of the twelfth baronet in 1809. The third baronet, Sir John Wray, of Glentworth, had an only daughter and heir, Elizabeth, who married the Hon. Nicholas Saunderson, eldest son of George, Viscount Saunderson, and had an only son, Wray Saunderson, who died without issue during the lifetime of his mother. That lady, by a deed dated October 29th, 1709, entailed her estates in Lincolnshire and Norfolk on her cousin, Colonel Christopher Wray, except the estate of Glentworth, which was conveyed to the Saundersons. There is a monument to Elizabeth, who died in 1714, aged fifty, in the church of Glentworth, opposite to that already mentioned of Sir Christopher. (While Burke gives the above information of the conveyance of Glentworth to the Saundersons as a note to his account of Sir John, third baronet, to that of his successor, he adds, "second Baron of Ashby, at whose decease the baronetcy of Ashby became extinct, while that of Glentworth passed to his cousin.")

The ruins of Glentworth still remain, forming three sides of a quadrangle, and presenting a fine specimen of the architecture of the sixteenth century, while the fourth side is occupied by a dwelling-house built in the eighteenth century.

The first of the Lincolnshire places mentioned in the list is Reresby, or Reasby, which is a hamlet of the next place, Stainton. It is mentioned four times in Domesday Book. First, in the land of the King "there are there 2 bovates, Soke of the manor of Nettleham"; also in the land of Earl Hugh, "there is in Rearesbi a Berewick of the manor of Stainton by Langworth, of 6 bovates of land rateable to gelt." There was also there land belonging to William de Perci, and to Gozelin, son of Lambert. On May 15th, 1569, a licence was given for John and Francis Carey to alienate lands at Reresby to Nicholas Saunderson.

It is strange and rather confusing that there should be a Stainton in each county belonging to Lord Scarbrough, but it is a very common name in the north, signifying "the town of stones." There are three altogether in Lincolnshire, but that belonging to Lord Scarbrough is distinguished by the name of Stainton by Langworth. In Domesday land there belonged to Earl Hugh. "Osbern one of the Earl's vassals has there 3 carucates and 5 villeins and 4 bordars, and 4 sokemen and 1 mill worth 12^d yearly and 80 acres of meadow and one hundred and forty acres of underwood. The annual value in King Edward's time was £3, and it is the same now." There is a monument to the Saundersons in the church. On November 8th, 1597, Nicholas Saunderson of Rearsbie let lands in Stainton to John Robinson.

Scothern is five miles north-east of Lincoln. In Domesday land there belonged to "St. Peter's Abbey of Burgh," or, as we now call it, Peterborough. "In Scotherne and Sudbrooke Holme there are 5 carucates and a half of land rateable to gelt. It is Soke of this Manor. The land is 6 carucates. St. Peter's of Burgh has in these places 32 sokemen and 8 carucates." "There is a church and a priest here, who has 1 carucate." Of this church Lord Scarbrough is now the patron.

Tetney had two manors mentioned in Domesday. "There is a mill worth 16/- yearly; also 13 salt works worth 12/- yearly and 140 acres of meadow." It is very often mentioned in the old deeds and leases. Thus, on October 1st, 1597, Nicholas Saunderson sold lands at Tetney; and on December 18th, 1597, John Kyngston sold lands there to Nicholas Saunderson of Fillingham for £220. On February 27th, 1601, William Grantham of Laughton let the manor, rectory, etc., of Tetney to Nicholas Saunderson for ninety-nine years. On May 12th, 1612, a licence of alienation was granted to the right honourable Edward Earle of Hertford to sell to Sir Nicholas Saunderson, knight and baronet, the Grange of Tetney with lands at Thedilthorp, Moreby, and Wiberton. In 1656, George Lord Vis-

count Castleton, was tenant there to James Gresham of the Inner
Temple, with whom he has a dispute.

Holton le Clay is a small place four miles south of Grimsby.
There was a manor there mentioned in Domesday Book and "the
site of a mill."

Willoughton, or Willerton, as it is often spelt, was a very important part of the estate, and the papers about it are innumerable.
There was an alien priory there, and a manor belonging to it was
granted by Henry VI. to King's College, Cambridge. In the reign
of King Stephen a moiety of the church and the greatest part of the
town was given to the Knights Templars, from whom it came to the
Hospitallers, and it is called in the papers "The Commandery of
Willerton or Hospital of S. John of Jerusalem." There is a very
interesting paper at Sandbeck copied from the original on June 26th,
1582. The beginning is torn, but it is docketed on the outside:
"This booke contayneth the possessions of the Comaundry of
Willoughton and sheweth what landes belongeth unto it at the tyme
of the suppression." Part of the original refers to 1524, but it is
evidently based on older documents, as in the Rental of Horkstowe
is written: " Hit appereth in an old parchment rental that there was
tempore Regis E. 2. theise freholders following." The possessions
comprise lands at Willerton, Ganesburgh, Blyton, Glentham, Bli-
burgh, Appulby, Saxby, etc. The earlier deeds are all connected
with the Sutton family, and a little later with " Susan Aiscoughe of
Blibourghe." The first mention of the Saundersons is in 1608, when
Stephen Bowyer Caistrope leases land there to Nicholas Saunderson
of Fillingham.

Blyborough, which is mentioned with Willoughton, is only a mile
away. Until the arrival of the Knights Templars, it was evidently
the more important place of the two. It is mentioned several times
in Domesday Book. Land there belonged to the Bishop of Durham.
Medulf had seven bovates of land there rateable to gelt. "The
monks of Durham have now on this land 2 carucates, 3 villeins and
1 bordar and 1 sokeman with 1 carucate and 20 acres of meadow;
and half the advowson of the church which belongs to and is divided
between the Bishop and Gozel the son of Lambert. The annual
value in King Edward's time was 20/-, now 30/-." There was also
land there belonging to Ivo Taillebois and to Geoffrey de Wirce.
" Lewic the Thane had 2 carucates . . . Robert, Geoffrey de Wirce's
vassal has there 2 carucates. . . . There is half a church and a mill
with 2/- yearly and there are 60 acres of meadow." Blyborough
belonged to the Southcote family before it came into the possession
of the Saundersons.

Hackthorn is a small place seven and a half miles north of Lincoln. In Domesday Book it is called " Agethorne." The land there
belonged to the Archbishop of York, who had half the church, to

Roger the Pictavien, to Colswain, to Gozelin, the son of Lambert, to Martin, and to Walden Ingeniator, who had "one carucate in demesne, and 3 villeins and 7 bordars who have 10 oxen and half the church and 1 mill worth 12^d yearly and 30 acres of meadow. Value 40/-." Paul Neale sold lands there to Nicholas, Viscount Castleton, on July 1st, 1639. There are several letters between George, Lord Viscount Castleton, and Francis Pickwell about land there.

Fristhorpe is a very small village also north-east of Lincoln. The name does not often occur among the documents.

Middle Rasen derives its name from being on the River Rase, between the town of Market Rasen and the village of West Rasen. It belonged at the time of the Domesday Book to Odo, Bishop of Bayeux. "Wedward the Bishop's vassal has there 18 villeins and 11 bordars who have 5 carucates. There is a church and a priest with 2 bordars. Of this land 1 bordar belongs to the church."

Moorby and Wilksby are near Horncastle. In Domesday Book the land at Moorby belonged to the king. "There is in the same place a church and 240 acres of meadow and 6 acres of underwood." In Wilksby the land belonged to Robert Dispenser, Steward of the Conqueror.

Fillingham was the original home of the Saundersons, and in the early deeds they are always called "of Fillingham." Robert Saunderson, who died in 1582, built a house there, which has now disappeared. There is a tablet in the church to Jane, first wife of Thomas Saunderson, third son of the above-named Robert, and also to Sir Cecil Wray, tenth baronet, who died in 1805.

The name Kursney must be a mistake. There is said to be considerable property there, and yet there is no place of that name in Lincoln, and it does not occur in the deeds. It is possibly a mistake for Friskney, about which place there are many papers.

Newton is a hamlet of Toft, both near Market Rasen. In Domesday Book the land there belonged to the Bishop of Bayeux. There is a deed between Robert Saunderson and William Yates about land there, dated 1576.

There are a great many very old deeds about Skegness, from 1313, all the earliest dated by saints' days. The name of Lord Castleton does not occur in them until 1678. The old family there seems to have been "de Westmels" or "Westemeles."

The earlier deeds about Saxby show that the principal landowners there in Henry VII. and Henry VIII.'s reigns were the Holmes. On May 20th, 1563, Robert Holmes of Tofte near Newton conceded lands at Saxby to Robert Saunderson.

INDEX

CHISWICK PRESS : PRINTED BY CHARLES WHITTINGHAM AND CO.
TOOKS COURT, CHANCERY LANE, LONDON.

WS - #0042 - 030124 - C0 - 229/152/24 - PB - 9780259508205 - Gloss Lamination